REFLECTIONS

REFLECTIONS

Topsy : It just grew

RUTH DRUMMOND

iUniverse, Inc.
Bloomington

REFLECTIONS
Topsy : It just grew

iUniverse books may be ordered through booksellers or by contacting:

iUniverse
1663 Liberty Drive
Bloomington, IN 47403
www.iuniverse.com
1-800-Authors (1-800-288-4677)

ISBN: 978-1-4697-9641-3 (sc)
ISBN: 978-1-4697-9642-0 (ebk)

Printed in the United States of America

iUniverse rev. date: 10/01/2012

This Book, REFLECTIONS, was like Topsy—it just grew. My youngest daughter said, "Mom, I don't want to sound pessimistic, but the chance of my children knowing their grandparents grows less each year. Would you please fill out this Grandma's Book for them?"

The first question required a one line answer, "What was your favourite subject in school?" Really!! I taught school for 33 years. Every subject I taught was exciting. You wouldn't expect me to answer that in one sentence!

I booted up my computer and wrote four pages, which I took to my husband Mac to read. "Well," he said, you should tell about this, and this and that . . ." My four pages became 15, and that's the way the book grew.

I would like to thank my husband, Mac, and my sisters Jean and Rosalind who filled in gaps in my memory. Special thanks to my daughter Jill for assistance in formatting and drawing the final manuscript together.

My Dear Family,

This has been a labour of love. It has been an enjoyable trip 'back to the future'.

It is said that we are a part of all whom we have met. I have found this to be so true. I trust that this chronicle may not only give you knowledge of where you came from, but also an insight into who you are and where you're going.

In spirit, we will always be together. To paraphrase The Twenty Third Psalm,

> Surely my grandmother will follow me all the days of my life, And we will dwell together on the Other Side forever.

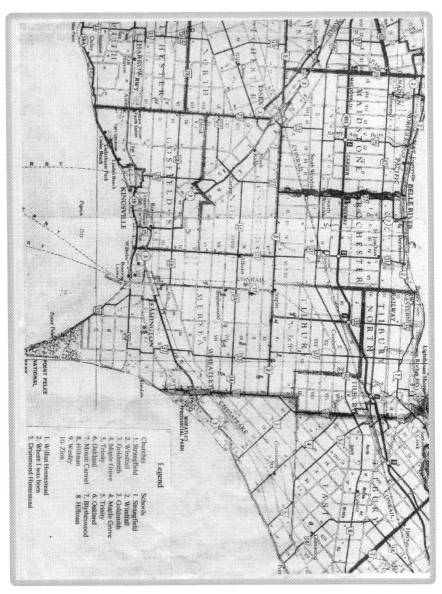

A partial map of Essex County where I grew up. Essex County, in the Province of Ontario, is the most southern part of Canada. It is surrounded by water on three sides. Lake St. Clair is the north boundary. The Detroit River on the west separates the Province of Ontario and the State of Michigan (Windsor and Detroit across the river from each other). The south boundary is Lake Erie. The legend shows the schools and churches which were the centers of community life for homesteaders.

SETTLEMENT BY THE PIONEERS

Essex and Kent Counties in southern Ontario were opened up for settlement after Colonel Talbot had built a road from London to Windsor to march soldiers to defend the borders of Canada from attack by United States during the War of 1812-1814. After the war, groups of people from England, Scotland and Ireland were encouraged to start a new life in Canada with the gift of 100 acres of land to homestead.

Areas were surveyed and divided into counties, townships and communities. Each community with a post office, church, and school. Homesteaders in each community were usually of the same religious denomination—Presbyterian, Methodist, Catholic, and some Quakers. Similar to giving your address to someone today, the pioneers identified themselves by the community where they had settled: Trinity, the 8th concession area; Goldsmith, to the west of Trinity; Windfall, on the line between Essex and Kent; Strangfield, west of Windfall, Maple Grove west of Strangfield; Coatsworth east in Kent County.

My Father's people, The Willan's, were in Strangfield. Mother's family, the Graham's, were next door in Windfall. When Mother and Dad were first married, they attended church both in Windfall and Strangfield each Sunday. After the Presbyterians and Methodist joined to form The United Church in 1927, our family went to Windfall Church. This meant that I went to Strangfield school, but Windfall Church, so I grew up with roots in both communities. (See the map at the front of the book.)

Most of the communities received their names from the people who settled there. Windfall, however, was named because a tornado had ripped out a strip of forest about a mile wide and five miles long. Now mind you, this was long before we worried about the destruction of the forests,

1

pollution, global warming, and El Nino. The swath cut out of the trees was identified as 'the wind fall'. The name stuck.

More prosperous communities set up saw mills and general stores. This land was covered with forest which had to be cleared for farming. Especially in abundance were great oak, maple, and elm trees which were in demand for furniture. At Staples, 5000 acres were given to the Menzies family. They established a store and saw mill. The dressed lumber was shipped to fine furniture makers in the north where oak was scarce. There were exotic trees that have long since disappeared, such as cherry and black walnut. The maple, elm, and fir trees were sawed to make the beams for barns and the logs for houses. Much of the smaller and scrub growth was burned since that was the easiest way to get rid of the roots so that land could be worked. The only tools they had were axes, saws, dynamite, oxen or horses, and a very strong back. It is no wonder that they hated trees!

It was necessary to have and to be a good neighbour. This amount of work could only be accomplished through cooperation, so neighbours worked in bees when a big job had to be done. Once the timbers were prepared, the neighbours for miles would come to help in the barn raising or putting up the logs and roof on a new home. At harvest time threshing bees started at one end of the road and continued until all the grain was in the granaries and the straw blown into huge stacks. The women helped each other prepare the meals to feed as many as 35 to 40 men at a time. That took a huge pot of potatoes and lots of pies! And, of course, if there were any kind of emergency, accident or death, the neighbours were the first on the scene to give support.

Once the land was cleared, families made a living with mixed farming—that is they raised horses, cows, pigs, sheep, goats, chickens, geese, ducks, and turkeys. In the fields, they planted wheat, oats, barley, buckwheat, rye, corn, and a large vegetable garden. These crops fed the animals and the family. A small amount of flax was grown to make linen. Sorghum, a crop much like corn, was grown as a sugar substitute. The stalks were stripped and sent to a mill where the sap was pressed out, then boiled down. The result was a thick, brown substance that resembled molasses. Mac's Mother made sorghum cookies and cakes that melted in your mouth. Hemp, called marijuana today, was grown, and sent to the mill to be made into rope, which was a necessary item on every farm. Yes, some of the farmers smoked it in their pipes. Hemp plants can still be found growing wild in many of the wood lots. A few tobacco plants were also grown. The leaves were stripped and hung to dry. Sometimes they were soaked in a molasses mixture. They were then rolled and twisted into a plug. After this had cured again, the tobacco would be cut off with a sharp knife to be smoked in a corn-cob pipe or chewed. If the farmer chewed his tobacco, that meant there was a spittoon in the house. That was an ugly, stinking sight!

The goal was to be self-sufficient. Cash was only needed to buy those things that you couldn't produce yourself—such as: machinery to work the land, pots and pans for the kitchen, shoes, fabric (other than wool or linen), and oil for the lamps.

Everyone in the family shared the work. If there were a shortage of sons in the family, then the daughters went to the fields. If there were a shortage of daughters to help in the house, then the sons were expected to pitch in. After supper Great Grandpa Hooker spun all the wool and knit all the socks and mitts for the family. It was said he did beautiful work.

Extra farm produce was traded with merchants. Mother used to tell the story of a woman who took her eggs and 9 pounds of butter into the general store to be traded for other groceries. On her list was 9 pounds of butter.

"But you brought in 9 pounds of butter," he said. "Why do you want to buy back 9 pounds?"

"Well," she replied, "A mouse fell into the cream so we just couldn't fancy eating the butter, and I felt that what other people didn't know wouldn't hurt them."

The grocer took her 9 pounds to the back of the store, changed the wrappers and brought them back to her order. "I just thought," he mused, "that what she didn't know wouldn't hurt her."

As more land was cleared, farmers began to produce more than they could use themselves. The surplus was sold, so that farm families had more cash to spend. Beautiful, big, brick houses replaced log living quarters. The standard of living improved steadily. This was the way my parents farmed when I was a kid.

The church was the centre of the community. There were morning and evening Sunday services. Most people attended both.

Social activities were mainly church hosted. Strawberry Socials were held in season to celebrate the abundance of home-grown strawberries served with home-made ice cream.

Box Socials were a fun way to raise money. Ladies packed tempting food into decorated boxes or baskets. There were to be no identifying markings on the item to show who had packed it. The men bid on the boxes, the highest bidder winning the privilege of eating with the woman who packed it. If two young men felt a certain young lady had packed a certain box, then the bidding could be exciting until one was forced to give in. Oh, dear. Sometimes the owner who stood up was not the young lady in mind!

Fall Turkey Suppers were held around Thanksgiving. Oyster Soup Suppers, (Oh, I hated oysters), were held in February when oysters were in season. The oysters were bought in gallon pails and cooked in a rich milk and cream broth. Sunday School picnics featured races for the kids followed by a ball game.

Afternoon Church Teas gave a winter diversion for wives. Women visited back and forth from community to community. The afternoon entertainment consisted of a short worship service, followed by musical numbers, skits or short plays, recitations and a guest speaker. Then everyone sat down together to enjoy a cup of tea and deserts.

Since the only entertainment available was what you created as a group, there was a lot of visiting and support from nearby communities. After a supper, or ball game, or any hosted event, those who could sing, play an instrument or recite were invited to make up the program that concluded the evening. Mother was an excellent elocutionist (someone who recited long, narrative poems) and was often asked to perform a number. I sang from before I can remember. My sister, Jean accompanied me on the piano. No, it wasn't rock and roll. Please don't laugh. Some of the titles were: *Is This The Train To Heaven, The Letter Edged In Black, May I Sleep In Your Barn Tonight, Mister?, Happy Little Country Girl, Somebody's Waiting for You, That Silver-haired Daddy Of Mine.* Oh goodness, they sound corny, even to me, now. But hey, I was in demand for socials, weddings and funerals.

Baseball was the favourite sport. Every community had a team and a field. Strangfield's was built in the corner of Gaines' farm which was next door to ours.

The rivalry was intense, and sometimes carried over to the street the next day.

House parties were the most frivolous of entertainment. Neighbours took turns hosting a party and dance. The furniture from the biggest room would be removed to make space to dance. There were always those who could play the fiddle, piano, and banjo. They provided the music. There would be someone who could call for square dances, and various numbers for 'round dancing'. Step dancing, which is similar to clogging today, was an art. Often a kind of competition arose to judge who could do it best. The whole family came. Children learned to dance at an early age.

Little ones were tucked into a bed when they got tired. There was no alcohol at these affairs. It wasn't needed to have a good time. Those attending brought sandwiches or cake for refreshments. Often the party would go on until the wee hours of the morning. Finally, parents would load up their brood, take them home in the horse and buggy, and tuck them into their beds. Then Mom and Dad would change their clothes and go to the barn to chore.

Fall fairs were big events. Leamington had one of the biggest and best in Southern Ontario. Winning a prize for an entry gave bragging rights for weeks. The competition to win the red ribbon for livestock was keen. That meant that you would proudly lead your prize winning animal in the parade that closed the fair on Saturday afternoon. There was a midway that included the latest of rides, and side shows. The spiel from a barker might go:

"Come and see the little man from Abyssinia—he walks, he talks, he crawls on his belly like a reptile".

How crude and cruel! Being politically correct was a long time coming. Neighbours and relatives planned their day(s) at the fair so that they could meet and have a picnic lunch together. Fried chicken was a must.

Music played a big part in everyday life. Children learned to play by ear if they were talented, or took music lessons from a travelling teacher. That is, the teacher came to your home to give lessons.

The most prominent itinerate music teacher was Ivan Coulter. (He was my Dad's first cousin. His Mother and Dad's Mother were sisters, but I won't bore you with more of that lineage.) Ivan was very accomplished, with music degrees just short of having a doctorate. He taught for 60 years so it was not unusual for three generations to benefit from his teaching. Mother, Jean and I took piano from him. I also took vocal instruction.

Nearly every home had a piano. During a visit, there was usually a sing-song around the piano. I remember at about age 7, wanting to be the one at the keyboard. I therefore took my lessons seriously and practiced without too much nagging. I never was good at playing by ear, but I did get good enough to play almost any piece of music placed before me, and I learned to sight read music.

This was the time of Shirley Temple and other child stars in the movies. Jean had a dream that she and I could make it big. She entered me in a talent contest that was held by the local radio station, CFCO in Chatham. I can't remember that, but I do remember being recalled, by popular demand, when I was about 6 years old. The studio was very plain with a piano and a microphone in the corner. Today it would remind you of a recording studio. I sang *THAT SILVER HAIRED DADDY OF MINE* which was a new country release. Jean tells me there was a similar talent show from a Detroit station which she also entered me in, but she got no reply from them. She thinks now that was because they didn't accept Canadian talent. There was, however, a school in Detroit that was looking for child stars. Talent scouts came down to see about enrolling me, but Mother and Dad would have no part of it. They did not like the way that child stars were handled. Years later when the truth was told, they were so wise. I was still too little to care or realize what was going on, but Jean was very disappointed, for if I had been put under contract, it meant that she would go with me.

Music always played a vital part of my life. It meant that I was invited all over the country to sing. It taught me to stand in front of people and perform without being nervous. I sang in church choirs from the time I was 10 years old, carrying either the soprano or alto part as was required to balance the harmony. Later I lead a number of children's choirs in church.

Music was an asset all the years I taught. When I was teaching in the Elementary school, I used music as a break time for classes. The teacher in the one-room country school was expected to put on the Christmas concert in the church. Because I could accompany my classes on the piano, I didn't have to depend on the music teacher being present for the concert. I had a group of bright little students in Grade 4 in Wheatley who learned to sight read music and sing in three-part harmony. They were called upon to sing at Parent Teacher functions and school programmes. They were exceptional performers. In Secondary School, I worked with the Glee Clubs, leading groups who won numerous festival competitions. For a number of years I travelled with the school band as the female chaperone. The glee club members came from the band as well as from the student body. Sometimes we sang with band accompaniment, sometimes a cappella, (without accompaniment). At the National/International Music Festival in Toronto (bands and choirs came from across Canada and the

US) the judges were so impressed with the girls, that they created a special category for them, and presented them with a trophy of recognition. I was so proud of them.

The piano has also a kind of therapy for me. When I was blue or discouraged, I could sit down at the piano and lose myself in the music. Today I do the same thing with the electronic keyboard, although you can't get the same release by pounding it's keys because that instrument does not respond to touch as the piano does. I also enjoy my CD player and the quality of the recordings available today.

Community bands were popular when I was a kid. In Wheatley, Ivan Coulter was the conductor. Mac took trumpet lessons from Ivan and played in the Wheatley Community Band. Band competitions called Tattoos were held throughout the summer. It would not be unusual to have as many as 25 to 30 bands participating. All bands were marching bands. They were judged not only on how well they played, but also on their marching manoeuvres. Wheatley held many trophies. At Michigan State Fair, Mac won the bronze medal for his trumpet solo.

Throughout the summer, band concerts were held in Wheatley every Saturday night, in a small downtown park with a band shell and benches for the audience. It became a ritual to hurry to town, complete your shopping, and then sit under a starry sky and enjoy a concert. Guest soloist were often invited. I was honoured at least once a summer to be asked to sing. The concerts continued until 1940 when many of the young band players joined the armed forces. After the war, Wheatley tried to reinstate the concerts, but by then people had many other interests. They couldn't get a crowd or young people interested in joining the band. Finally the concerts were discontinued.

Gaines took violin lessons from Romannelli (that's a phonetic spelling) who was a stern, demanding man of German descent. I can still hear Gaines tuning up his fiddle with *Old Kentucky Home*. Sometimes he didn't get much farther than that. Rosalind took some violin lessons from Mrs. Julian. She was an austere, stone-faced woman who could take the play out of playing an instrument. Her idea of perfection was 10% talent and 90% hard work. Rosalind, who also had a beautiful voice, soon dropped the violin in favour of singing. She, too, was frequently asked to sing for concerts and special occasions.

A child always felt safe in the community. Neighbours looked after neighbours. On the other hand, if you were misbehaving, a neighbour would catch you by the collar and remind you that you had better straighten up your act or your Dad and Mother would hear about it. Believe me, that was next to being caught by the police. You were stupid if you didn't take heed. I remember being at a picnic where I was running pretty uncontrolled. Our next door neighbour, Lewis Forrest, caught me by the shoulder and firmly reminded me that Mother and Dad would not approve. That was enough to slow me down! No, he didn't tell on me, but I'm sure he would have if I hadn't taken the warning.

Does this sound like everything was love and roses in every community? Well, not really. There were usually one or two families who were different and required kid-glove treatment. For the good of all, they were tolerated and included even when it was difficult to accommodate their moods.

Laziness was frowned upon. How lazy was he? This is an old joke that defines laziness.

There was this farmer who was so lazy that his family was starving. The neighbours got tired of providing them with food and decided that his wife and family would be better off without him. So they built a coffin and carried him off to the cemetery. On the way, their consciences began to bother them.

"It's too bad to bury him alive without providing him with something to eat," one man reasoned.

"I have a few ears of corn left in the crib," another offered. "We could put that in with him."

At this the man in the coffin opened his eyes and slowly asked, "Is it shelled?"

"No," was the reply.

Then said the man, "Drive on."

In Mac's community of Maple Grove, the McCrackens and the McKeens came from Ireland, settled side by side and forgot to leave their Irish tempers in the old country. It took real diplomacy to keep peace at times. They would fight at the drop of a hat, No holds were barred. Folks held their breath when a fight broke out on the street. To interfere meant having to fight them both. The last I heard, the fourth generation is still at it.

By 1925, the farm community had become prosperous. When I was 2 1/2 years old, in October, 1929, tragedy hit!

THE GREAT DEPRESSION

As I said, prosperity was on a roll. Everyone had money. The stock market was a household word. At first, a little of your extra cash was invested. When that made big profits, more was invested. With luck, you could become rich over-night. Farmers bought more land where they borrowed the money at high interest rates (8%). Those who became addicted to the markets gambled with their assets to invest more. It was a bubble that burst with an enormous bang.

The stock market crashed. Suddenly everybody was poor. Stocks that were highly valued became worthless over night. Industries, businesses and companies went bankrupt. The ripple effect hit everyone. Jobs were lost. People were left with big mortgages while the price of farm produce dropped to pennies. Eggs sold for 12 cents per dozen, that's one cent per egg. A crate of eggs, 36 dozen, sold for $4.32. That was the cash Mother had to run the house for a week. Her grocery purchase was standard—25 cents worth of oat meal, 25 cents worth of white beans, and 25 cents worth of brown sugar.

Many farmers lost their land. It became a common occurrence for a family of kids to come to school in tears. Their parents had lost the farm and they were forced to move. Sometimes it would be in with aunts and uncles or grandparents, sometimes to the city to find employment. It was the dark cloud that hung over everybody's head. You knew it could happen to you, and in some way, you felt guilty that you were still there. There was no disgrace in being poor. All your friends were poor, too.

Unemployment was country wide. Hobos and tramps, men who were destitute, rode the rails, meaning they hitched rides on the railway trains, or tramped the countryside looking for whatever work they could find. Two or three times a week, Dad and Mother would take in a 'bum' for the night. These men never expected a hand-out without doing chores to pay for a meal and lodging. They milked cows, chopped wood, whatever, in the evening and in the morning in thanks for the generosity they had received. The country music hit of the day was *MAY I SLEEP IN YOUR BARN TONIGHT, MISTER.*

Sharing was an expression of real generosity. Farm families had barely enough to feed themselves. A meal often was no more than potatoes, eggs and home-made bread. I marvel now at the honesty of the hobos. They never stole from the hands that fed them. Hands were needed for harvest, both at home and in the west. Train loads of men went west to help. A few stayed. Dad hired young men from Windsor. Monthly wages were: $25 in cash, room and board, and one week-end off per month.

People who survived on their farms were those who became creative in recycling and reusing. Nothing was thrown out. Kitchen waste was collected in a big pail to be fed to the pigs. The unworn parts of adult clothing were remade to fit the children. Patches were taken for granted. An old saying—A patch over a hole is thrifty. A patch over a patch is miserly. That was poor! Darning a hole in the toe or the heel of a sock became an art. Underwear, tea towels, pillow cases, and men's shirts were made from heavy, cotton flour bags that has been bleached to remove the brand name. Some were dyed to the desired colour. Two flour sacks would make a man's shirt, if he wasn't a big man.

Children only wore shoes in the winter and to church. The rest of the time, they went barefoot. Each child got a new pair of shoes in the fall to go back to school. These were usually black because the scuffs on black would polish up better than those on brown. By spring, the leather soles would be worn through into holes. Before you went to bed, you cut out insoles from cardboard or newspaper to keep the stones and gravel out for another day. And, of course, by spring, the shoes were too short for comfort so you looked forward to the 24th of May, the set date when you could kick them off and go barefoot. It would take 4 or 5 days for the bottom of you feet to toughen up so you could walk on the gravel roads comfortably. Then there were thistles to contend with. These would fester and get sore when they worked their way into your flesh. The only treatment was extraction of the offending barb with a needle. My Dad was very good at this. Don't you dare move!

I have taken some space to describe the community connection because Mac and I grew up in that kind of tight, loving, safe environment.

It remained with little change until the servicemen returned from World War 11 in 1945.

As some communities grew, others became less defined. The post offices were the first to disappear shortly after World War 1 when Rural Mail Delivery was brought in. In 1968, with the establishment of District School Boards and bussing, the one-room country schools disappeared. Progress in the development of mechanized machinery has made it possible to turn most of the 100 acre farms into 400 to 500 acre holdings. This meant a drop in rural population, so many of the church communities have amalgamated or closed. Of the dozen or so we used to visit, only Strangfield, Trinity and Goldsmith are alive and well. For the most part, the sense of identity with your place in your community family has been lost to history.

WILLAN/ HOOKER

Married: Nov. 22, 1882

Isaac Hugh Willan
Born: Oct. 8, 1861
Died July 3, 1828

Etta Samantha Hooker
Born: Apr. 27, 1865
Died: Aug. 20, 1926

These were my Grandparents: their children were my aunts and uncles
And their grandchildren were my first cousins

Orphy (Mahlon) Keith	Effie (Norman) Whittal	Winfred (Alvin) McIntosh	Earl Austin/Muriel Irene Graham	Russel
Alice	Marjorie	John (Jack)	My Father and Mother	Died WW 1
Died in infancy	Mildred	Donald	See My Family Tree	
Harold	Rose 1	Murray		
Jean	Albert	William (Bill)		
Retta (Bill) Tetzhff	Bertha (Ray) Beacom			
Edwin	Betty			
Died WW I	Robert (Bob)			
Wilbur	Ronald			
Kenneth	Rosemary			
	Linda			

Standing: Grandmother Etta (Hooker) Willan and Grandfather Isaac Willan
Seated: L.R. My great-grandfather, Francis Hooker, Aunt Orphy holding Marion,
and my great-great grandmother Roxanna Healy Willan. Circa 1908

MY GRANDPARENTS—THE WILLAN/
HOOKER SIDE

M Y FATHER WAS THE FOURTH child and first son born to Etta Samantha (Hooker) and Isaac Willan. William Willan (from England), David Reid (from Ireland, via Quebec, and on to Essex County in 1854, with his mother, three sisters and two brothers), Frances Hooker (from England, born in Quebec, on to Ontario 1861), and Duncan Drummond (From Scotland, born in Glengarry County, Ontario) had homesteaded side-by-side on the eighth concession of Mersea Township, Essex Country. The Hookers were Quakers, the others Presbyterian and Methodists. Aren't you impressed by the daring, courage, and faith it took to continue to venture farther into the bowels of a strange country, covered with huge trees, extreme cold, deep snows, and occupied by Indians? It was common to plough up arrow heads in the fields 100 years later.

It was very common in those days to marry the girl/boy-next-door or from a neighbouring community. Marriages were mostly arranged by the parents. So, at age 17, Etta Samantha Hooker married Isaac Hugh Willan on November 22, 1882. They took up a homestead in the Township of Tilbury West on the Essex County 'Township' line in Strangfield community. They had nine children. The first-born, Alice, died in infancy. They were married 44 years and both died in their early 60's. Dad and Mother bought the farm from Grandpa and Grandma. Today it is owned by Rosalind, my sister, and her husband Harold Dundas. It is registered as a Centennial Farm, having been in the family for more than 100 years.

I have mentioned that very often you married the girl next door. Sometimes this presented an interesting situation. My Grandma Willan's father, Frances Hooker, after his first wife died, married my Grandpa Willan's sister Elizabeth Willan. This made Grandma's father

her brother-in-law. Her sister-in-law Elizabeth became her step-mother. When Elizabeth and Frances had a son, Milton, he became his own uncle. Confusing? I guess so. No doubt this is the situation that prompted the song, *I'm My Own Grandpa*.

My Grandma Willan died about 6 months before I was born, so of course, I never knew her. But Mother always spoke about her with love and admiration. She had the ability to pour oil over troubled waters, helping life run more smoothly. That would definitely be a plus with 8 children and a husband who reportedly could pout if he didn't get his own way. Dad often spoke of his mother's ability to read minds and foretell the future. He said no one told her a lie, because she would know the truth. Often she knew when uninvited company would show up after supper, or who was knocking behind a closed door. This was not something that people often talked about because society, at that time, thought this sort of ability was from the devil. I always felt that Dad inherited some of her psychic ability.

Grandpa Willan died when I was about one and a half years old, so I have no memory of him either. I have been told that Mother wanted to name me 'Etta Samantha' after Grandma, but he knew that she didn't want any of the grandchildren named for her and suggested that I be called 'Ruth'. The story went that he willed himself to die after Etta's death.

GRANDPA GRAHAM

My mother, Muriel Irene Graham, was the adopted daughter of Gaines and Annie (Cottingham) Graham, in Romney Township, Aug.14, 1895. I know very little about his family. Because he was a devout Methodist, I presume the family came from Scotland. Apparently, there was a large family of boys, Grandpa being the oldest. I heard this story from Mother. His father was a mild mannered man, but on Saturdays he would go to town and come home drunk. He would beat up his wife and children and then pass out in the bed. One day, his wife had had enough. She sent the boys to the barn for rope, tied him hand and foot spread eagle to the bed, and left him to sober up. Then she sent the boys to the barn for the buggy whip. Each child who had been beaten the night before used the whip on him. When they were finished, they said, "That's what you do to us when you are drunk." How's that for just and immediate punishment! It was said that he never took another drink. He was no dummy.

Gaines Graham left quite a legacy. He was a prosperous farmer, farming a homestead in Romney Township on the county road separating Essex and Kent Counties in Windfall Community. Their house had running water! In the attic, there was a large cistern which was kept pumped full of water. This was piped down through the house and ran by gravitation to the kitchen and bathroom. That was pretty unique in the early 1900's. He also owned one of the first cars in the community.

Grandpa Graham was a lay preacher for the Methodist Church. Ordained ministers travelled from church to church, preaching every 4th to 6th week, depending on the size of their territory. On the other Sundays, upright, good speakers, well-thought-of persons, (These were always men!) took the services and taught the adult Bible Study classes. These men were known as lay preachers.

Gaines Graham practiced what he preached. Nothing was done on Sunday that could be looked after in advance. The feed for his animals was put in front of the mangers on Saturday, so that it only had to be forked in on Sunday. Sunday dinner had to be prepared as much as possible on Saturday. You were allowed to kindle a fire to cook on Sunday. Sundays were days of worship and dedication to church and visiting. Mother said that this caused her to 'sin' many times. The only reading allowed on Sunday was the Bible or Sunday School papers. Mother, who loved to read, would hide a book under her mattress, escaped to the privacy of her room, and read the forbidden book. Grandpa Graham served as Reeve of Kent County for several years. His picture still hangs in the County Building in Chatham.

In the early 1900's there was a lot of poverty in England. When a family couldn't support a child, (s)he was put in an orphanage. Farmers in Canada would apply to get one of these children, usually boys. They were referred to as *Home Boys*. Passage was paid by the sponsor. After arrival, the child was expected to work long enough for the family to pay the expense incurred to get him/her to Canada. This was called Indentured Service. Some children got good homes. There were, however, families who were looking for cheap labour. The children they got were ill-treated and abused.

This was the situation for Stanley Stevens, age 13. He was indentured to a farm family named Glazier. They did not give him enough to eat or clothes to keep him warm. He was forced to sleep in the barn. After a beating, he ran away. Imagine Grandpa Graham's surprise one morning to find him hiding out in his barn. Gaines Graham was appalled at this. He bought Stanley's indentureship from the Glaziers, then cancelled the debt to the boy. Stanley lived with the Grahams, going to school and helping on the farm until he was 18. He lived in Windsor, married and raised a family. He remained in contact with Grandma and Mother all his life.

Grandpa Graham died in 1919 following a heart attack. Grandma married Garret Dean in 1927, the year I was born. Grandma and 'Uncle Garret' were the only grandparents I knew.

THE MELLISH CONNECTION

THE MELLISH FAMILY WERE PENNSYLVANIA Dutch who fled to
Canada during the American Revolution because they were United
Empire Loyalists, that is they didn't wish to separate from England. They
were Jews with money, educated, and considered themselves to be part of the
upper class. They established a jewellery shop in Chatham. The Funstone
family came from Ireland and had settled in Tilbury. Mabel Funstone
worked as a housekeeper for the Mellish family. When Will Mellish, a
spoiled and pampered son, became interested in Mabel, the Mellishes
were not pleased. When Mabel became pregnant, Will was shipped back
to Pennsylvania. Mother was born May 1, 1897, an illegitimate child.
People at that time considered illegitimacy a sin that was carried over and
imposed on the child.

The Funstones raised the baby for a year or more. Mabel and Annie
Graham were good friends. The Grahams were married and couldn't have
children. A legal adoption was arranged. Mother became Muriel Irene
Graham. Now she would have 'respectability' in the community. This
was something Grandma never let Mother forget. That was not cruel on
Grandma's part. It simply was the thinking of society at the time.

Will Mellish returned to Chatham shortly after this. He and Mabel
eloped and went to live in Detroit where he set up a jewellery business.
They had a second daughter, Amy, Mother's full sister.

When Mother was about 10 years old she was told that Aunt Mabel
and Uncle Will were her birth parents. They begged for 2 years to have her
back. Finally, Grandpa Graham agreed that Mother could live with them
in Detroit for 6 months. At the end of that time, she would decide which
parents she wanted to live with. Mother lasted in Detroit for 3 months.

The Mellishes fought like cat and dog, something that didn't happen in the Graham household. She was often left alone in the apartment with little Amy. The city was strange to her, the new school was foreign, and she had no friends. When the Mellishes went to Tilbury for a family funeral, Mother ran away and called Grandpa Graham to come and get her, which of course, he did—tout suite! The story goes that he ran to the barn. harnessed his team, hooked them to the buggy, and raced to get her. He had to take all the back roads home to avoid a search party. Let your imagination run here and you have a great soap opera.

The Mellish family moved to Chicago where Mr. Mellish owned a jewellery store. They divorced. Mrs. Mellish had custody of Amy. I don't believe there was such a thing as child support in those days. Or maybe, Mrs. Mellish, being the person she was, wouldn't accept it. She was a dress-maker and seamstress. She could copy or design whatever her clientele wanted. She also did costumes for the ballet and the theatre. Even when the depression hit, she was able to make a comfortable living.

Amy grew up. When she was 17 or so, she fell out of an apple tree. From that time on she suffered from Grand Mal seizures.

After Mother and Dad were married, Mrs. Mellish made contact with Mother again. She and Amy made periodic visits. As I remember, these were always stressful times. Mrs. Mellish was loud, brash, opinionated, domineering, outspoken, short and fat. That was the assessment of a child, so it may be exaggerated a little. Dad was not one to lose an argument or to accept criticism. He would take offence and stomp off to the barn to pout. Mother was caught in the middle trying to keep peace.

Amy married Cal Danielson and Bill was born March 14, 1932. The marriage didn't last long after that. They divorced. (Dad often said that this was bound to happen because Mrs. Mellish couldn't keep her nose out of the marriage.) Cal made several attempts to see Bill and get custody. Each time this happened, Mrs. Mellish would pack up Amy and Bill, come to visit, and leave Bill with Dad and Mother. When things quieted down, they would come back to get Bill. Bill was shuttled back and forth between Chicago and Canada three times that I can remember.

Amy married Oscar Peterson. When Bill was about 8 years old, he returned to Chicago to live with his mother and Oscar. We thought Bill would finally have a stable home life. Later we learned that Amy's epileptic seizures had increase in strength and frequency. Often Bill would come home from school to find the door locked. Amy would be in the deep sleep that followed an attack, and not be able to get up to let him in. Oscar worked night shifts. Bill would be on his own until midnight when Oscar came home. He learned to do whatever it took to survive on the street.

When Bill was about 12 years old, Amy died in a epileptic seizure. Mother and Dad went to Chicago to settle her estate. Oscar was not prepared to take on the responsibility of a son. Mother and Dad brought Bill home for good. They wanted to adopt him, but the red tape was daunting. First was the fact that he was born in United States. Second, they had lost contact with Cal who would have had to agree. They were afraid that if they started legal proceedings, they could lose custody. Canada did not keep close track of immigrants, so nobody investigated. Bill became accepted as our brother.

When Bill was about 15, Cal Danielson came to visit him at Mother and Dad's. Memories of Cal's treatment of his mother kept the relationship strained. Oscar and his second wife contacted Bill later. This became a good friendship. They kept in touch throughout the years.

In 1967, Canada offered amnesty to persons living illegally in Canada. Bill applied and received his Canadian Citizenship.

Mabel's sisters also made contact with Mother, accepting her as their niece. I can remember visiting with Aunt Clara Roberts in Chatham. As usual, I had been well warned as to proper behaviour. I sat in a beautifully decorated living room afraid to move or speak, and that was hard for me. Aunt Edna Maltby lived in Richmond Hill. Meeting her was like seeing Mother's image, they looked so much alike. Then there was Aunt Ruth and Uncle Russell McTaggart. They owned a hotel in Lindsay. They had money and no children. Aunt Ruth was short and stout and ever so jolly. She always came bearing gifts. I felt favoured because I was her name-sake. It was such a delight to have them visit.

About 1933, Mr. Mellish also contacted Mother. In his own way, he claimed Mother as his daughter. It seemed he wanted to say he was sorry and to apologize but didn't know how. I remember him as an old man who was slightly crippled from a stroke. He was austere and unapproachable. Since I was an out-going kid who liked everybody, my opinion here could say a lot. The closest he came to admit his feelings was to make Mother the executor of his will when he died in 1937, just 6 months after Mrs. Mellish.

An interesting irony just struck me here. The Mellishes must have had deep feelings for each other but they couldn't live together. Their final wishes were to be cremated and their ashes buried together in a plot of land they had purchased together.

The Mellish connection influenced Mother's thinking all of her life. She never got over wishing for things that might have been.

THE COTTINGHAM TREE

Henry Cuttingham married Sarah Anne Caster
Immigrated from England to Canada about 1882

These were my Great Grandparents
Their children were my great aunts and uncles: their grandchildren were my second cousins.

Rose	Gertie	Annie	Lillie	Minnie	Mary	Ray	Fred	George
Smith	McPherson	(Gaines)	(Art)	(Tom)	(Jim)			
		Graham	Bowles	Mills	Graham			

Gertie McPherson —
Adopted
Murriel Irene
Mellish

Grandpa
Graham died
Grandma
married

Garret Dean
(Uncle
Garret)

THE MELLISH CONNECTION

Will Mellish/ Mable Funstone

Muriel Irene
(adopted by
Annie &
Graham)

Amy married
Cal Danielson

Bill Danielson
Born: Mar 14, 1932
Married: Feb. 2, 1952

Maxine Mc Donald

Children:

1. Dianne (Perry)
   Thomas
2. Pamela (Gene) Pulley
3. Tal

THE COTTINGHAM RELATIVES

Annie Cottingham was born June 2, 1877 in Sheffield, District of Brightside, County of York, England. She was the daughter of Sarah Anne Caster and Henry Cottingham. The family immigrated to Canada about 1882 taking up residence in the little settlement of Coatsworth. Grandma had a club foot which kept her from attending school because she could not walk the 2 miles to get there. Her Father, being a blacksmith, forged a kind of brace which he refitted regularly to force her foot and ankle to grow straight. Wearing this crude contraption was real torture for her and certainly must have contributed to her determination. One of her much repeated remarks was, "I won't let it beat me." The brace did straighten her foot enabling her to walk without a limp when she grew up. She attended school enough to learn to read, write, and do 'sums', a good education for girls in 1890. When she was about 10 years old, she worked as a maid for the Geddes Family who owned the General Store and had a big family. (She might have written Anne of Green Gables.) Grandma did not speak kindly of Mrs. Geddes!

Grandpa Cottingham soon left Coatsworth to open a smithy business, The Cottingham Harness Shop, in Tilbury. (Grandma (Annie) and Mabel Funstone operated a dress making shop in the back of the store.) When automobiles became popular, he became the mechanic who could keep them running. I can remember visiting his garage, one of the largest businesses in town. His sons and now some of their children still own and operate 'Cottingham Tire' which has grown to compete with Canadian Tire. Grandpa Cottingham died in his 99th year. He had a valid driver's license until he was 92!

There was a large Cottingham family. Large families were considered a blessing in early days. The more children you had, the more hands were available to help make a living. That meant, there were a lot of great-aunts and great-uncles in your extended family, as well as aunts, uncles, first cousins, first cousins once-removed, etc. You had to be careful what you said about someone because, sure enough, they could be related to the person you were talking to. Stammers, stutters and apologies were well practiced. Grandma's sisters were my great-aunts.

Aunt Rose Smith was the oldest in Grandma's family. She lived in New York State so it was always a special occasion when she came to visit. She looked so much like Grandma that they might have been twins.

Then there was Aunt Gertie McPherson. She had a twin brother who died on the ship coming to Canada. He was buried in Halifax. Aunt Gertie lived in Windsor. It seemed to me that she was 'well-off' (had money) perhaps because of her regal personality and clothing. Annie (Grandma) was the third daughter.

Aunt Lillie and Uncle Art Bowles visited Grandma a lot. They had a crippled, quite deformed, and mentally retarded son, Belvie, who couldn't walk or make himself understood. Belvie had been very ill when he was one or two years old. It was believed that it was this illness that left him crippled and mentally handicapped. We were well cautioned how to treat him, not to ignore him, and not to tease him. He seemed to enjoy kids so I would sit on the floor and show him a toy, talk and smile with him. Although I never knew if he understood, I was sure that that little bit of attention brightened a spot in his life.

Aunt Minnie Mills was the next sister. When the Mills retired from the farm, they moved into Wheatley just a few doors down from Grandma. I loved Aunt Minnie. She was so good humoured and understanding. She had the ability to listen and truly be interested when you talked to her.

Aunt May and Uncle Jim Graham lived in the Windfall community. This was another case of brothers marrying sisters. Jim Graham was Grandpa Graham's brother. Their children (first cousins once removed) were the same age as my brother Gaines and sister Jean, so we visited with them a lot.

There were three Cottingham boys, Ray, Fred, and George who continued to run the garage and tire business in Tilbury. Other than recognizing who they were, my memories are mostly connected to seeing them in the store.

LIFE WITH GRANDMA

Aᴄꜰᴛᴇʀ Gʀᴀɴᴅᴘᴀ Gʀᴀʜᴀᴍ ᴅɪᴇᴅ, Gʀᴀɴᴅᴍᴀ sold the farm to George Dunmore and moved into a new house that she had built in Wheatley. Shortly after that, she married Garret Dean, an arrangement set up by mutual friends.

Uncle Garret (we never did call him Grandpa), was a dear, sweet man who adored Grandma and waited on her hand and foot. He had a good job with Canada Bridge and Steel Company in Windsor, and owned a home on Moy Avenue (Now, why should I remember that? I'm sure I couldn't find Moy Avenue today.) Mother and Dad took chickens and eggs to the market nearly every Saturday. We always stopped at Grandma's before we came home. Old Mr. Dean, Garret's father lived with them. Grandma referred to him as 'the old gent'. Can you remember how cruel you could be as a child? I'm afraid I'll have to admit that I delighted in teasing this poor old man who had his place in an arm-chair behind the kitchen door. It was amazing the number of things that could be shoved through the crack between the door and door jamb.

Grandma Dean was a strict Victorian Lady who lived by the Victorian morals of the times. She was not backward about quoting these as gospel. How often did I hear:

> *It's a good thing those two married for it would be a shame to spoil two families; It's not enough to clean the outside of the cup only;*
> *Beauty is as beauty does;*
> *It's not enough to be good, one must appear to be good as well;*
> These three emphasized inner beauty but at the same time discouraged vanity.

The devil finds work for idle hands; Better not ever say, "I'm bored!"

Love goes where it's sent; Marriages were arranged. Make the
most of it.

A place for everything, and everything in its place; This asked for
more than just tidiness.

The road to hell is paved with good intentions; and

Never put off until tomorrow what can be done today; Warnings
against procrastination!

Familiarity breeds contempt;—A saying to keep you from
forming bad habits.

Waste not, want not—and

A fool and his money are soon parted,—lessons in thrift.

Don't wash your dirty linen in public;

Don't tell tales out of school; These two kept one from tattling
and gossiping.

Don't borrow trouble; You know, don't worry, be happy!

One task at a time, and that done well;—a lesson in order and
responsibility.

Cleanliness is next to godliness;—shall I go on? The next one
always hit me hard.

Children should be seen and not heard. That was an impossible task for
me. My feet wouldn't stay still and I never knew when to stop talking. One
look from Grandma could freeze me in my tracks. I walked on egg shells
when she came down to the farm. Mother worked outside in the barn
and in the fields a lot. This meant that the house was often 'neglected' as
Grandma would put it. Are you ready for this one?

An orderly house indicates an orderly mind. Grandma would come down
hard on Mother for not being a good housekeeper. After all, a good wife
was judged by the spotlessness of her housekeeping. Is it any wonder I felt
sorry for Mother and a bit afraid of Grandma's tongue?

May I digress for a minute?—It wasn't until I recalled these sayings
that I realized how much they shaped my personality and opinions as I
developed into the person I was to become. Did I chafe at some of the
stricter ones? Did I feel like rebelling sometimes? Of course I did. Why
didn't I? Well, first of all, it simply wasn't done. Secondly, I wanted to
go to school so I didn't do anything that would jeopardize that. Much
later I realized that I had used those rules to provided a safe wall that was

respected by my peers. Many times I said, "My Mother won't let me," when I hadn't even asked. It was a response that my friends respected, and it allowed me to save face in my refusal to go along with the crowd.

The discipline of the sayings became automatic to behaviour. I'm sure that they taught me how to assess, organize, prioritize, plan and persist in the job at hand. I must tell you how ingrained this became. This is the year of Harry Potter. I got the set of four books for Christmas. My neighbour, Grace asked me how I liked them. I answered, "I'm so upset with my Mother. She wouldn't let me start something new until I'd finished what I had started. So I have to finish the book I'm on before I can start Harry." We both enjoyed a good laugh over that. Yes, I did finish the other book first.

I can't remember ever being told that I couldn't try something new, or that I couldn't do something because I was a girl. The only stipulation was, "If you start it, you must finish it." This may have been some of Mother's sort of rebel nature that encouraged me to expand my horizons of existence. (Mother was one of the first farm wives to drive a car.) Those are assets that helped me succeed in the choices I made for my life.

Back to Grandma—Being English was a fact Grandma was very proud of. She always dropped her h's in words that started with 'h' and added an 'h' to a word beginning with a vowel. Harold was 'Arold' and Earl was 'Hearl'. She liked a drink of 'spirits'. This was forbidden during Prohibition (there's a period of history I'll leave you to research for yourself), so she made her own dandelion wine. No, I was never allowed to taste it although I often had to help gather the dandelion heads required to make it. Her liking for a whiskey night-cap was a ritual that the doctor approved as medication until she died.

Uncle Garret made very good wages so they had money to travel, spending some winters in California. Then the Great Depression hit. The company went bankrupt so he was without a job. Finally, they sold the house in Windsor and moved into Grandma's house in Wheatley. Garret did whatever jobs he could find to supplement their living. He swept streets, shovelled snow and dug graves. This was quite a come-down for someone who had been making a good salary, but I can't remember him complaining or feeling sorry for himself.

When I was 16, going into Grade 13, my last year in high school, I transferred from Comber Continuation School to Wheatley Continuation School because I could get the 9 credits required to go to Normal School in one year there. I stayed with Grandma and Uncle Garret. This was a big step for Grandma because she considered it a waste to educate a girl who would just get married anyway.

Grandma believed that praising a child taught them to be too proud, and pride was a sin. That could certainly put a damper on a child's spirit. Success had to be celebrated silently. Garret was always generous in his praise of my school work while Grandma always said, "You can do better." However, when her friends came in for an evening, (I was expected to disappear) I once overheard her telling them how dedicated I was to my studies.

There were some pretty strict rules at Grandma's house. I was expected to come home from school without dawdling along the street. Nor was I allowed to leave the house after school unless it was to run an errand for her. Don't leave anything in the bathroom, and be sure to scrub off the ring in the tub. Hang up the towels to dry, hang up your clothes, and keep your bedroom picked up, left no room for argument or excuses. I appreciated the chance to stay there to go to school so much that I did my best to toe-the-line.

I loved Garret who quietly did his best to temper Grandma's domination. He had Irish sayings that I considered pretty unique:

> The sun, the sun, the beautiful sun,
> That shines on the rich and the poor!
> > and
> If bread is the staff of life
> Whiskey is life itself!
> > and
> `That's a lazy wind today
> It's too lazy to go around, so it goes through.

I believe Mother paid Grandma about $2.00 per week for me to stay with them, plus fresh eggs, butter, cream and milk to help off-set the cost of food.

Grandma always did her housework in the morning. After lunch, she would dress up, complete with earrings and beads to receive callers. She pieced quilts, and did beautiful knitting, crocheting and tatting. Oh, yes, she made soap that could get socks as white as new. Your mothers will remember that. When they were teenagers, they used Grandma Dean's soap to scrub their white socks clean. Grandma loved to go to auction sales. She had an eye for fine things as shown in the art, lamps and glass that she collected.

Uncle Garret became ill to the point where he couldn't drive. At age 50, Grandma learned to drive their 1932 Chevrolet Sport Coupe with a rumble seat and wooden-spoke wheels. (Pretty classy even then). She drove that car all over, including to North Bay to see the Dionne Quints. The distance at that time would take 5 or 6 days each way. She never drove faster than 30 mph, (the speed limit was 35) which was fine with most drivers because many people thought that 35 was a break-neck speed anyway. Road rage was unheard of!

In 1951 Uncle Garret died of Pernicious Anaemia—today it would probably be identified as Leukemia. He never lost his positive attitude or appreciation for each day's blessings. To Grandma's credit, she did a complete turn-about-face. For years he had jumped at her every whim and demand. During his illness, which became debilitating to the point where he couldn't get out of bed, she looked after him with great care, love and devotion.

In 1957-60, we lived in Wheatley across the street from Grandma Dean. Erla, Debby and Jill often ran errands for her. She paid them with pans of fresh, home-made buns hot out of the oven. This was such a special treat when served with real butter that they used to argue about who would go. She enjoyed going on Sunday drives with us. I marvelled at the change in her attitude about children. She never complained about being in the back seat with the three girls. Just don't get home before 4 o'clock, for any time before that was too late to start something and too early to get supper.

Grandma was proud of the fact that she lived in her own home and looked after herself until she was well past 80 years old. She lived in the Home for the Aged in Chatham and enjoyed being the grand old lady with the nurses. When she realized the strain it was putting on Mother to make the trip to Chatham every week, she had herself transferred to the Home in Leamington. She lived long, as her father had done, passing away in 1975 in her 99th year.

MY FAMILY TREE

Earl Austin Willan	married	Mariel Irene Graham
Born: Mar, 2 1982	Sept. 22, 1915	Born: May 1, 1896
Died: June 21, 1972		Died: Mar 12, 1982

Anna Jeanne	Russel Gaines	Edwin Earl	Ruth Irene	Elinore Rosalind
Born: Oct 18, 1916	Born: Jan 15, 19818	Born: Mar 14, 1922	Born: Feb 4, 1927	Born: June 13, 1937
Died: Oct 20, 2007	Died Jan 8, 1997	Died: Oct 20, 1998		

Married:	Married:		Married:	Married:
Aug 31, 1935	Oct 12, 1937		Jul 18, 1946	June 13, 1959
Harold Sova	Jean Knister		Mac Drummond	Harold Dundas
B: Sept 15, 1912	B: July 9, 1918		B: Sept 22, 1920	B: Jan 15, 1934
D: May 13, 1985	D: Oct 21, 1997			

Children:

1) Dee Ann
(Ken) Johnson
    Tyler
    Erin

2) Barbara
(Doug) Ross
    Jeannine

    Brandon

Children:

1) Donald
(Gerry Hickson)
2) Shirley
(Larry) Belanger
    Donna Kaye
    Christine
    Kelly
3) Donna (Ken)
Hartley
    Kyle
    Tricia
4) Linda
(Gordon) Ciliska
    Michael
    Divorced, married
    Donald Clark
5) Leonard
(Trudy Lansue)
    Wayne
    Lynn
6) Robert
(Janis Bailey)

    Ryan
    Tyler

Children:
See your tree

Children:
1) Fred (Wanda)
    Maria
    Molly
2) Susan
(Greg) Platsko
    Twins: Maxwell
    Valerie

3) Hal (Christine)

    Connor
    Dylan
4) Heather
(Brad Cobby
    Andy
    Divorced, married
    Mike Rupert
    Donovan
    Calvin
5) Neil (Angie)
    Olivia
6) Kenneth
(Christine)
    Lorrayne
    Divorced, married
    Maggie Rivait
    Willow
7) Garnet
Heather Page

My mother, Irene, and father, Earl in their wedding photo, 1915

THE WILLAN CLAN

WHEN DAD AND MOTHER MARRIED September 22, 1915, the extended Willan family became a part of my ancestry. Dad had 5 sisters and 2 brothers. His brothers, Uncle Edwin and Uncle Russell were killed in World War 1. (See their story titled Ghost Brothers)

Theirs was a family with very close ties. As a child. I have fond memories of visiting with his sisters, who were my aunts, and their families: Aunt Winnie and Uncle Alvin McIntosh (children: Jack, Donald, Murray, Bill), Aunt Orphy and Uncle Mahlon Keith (children: Marion, Harold, Jean), Aunt Effie and Uncle Norm Whittal (children: Marjory, Russell, Mildred, Albert), Aunt Reta and Uncle Bill Tetzlaff (children: Wilbur, Kenneth), Aunt Bertha and Uncle Ray Beacom (children: Betty, Bob, Ronald, Rosemary, Linda). That's 18 first cousins. This kind of family is called an extended family.

All my Aunts and Uncles lived within 10 miles, (16 Kms.), of each other. Either we visited them or some of them came every week to play cards, or to eat ice-cream made in our ice-cream maker. Dad had an ice house; that is a building where, during the winter, blocks of ice were cut from Lake Erie or Lake St. Claire, hauled home, and packed in saw dust, to be dug out in the summer for the ice-box, (no refrigerators), to chill summer drinks, (didn't have freezers), and to make ice cream.

Making ice cream was a ritual! Everyone accepted Mother's recipe as the best in the country. I think the secret was fresh eggs and real cream, or perhaps the fact that she never had enough wood to over-cook the ingredients—but that's another story. The cooled mixture was put into a 2-gallon stainless steel canister which had a wooden beater in the middle and a square metal axle that protruded through a hole in the lid. The canister was centred into an oaken bucket. The end of the axle fitted into cogs that turned the paddle when you turned the handle. Then crushed ice mixed with salt was packed between the canister and the bucket. Several someone's had to turn the crank and keep adding ice until the cream inside was frozen enough that you couldn't move the handle. More ice and salt were packed around and over the bucket, then covered with heavy rugs to keep it cold until you HAD A PARTY! Dare I say that making the ice cream and anticipating the eating was also fun? Anyway, it seems that it was.

Uncles Bill, Norm, Ray and Dad were all very good barbers, so when it was time for a haircut, it was time for a family visit. Most folks couldn't afford to go to a barber. It wasn't unusual for one or more family members to master the art. The joke was if you got a bad cut, wear your hat for a couple of weeks. Maybe that's why you see men wearing hats in so many of the old pictures.

Then, of course, each spring and fall, there were the bees for killing the beef and pork for each family. Seldom did you buy meat from a butcher. You raised and slaughtered what you needed twice a year. Dad and the Uncles gathered at the barn where the 'meat' animal was killed, hung up, skinned out and eviscerated. The heart and liver were saved. In the case of pork, the head and feet would also be save and later cooked up to make head-cheese. Sometimes the intestines would be emptied, turned inside out, thoroughly washed and used as casings for sausage. Little was wasted. The hides were sent for tanning or traded for finished leather that was needed to keep harness in repair. I just realized how gruesome all this sounds today, but it was a part of life on a farm at that time. Few people realize this is done in an abattoir today—nice and clean, and hidden away from the eyes of the shopper in the super market or deli.

But hey, that was only the beginning. In the house, Mother and the Aunts started the job of preserving the meat—remember, no refrigerators or freezers. Beef was packed into glass jars, covered with salted water, lids put on loosely, inserted into a boiler of water and cooked for several hours. The jars were removed, sealed tightly and stored on the shelf. The pork was usually 'fried down', that is cut into slices, the fat cooked out, the meat packed in a crock and covered with the rendered lard. When the job was completed at our house, then the crew moved on to the next uncle's farm. Wow! talk about cholesterol! Makes McDonald's food look pretty good.

If no one was at my house after school, I would walk to Aunt Effie's, which was a real treat. Her kitchen was always warm and smelled of fresh-baked cookies. Cookies and milk remind me of her to this day.

I liked visiting with all the aunts and uncles, but I think that Aunt Bertha and Uncle Ray's home was the best. Of all the relatives during the depression, they were the poorest. He was an itinerate worker doing whatever work he could find. He was a butcher in a slaughter house and a share-crop tobacco farmer. Finally he got a job as a gardener for a man with an estate in Kingsville. This man appreciated the love Uncle Ray put into his work, hiring a young man to help him when he got older. When it came time for Uncle Ray to retire, this generous man gave him a pension and a life lease on the pretty little gardener's house. Though there were hard times and very little money, there was always so much laughter and love in their house. Uncle Ray had a wonderful sense of humour and could make a joke and have fun with the simplest of situations.

1ˢᵗ Row: Grandpa Willan, Uncles Edwin and Russell, Aunt Effie, Aunt Retta, Grandma Willan with Aunt Bertha on her lap.

Standing: Aunt Winnie, Aunt Orphy, My Dad Earl Circa 1904

THE GHOST BROTHERS

(This is the story I gave to Barbara Smith who writes books of ghost stories. An edited version appears in *Canadian Ghost Stories,* page 171)

U NCLE EDWIN AND UNCLE RUSSELL enlisted in the Canadian Army in 1916. Uncle Edwin was killed in the spring of 1918 and was buried in France. Uncle Russell was listed as missing, presumed killed in action, just a few days before the Armistice, in November, 1918.

Grandma and Grandpa Willan had pictures set in those beautiful oval frames with the convex glass that were popular at the time. When Mother and Dad took over the family farm, the pictures remained in the parlour, under their care. I was raised with the pictures of these treasured uncles. I found them fascinating, with the hint of impish mischief that played at the corners of each mouth, and eyes that followed you no matter where you were in the room—a feature typical of pictures in the early 1900's.

Eventually, Mother and Dad sold the farm and moved to a new home in Wheatley. The pictures went with them, again hung in a corner, facing each other, as they had always been. In 1978, after Dad's death, when Mother could no longer remain by herself in her home, there was a question of who would take care of Uncle Edwin and Uncle Russell. Eventually, they ended up with Leonard Willan, Gaines' son and his wife Trudy. Trudy, who treasures family history, proudly hung the pictures side by side in their living room.

In 1991, when Trudy and Leonard were visiting us in Sundridge, Trudy asked me if I believed in ghosts. When I hesitantly said, "Yes," she told me what had happened while the pictures hung in her home. She has been reluctant to tell the story, even to other family members.

Within a month after the pictures were hung in Leonard and Trudy's home, Leonard got up one morning and announced that the pictures had to go.

"Those two boys ran through the house all night," he said. "I didn't get any sleep."

After a few days, when he became more agitated and insistent, Trudy decided to move the pictures deep within their daughter Lynn's closet. No one knew that she had put them there. The following morning, Lynn complained at breakfast that she couldn't sleep all night because those two boys in army clothes made too much noise playing games and chasing each other around her bedroom. It was then that Trudy decided to pass the pictures back to Gaines. She didn't tell him why she wasn't keeping the pictures. Having no suitable spot to hang them, he tucked them into a cubby hole under the eave in his home.

Some time later, Gaines's daughter Linda came home for a visit. She slept in the bedroom next to the hidden pictures. The next morning, she went to Trudy's for coffee and complained that she hadn't slept well because these two kids in army uniforms had chased each other through the upstairs all night. From that time on, whenever Linda stayed over night, she refused to sleep upstairs, choosing instead to curl up on the chesterfield.

I then provided Trudy with some background about the uncles that she did not know. Uncle Edwin and Uncle Russell joined the army when they were still kids, just 17 years old. The boys were almost like twins, 10 months apart in age, and usually inseparable. Tales of their pranks on each other and unsuspecting members of the community were often repeated and enjoyed by those who escaped their wit.

One such prank, that Dad liked to tell, involved a neighbour who was not very well liked in the community. He had no patience with 'kids in the field'. It seems there was a threshing bee at this neighbour's farm. A load of sheaves had been left pulled up to the threshing machine, ready for an early start the next morning. There was a full moon that night. The two brothers, with a couple of like-minded friends, went over after midnight. They unloaded the wagon, tore it down, took it to the top of the barn roof and reassembled it straddle of the ridge board. Then they hauled up the sheaves and completely reloaded it. What a sight for the men the next morning when they returned to finish the threshing!

Back to the pictures and the rest of the story. In 1992, when Jean and Gaines retired to Wheatley, again the question was, what do we do with Uncle Edwin and Uncle Russell? The family decided to donate the pictures to The Royal Canadian Legion in Wheatley. The Legion members graciously accepted the gift and hung the brothers, with an identifying bronze plaque, in the Legion Hall. Shortly after that, the Legion building mysteriously caught fire and was badly damaged by smoke and water. Did the displaced brothers have anything to do with it? Who knows?

Who has the pictures now? Bill Danielson has a passion for antiques and family heirlooms. In the spring of 2000, he went to the Legion, found the pictures tucked away in a cupboard, and brought them home with him. He says the photographs and glass are still in good condition, but the wooden frames are warped and the finish is peeling. They are packed in his storage room with other antiques waiting to be restored. Since he too was raised with the pictures and doesn't believe in ghosts, he and his family have experienced no further antics from the brothers.

MY DAD, EARL AUSTIN WILLAN—(Your Great Grandfather)

H IS FAMILY WAS DAD'S LIFE. He kept close ties with his sisters and their families. He loved his children. He loved to rock his babies, and to hold them on his knee. The baby always sat on Dad's knee at mealtime so that Mother would be free to serve the food. This is where we learned to taste food. A tiny bit of mashed potato, carrots, a crust of bread dipped in fruit juice would find its way into a baby's mouth. I guess that's why they never fussed. Nutritionists today would have a fit, wouldn't they? When the youngest baby was replaced by another, or grew old enough to sit on a chair, he/she was placed at Dad's right side. He filled your plate and saw that you ate. I mean ate—whatever he put there! If you didn't like it, you ate a small spoonful for medicine. Of course, you didn't refuse medicine. I hated carrots, but had to at least taste them. Wonders! Today carrots are one of my favourite vegetables.

Although Dad had a limited education, equivalent to Grade 4 today, he read a lot and was a deep thinker. He opened himself to children who were not critical or judgemental of the thoughts that ran around in his head. Perhaps some of them came from his psychic mother. He was in awe of the size and distances in the expanse of space in the sky above his head. Long before airplanes were a common sight in the sky, he believed that man would one day walk on the moon. When that became history in 1958, he was literally glued to the television. He believed that there was a strong possibility of extraterrestrial life in the universe. He would muse, "Mankind is pretty egotistical to think that he is God's only creation in the vastness of space." Satellites into space and the Hubble Telescope, along with investigative studies that force new space premises, seem to support that fact, even though there are still those who are sceptical.

Dad had his own interpretation of the scriptures. He believed in life after death but thought that 'fire and brimstone' sermons frightened people away from a God that he saw as the model of love. He never argued about scripture, even though he seldom passed up an opportunity to argue in other areas. He believed that the Bible was so written that the answer and strength you needed for any situation or problem could be found with your own reading and understanding. Perhaps that came from his Quaker heritage. He neither drank alcohol nor smoked tobacco or hemp. He seldom missed going to church, believed it was wrong to take God's name in vain, and found it hard to tolerate a liar or a gossip. If he worried, it seldom showed, for he believed that God was in control of the universe. I remember him giving me this advice,

"Ruth, what are you worrying about? Are you sure it will happen? If the answer is yes, then prepare yourself for it. If the answer is no, then don't borrow trouble. It may never happen."

Dad found it difficult to work alone, so he welcomed anyone who would tag along, even if they were too small to help much. You were a handy 'gofer'. We were encouraged to do what we could to help with the chores. I started by feeding the chickens. There was a feisty little rooster in the flock. He would come up behind you, and fly/jump to the nape of your neck flogging you with his wings. It was hard to have eyes in the back of your head. One day I heard him coming, and swung around with the pails I had in each hand. I hit the monster in the head, oops, and killed him. We had chicken for supper.

Then I was promoted to gathering the goose eggs from the coops in the orchard. The eggs were carefully gathered and stored until there were enough to go into the incubator, where Mother would monitor the temperature and turn the eggs every 24 hours until the goslings hatched. So gathering the eggs without cracking the shells was a very important task. The problem—the three or four ganders kept with the geese to make the eggs fertile. Ganders are very protective and fight fiercely to establish their territory and to guard their flock. An attack on a careless intruder meant beating with powerful wings that could leave you well bruised. So it became a test of who could outsmart whom. I would wait until the ganders were in the far corner of the orchard, dart through the gate, crawl head first into the coop, carefully deposit the eggs in my basket, check to see if I was still safe from the ganders, head for the next coop, crawl in, gather, crawl out, next coop, until I had finished. Then I headed for the gate to escape with a few feet to spare before the ganders came hissing with outstretched necks in protest.

Dad took great pride in his horses—like a man takes pride in a beautiful car today.

For several years he took in horses for Mr. Burgess who had a ranch in Alberta. The range-wild animals were shipped by rail to Tilbury in the fall. Dad would get 6—three teams—which were to be broken to harness by spring. This was a winter project for him and brought in some extra, much needed cash. Sometimes it took several weeks just to quiet them enough to get them harnessed. With the first heavy snowfall, a team would be hitched to the bob sleighs and driven in the 25 acre field beside the barn. Of course they ran, but where could they go? With the snow and weight of the sleigh, they soon gave up. Within a week they would behave like a well trained team. Farmers liked to get a team he had broken to harness because he never mistreated his animals, who in turn, trusted their driver.

A beautiful, fine featured horse came from the west. She was too light to be a work horse. Dad and Mother bought her for me for my 12th birthday. I think they paid $50.00 for her. She came complete with a brand, mange, lice, and total fear of humans. Once the mange and lice had been eliminated, I spent the evening chore time gaining trust and making friends with Nancy. That's what I named her.

By spring, it was time to break her to the second-hand western saddle that Dad had bought for me. The fun began! As I have said, I was tiny for my age. My legs barely came two thirds of the way down the barrel of her stomach. That didn't give much purchase to hang on with. Dad put her on a lunge line and I climbed aboard—for a minute, before she bucked and I rolled off on the ground. The family directive to try again put me back up, and then off, and back up, and then off, until she decided I could stay up. We became buddies after that. She was a women's mount. She wouldn't tolerate a man on her back. She was a 5-gaited little mare, perhaps with some Tennessee Walking Horse somewhere in her breeding. Smooth! A ride on Nancy was like sitting in a rocking chair.

Dad, who had a good eye for fine horse flesh, showed his horses at the country fairs for many years. At first he had grade animals. As he learned the tricks of picking good horses and showing them to advantage, he was a regular winner and became known throughout Essex and Kent Counties for his foals, yearlings, and teams. A horse from his barn always brought a good price. After Gaines was married, he quit going to the fairs to help

Dad show. I was next in line. It was a lot of work getting horses ready for the show ring—training, bathing, currying, braiding. I learned to put in some neat braids done with ribbon made from strips of broadcloth, and crepe paper roses made by hand weeks before fair time.

Besides showing the draft animals, I showed Nancy. There was a wealthy riding club from Windsor dressed in expensive habits, who came in to show expensive horses with expensive tackle. They were not impressed when this whippet of a farm girl in home made jodhpurs, who had never had a riding lesson, on a horse from the prairie with a brand yet, sitting an unadorned second hand saddle, cantered into the ring and took the prize in each class. Nancy would go into the 5th gait, dance smoothly on the spot if you asked her to, and catch everybody's eye, including the judge's. After one class for horsemanship, one of the riders complained to the judge. Dad heard him reply, "Lady, you couldn't handle the horse flesh that little girl is riding. You don't have the hands."

After I married and left home, Rosalind helped Dad show the horses. She had a little Indian Pony named Dixie who loved to jump. English riding with jumps was just beginning to get popular. She and Dixie were a matched pair—she said, "jump", and Dixie said, "How high?" They were winners. Again, the club from Windsor hated being beaten by a little, untrained, country girl who rode by the seat of her pants. Somehow, someone got into the stable just before a competition and gave Dixie a needle filled with a drug. The gallant little horse became confused and uncooperative in the ring. She refused to take a jump, tossing Rosalind head first into the poles. She suffered a concussion. Dad found the spot on the pony's shoulder where the needle had been injected, called the vet, and laid a complaint. Nothing could be proven. No one was caught. Dixie refused to ever jump again.

Dad had a small draft team of Belgian mares that were absolutely striking, Perfectly matched, they were the colour of burnished copper. He named one Penny, the other Goldie. This little team won ribbons everywhere they went. Silverwood's Dairy in Windsor bought them for Dairy Delivery Wagon horses. Twenty nine years later when I sat in the staff room at Almaguin talking to Walter Streich, another teacher who had come from Windsor, I mentioned this team. It's a small world.

"Yes," said Walter, "I knew those horses well. I delivered milk during the summers and on week ends to work my way through university. I drove Penny. She had the original computer brain. She knew every street and every stop. She did everything but carry the milk to the door. When the company took the horses off the street, she was turned out to pasture where she happily spent the rest of her life."

"Do you know what happened to Goldie?" I asked. The answer was not so happy. Goldie had been equally as faithful for many years, until, one day, a car went out of control, hit her, and she had to be put down. As long as Silverwood's was in business, photos of these two horses hung in the offices.

Dad's dream was to one day show horses at the Royal Winter Fair in Toronto. This was, and still is, THE fair of all fairs in Canada. A horse good enough to win at that level had to be a registered pure-bred animal. He bought a 10 year old, Clydesdale mare, Lady, and took her to Lindsay to be bred by a top, prized stallion each spring. Over the next 7 years, Lady presented him with 7 filly foals, each perfectly matched with the other. Did they win? Indeed they did. The year before he retired, he took a team and a 2-year filly to the Royal. He won prizes with all of them, but in addition, one filly won the Reserve Grand Champion ribbon! A dream come true.

When it came time to quit farming, Dad had Lady and 3 of her foals left in the barn. He took them to the horse auction in Lindsay where he knew buyers would recognize the breeding. At that time, Carlsburg Brewery, from United States was planning to expand their 6-hitch show team to an 8-hitch. The horses they had were all half-sisters, being off-springs from the stallion Dad had used for breeding Lady. The Mennonite farmers had come to buy horses. Now, they knew fine horse flesh when they saw it, and wanted at least one of those mare. They didn't have the kind of money that backed the brewery so they finally had to give up the bidding. The three mares sold for an almost unheard of price at that time—nearly $2000 each. Lady was 18 years old. The Mennonites bought her for $600, still a big price for an animal that old, but they thought that, with good care, she would give them one or two more foals. All's well that ends well!

Dad never showed cattle at the fairs, but he did become interested in raising registered Guernsey cattle. About 1947, he and Mother started with a small herd which in time grew to about 30 registered animals. They worked hard and took a great interest in these cows, going through all the red tape it took to have them listed as an *accredited herd*. Accreditation meant that each cow in the stable was blood tested every three months to guarantee that the herd was disease free. The stable was checked at the same time for cleanliness.

Tuberculosis was a dreaded disease in Essex County. It is very contagious so infected patients were sent to a large sanatorium (hospital) in Windsor to recover. There was little medication at that time. Treatment was mainly fresh air and unpasteurized milk from accredited cattle. For several years a refrigerated milk truck from the sanatorium picked up the milk from the cooler at Dad's farm.

A government milk tester came once a month to weigh each cow's production and to check the level of butterfat in the milk. One cow set the record for butterfat production by a Guernsey cow in Ontario three months in a row. That was like winning a gold medal at the Olympics! She was now a very expensive animal which a lot of top breeders wanted in their barns. Yes, Dad sold her. He felt she was too good to stand in his lowly stable.

Dad always suffered from what was commonly called sick headaches. When he did heavy work, he would have a headache that brought on debilitating nausea. Because he looked healthy, many people thought he 'put it on' to get out of work. He had taken out a disability health policy when these were first introduced. By the time he was 40, his headaches became so bad that the family doctor suggested that he apply for the disability payment of $30. a month. The insurance company, of course, didn't want to pay it. They sent him to specialists all over Canada and United States. The diagnosis was always the same. He had arthritis in his back which pinched nerves causing the headaches and sick stomach. He should never do physical work for the rest of his life. The company kept pressing him to take a cash settlement. When the amount grew to a sum that would pay off the mortgage on the farm, he decided to take it. This took some of the strain off the family during the depression and made it possible to hire help with the heavy work.

In time, Dad's back and neck grew solid with arthritis, restricting movement in his neck and back. When that happened, he no longer had headaches.

Now, doctors know a lot more about arthritis, the causes and treatment. However, it is not completely understood why it is inherited in some families. In my family, all 5 of us have arthritis in some area of our bodies. This is unusual. Perhaps the advancement in gene studies will one day provide the answer and cure.

MY MOTHER, MURIEL IRENE (GRAHAM)
WILLAN—(Your Great Grandmother)

MY MOTHER WAS A SMALL, (5'4") very pretty woman. She had beautiful brown hair with highlights that caught and reflected the colour. It turned prematurely white by the time she was 40. Her eyes were the deepest brown I've ever seen, and at times could dance with humour. I was always a little disappointed that I did not inherit her eyes. Her complexion was flawless. Women of her time did not wear make-up. Her only cosmetic was a bit of cold cream. When she worked out in the sun, she kept her arms covered and wore a large straw hat. A summer tan was not fashionable. Perhaps the protection from exposure to ultra violet rays contributed to her eternally youthful face. Although her hair turned white by the time she was 40, I can't remember her with wrinkles.

Mother loved her children dearly but was brought up not to show affection openly for fear of spoiling your child. This was the Victorian role for a woman instilled to the bone by Grandma Dean. When she hugged or kissed me, I sensed a kind of embarrassment on her part, which made me feel a little sad for her. A woman's success and worth were judged by how well she looked after her house, husband and children. Super Woman—that's right. It was part of your role to solve every family problem. Mother took it seriously. She tried to show her love with a dedication to being a good wife and mother through hard work. And she worked hard all her life!

Mother always seemed to be on the run, trying to catch up with herself. We used to say her feet ran to keep up with her head. A fourteen to eighteen hour day was never long enough. She would come in from doing barn chores and after supper, when everyone else had settled down, she would clean up the kitchen, do the dishes, maybe scrub the floor, do the ironing, or catch up on the house work that was still there to be done. The men never dreamed of pitching in. You know, even as a 10 year old, I thought there was something wrong with that picture. When I think about it now, I regret that we took her dedication for granted. We didn't say 'thank you' often enough.

Mother always had one more thing to do. That usually made us late when we were going somewhere. How I hated being late! I thought that if I did more to help it would solve the problem, so I took over dressing Rosalind to go to church. Jean made Rosalind pretty little dresses from lace and taffeta which showed her off like a precious doll. It was a thrill to dress her up, complete with matching panties, socks and hair ribbons. One Sunday, she toddled out of church and fell down on all fours. The skirt of her dress came up over her head revealing the heavy, faded, blue panties that were her everyday wear. I had forgotten to put on the ones to match her dress. I felt Mother's embarrassment as my own. I'm glad it wouldn't mean that much today.

Mother did house work because it had to be done, not because she liked doing it. One reason may have been that she had very little to keep house with. There was little money to buy groceries, and as a good wife, she was expected to make do with what there was. She was a good cook but there were limited supplies in the cupboard to cook with. She made wonderful biscuits that almost made the meal when they came hot out of the oven. When asked for the secret of good biscuits, she would say, "You have to make them quickly and get them into the oven immediately." That must have been true. Mother never had time to dawdle over anything!

Three times a week, she made bread, four to five loaves at a time. Fresh from the oven, it was delicious. I hated sandwiches made from it when it was two or three days old. It had dried out by then, there being no waxed paper or air tight containers to store the loaves. I used to trade my sandwiches with Maxine Stratford who had sandwiches made from store bought bread. Her mother didn't bake bread, and mine never bought bread. We both thought it a fair deal. My lunch would consist of a sandwich made from cold meat left over from last night's meal, or if that wasn't available, brown sugar or a hard boiled egg. Do you know that baked beans spread on bread make a great sandwich? So do mashed potatoes. There was seldom any baking, but usually there was a carrot and an apple from the winter storage pit.

Fresh bread usually came out of the oven late on Saturday night, and would be left to cool on the table until morning. Before Jean and Gaines were married, they came home with their friends one night, found the bread cooling on the table, and decided to have a snack. An argument arose over who would get the choice crust slice. To keep everyone happy, they cut a round loaf, that is they cut six slices from around the sides, plus the top and bottom. It was really quit ingenious! Everybody got a crust. The soft inside sat on the table the rest of the night to dry out. Mother was irate—not that they had eaten the bread, but rather that they had wasted the rest of the loaf.

Mother cooked on a wood stove. More times than not she would have to scrounge for wood chips or wait for Dad to cut and split a log before she could cook a meal. Somehow, she managed to have something ready to eat at noon each day.

When company would show up unexpectedly, Mother would put on the tea kettle and disappear out the side kitchen door. She would go to the hen house, catch two or three chickens, and holding them by the legs with one hand, she could flop the heads, one at a time, over the chopping block at the wood pile and in no time have them dressed and ready to be cooked.

—Let me tell you.—Years and years later, when Mac and I moved to the farm on 124, one Saturday, I decided that I would dress out three fryers (that's chickens grown big enough to cut in half and fry) for Sunday's dinner. Now it had been some time since I had dressed a chicken, but hey, it's like riding a bicycle, you never forget—eh! So, there I was, all alone, with three chickens held by the legs in one hand, at the chopping block, with the axe in the other. I made one whack and started to laugh. I saw my mother all over again!

Mother much preferred to work outside. She went to the barn to help with the milking every morning and night. Each animal in the stable was special. There were often cows that would only tolerate her hands. Farming, of course, is a business. Animals are bought and sold. Every time a cow or horse was sold and left the barn, Mother would stand in the kitchen door and shed a tear.

Mother took as much delight from seeing the horses win at the fairs as Dad did. Showing took as much dedication on her part as on his. When he was at the fair, the barn chores would all fall on her shoulders. Then she would rush to pack a big lunch and get to the fair in time to see the horses shown. The evening chores and milking had to be done when she got home.

She seldom went to the field except to husk corn in the fall. Her job was to plant and care for the kitchen garden, growing the vegetables for summer meals and winter storage. The land on the farm was hard clay, and although Dad would do the basic preparation with the team or tractor, it still took a lot of thumping to find enough soil to cover the seeds. Hoeing and weeding were a constant challenge. Besides the vegetables, there was the strawberry bed to tend, along with raspberry, currant bushes and quinces. Dad and Mother had planted an orchard which provided apples, grapes, pears and plums. Mother saw that none of this went to waste, so there were hundreds of cans of fruit stored on the shelves each fall.

Our orchard did not brag a cherry tree, so in early July, when cherries were ripe, we would pack pails and ladders into the car and head for a cherry orchard around Leamington. You could buy a 'tree' for $3.00—that is, the cherries on a tree. Then you wrestled out the ladders and pails and picked until the tree was bare. There could be as many as 5 large pails full. Home you would go, wash and pit ready for canning. Of course, you ate while you picked, and you ate while you pitted, and expected the stomach ache that was sure to follow. But, oh, they were so good.

When Dad bought the threshing machine, he would be away from mid July until late September doing custom work. He was fed where he worked, so Mother enjoyed this time because it meant that there was no need to prepare big meals at noon or in the evening. We lived on green corn and tomatoes. Sweet corn as we know it today, had not been developed. We ate the regular field corn in the milk stage (hence, *green*), picked, husked and cooked for the table. I think we must have started the craze for toasted tomato sandwiches. By Thanksgiving, everyone was thankful that neither green corn nor tomatoes were fresh vegetables available in winter.

A need for ideas to add money to the meagre income was important. There was a salesman who painted a picture of profit from raising beautiful, big, Australian White Rabbits. You bought breeding stock from him, and because of the rapid multiplication of rabbits, you would have a product ready for the market in no time. Great idea! Too good to be true? So it seemed. Mother bought rabbits, soon had a house full, and no sale for the bunnies. Some she dressed and took to the market in Windsor. The rest ended up on our dinner table. Mother was creative. She could make rabbit taste like chicken, fried or roasted, and her rabbit stew could taste like pork.

The money to run the house was usually collected from the hen house which held 100-125 laying hens. Mother raised register white Leghorns, with roosters, to produce eggs for Neuhauser's Hatchery in Essex. Leghorns were hard to raise. If one bird got any sort of injury, the others would peck it to death. So we had a yard full of hens wearing 'specks', a small bit of coloured plastic-like apparatus that fitted over the bird's beak so that they couldn't see blood, and hence would not peck each other. Pretty ingenious, wasn't it. Soon, however, they changed to white Plymouth Rocks, which were bigger, heavier birds that were content to eat, lay eggs, and dust themselves in the dried dirt of the hen yard. Two to three crates of eggs (60 to 90 dozen) had to be taken to the hatchery once a week. The extra bother of raising nursery stock brought in 50 cents more per dozen for the eggs.

The young cockerels, i.e. roosters, made up about half of a hatch. These were not raised, because of course, roosters do not lay eggs. You could buy them for 1 cent each, and for another cent have them caponized (neutered). These birds would then grow to the size of small turkeys. Mother use to raise capons because they were in big demand at the market. Now there is a trivial question for you—what is a capon?

When winter settled in, Mother caught up on her sewing, a talent that was very useful. I remember Dad needing an overcoat. Mrs. Mellish had sent a bale of used clothing. One article was a well worn, heavy, woollen overcoat. Mother carefully ripped it apart, washed it by hand, pressed it and sewed it up wrong side out where the material still had a nap. It looked like a new coat and served Dad for several years.

When I was in high school, full, pleated, plaid skirts were in fashion. Mother wanted me to have one. She found red McIntosh plaid at a fire sale, at a price she could afford. When she got it home, there was less material than had been marked on the piece. The only way to get a skirt and match the plaid was to drop it on a yoke at the waist. With a red, wool sweater worn over it, no one knew about the yoke. Mother always felt badly about it, but I wore that skirt proudly for five years. In fact, it was still part of my wardrobe when I went to Normal School. When I took it off one day and held it up to the light, the material was so thin you could see through it. After that I only wore it if I was not taking off my coat.

Mother and Jean sewed quilt blocks in the winter evenings. Some of these were pieced, some appliquéd. The work was all done by oil lamp light, and sewn on a New Williams treadle sewing machine. Sometimes they quilted them by themselves, and sometimes they had a bee of neighbours or aunts to help. The frames would be set up in the dining room for three or four days. It was tempting to play under the quilt. If you got too active and bumped it anywhere, the women picked their fingers and you were pulled out by the ear from under it.

Mother either couldn't or didn't like to knit, but she did beautiful crochet work. She made doilies, table clothes, and afghans that family members prize today. Jane and Will have one of the last quilts, pattern "Tree of Life", which she pieced when she was 80 years old. The younger grandchildren have baby afghans which I crocheted from her Basket Weave pattern.

Each of us was expected to learn to sew at an early age. Before you were allowed to touch the sewing machine you had to be able to sew well with a needle. You usually started with embroidery stitches. My first pieces were done on bleached flour sacks with pictures I had drawn myself. Because I was home a lot, I had 20 or so of these squares done before I was 12 years old. When Erla was born, Mother set the blocks together to make a crib quilt for her. The print used to do this, and the lining have worn out, but the cotton in the blocks and the embroidery floss are still in good condition. Like Mother, one day when I have time, I will take it apart, and reset it with new material. In the mean time it remains stored on a closet shelf waiting for someday . . . .

Knowing how to sew has been an asset to all of us, helping us to dress our families. Rosalind has honed her skills and is qualified by the Canadian Heritage Association to reproduce and/or copy costumes for museums. She also has a clientele from Windsor who pay well for reproductions or new designs. This talent continues down the line. Rosalind's daughter, Susan has a diploma in design from Seneca College and does beautiful, original creations. Jill's Beth, is also studying along these lines.

Mother liked to play Bingo, and often won. She limited herself to Bingo because she realized the trap of gambling. One time at Leamington Fair, a Barker pulled her in to play the wheel. He let her win for a few turns, then took all her money—the $20.00 she had for the week's groceries. From that time on, we were all warned about the dangers of addiction and the unreality of expecting to win easy money.

Mother was a very talented woman. She played the piano and had a good singing voice. She sang in the church choir and sometimes sang the solo part. Jean tells me Mother sang when she went to the hen house, and the chickens would all start to cackle and sing back. I can remember her singing bits of songs to get a point across. When I would complain about a perceived injustice, she would sing,

"Oh, they always pick on me.
Never, ever let me be.
I know what I'll do
It ain't no joke.
I'll swallow a frog
And then I'll croak.
And when I'm gone
You just wait and see.
You'll all be sorry
That you picked on me!"

I have already mentioned that Mother used to give 'recitations' at special entertainments and programmes. I marvelled at her ability to quickly memorize long narrative poems, many of which she could still recite when she was 80 years old. With the energy and expression she put into her delivery, she could have been an actress.

With encouragement, Mother could have been an author. She had graduated from Public School, (Elementary) with a High School Entrance Certificate. That would be Grade 8 today. That was a lot of education for a girl in those days. It meant that she was an excellent speller, knew perfect grammar and sentence structure, and had command of an extensive vocabulary. She had a wonderful imagination which she was afraid to put on paper. Mother could write the most interesting letters. Her sense of humour came out in a letter she wrote to me when I was in Normal School. The letter was all in rhyme and made light of everyday things that filled our lives. She was also a whiz at cross-word puzzles.

I don't know when Mother found the time, but she read a lot. We were one of the few farm families who had a daily delivery of the *Windsor Star* newspaper. One of her few self-indulgences was the *True Story* magazine. She felt the stories had too much sex (oh, dear, forbidden knowledge) in them and would corrupt a teenage mind. She would hide the magazine in a draw-string bag that hung on the back of her bedroom door. I hate to admit it, but, when I was alone in the house, I would sneak out the magazine and read the stories quickly, replacing the book before she missed it. This makes me smile today. The 'sex' in those stories was little more than passionate kisses. I wonder where Mother might have hidden a Harlequin Romance! Or better still, could she have written one?

Dad and Mother sold the farm to Harold and Rosalind. They built a beautiful brick home in a new sub-division in Wheatley and enjoyed several years of retirement there. Dad took pride in his tea roses. Mother enjoyed travelling and seniors' activities.

During this time, they rented Mrs. Bell's little house in South River from May until Thanksgiving for two or three summers. Your parent will remember these visits well. They were special.

Dad died from heart problems and cancer in 1972. Mother was able to live on in her 'house that Dad built' for 6 more years until her health and memory began to fail.

She moved into the Senior's Home in Chatham where she spent, on the whole, a comfortable, happy time until she died from heart problems in 1982.

Seated: Mother Muriel Irene (Graham) Willan, and Father, Earl Austin Willan.
Standing: L.R. Ruth (that's me), Jean, Gaines, Edwin and Rosalind. Circa 1949

MY BROTHERS AND SISTERS

A NNA JEAN WAS THE FIRST born, October 18, 1916. Two years later, on January 15, 1918, Gaines Russell came along. Edwin Earl was the third child who showed up on Mar 14, 1922. Yours truly dropped in February 4, 1927. Elinore Rosalind took some thought and waited 10 years before joining us on June 13, 1937. Mother had Jean at 20, me at 30 and Rosalind at 40, so it was always easy to remember her age and ours.

Stories I've heard can be repeated here, I think. Jean and Gaines, being just 15 months apart, could think up all kinds of mischief—you know, two heads are better than one. Dad told them they could have only rusty nails to build their forts, whatever. It seems they had a big project and not enough nails, so they filled a pail with new nails, put that under the eave trough to fill with water. Right, in 3 or 4 days—rusty nails! They liked to play in the hay mow in the barn, jumping down to the thresh floor into a pile of hay. That's quite a drop and took a bit of nerve. Gaines was standing in the mow waiting to jump. Jean thought he was too slow and gave him a push. He hit the back of his head on the way down, waking up several hours later. We often used that bump to taunt him later when he did something foolish.

The hens were treated for lice in the fall before they were housed for the winter. Sometimes they were dipped in a solution as part of the treatment. One winter afternoon, when Jean and Gaines were playing in the barn, they caught 5 hens that were in the stable and proceeded to treat them for lice by dipping them in the potash kettle. Oh, oh! When Mother and Dad came to do chores, they found 5 very cold, wet, bedraggled hens, and a couple of kids were lectured—and maybe "OUCH"!

We were always short of water on the farm. There was a drilled well with a windmill back the lane, but the meagre stream of water it pumped was not enough for the animals. The eave troughs on the barn roof collected rain water into a large cistern at the corner of the barn. Water could be hand pumped into a large potash kettle inside the stable. (A potash kettle was made from heavy iron, shaped like half a sphere, and stabilized with three or four feet. It was used to boil the lye out of ashes. Lye was needed to make soap. The potash that was left was used as fertilizer.) In the spring, there was a good supply of water, but during the dry spells of the summer there was always a shortage.

In the corner of the field across the road there was a big pond. The farm was owned by Cates so the pond was referred to as 'Cates' Pond. My goodness, how original. Anyway, Dad had permission to draw water from the pond. Four wooden barrels would fit in the wagon. When full, each would be covered with a sack held in place by a stave to keep the water from sloshing out. A load of water would be drawn first thing in the evening to water the animals at supper time. After supper, the horses would be hitched to the wagon again to get another load ready for morning feeding. It was pretty tempting not to flick water at each other. That had a tendency to develop into a water fight. One really hot summer night, after Jean and Gaines had drawn the last load and turned the horses for the evening, the flicking got a bit out of hand and progressed to pails. They emptied all four barrels on each other. As a 5-year old standing in the shadow of the garage, I thought it looked like great fun. Dad thought otherwise! They had to bring the horses back into the stable, harness them, return to the pond and bring another load. As I remember, there wasn't much water spilled that time.

Baseball was the sport everyone played. Gaines played hard ball, Jean played soft ball. They said she could hit a ball as far as any man. She and her friend, Lena Robb played on the Leamington Women's Team. I don't remember seeing her play, but I do remember the uniforms. This was before it was fashionable for girls to wear pants, so the uniform had to keep the girl modestly covered, with room to play, and at the same time not seem too risqué. They wore blue wool serge bloomers that fitted below the knee with wool knee socks, and heavy white cotton middies with long sleeves. Imagine sweating in this outfit in the heat of a summer ball game! Only the catcher had a glove—well it *was* called *soft ball*—so you had to learn how to catch and give with the ball. Jean often came home with a sprained finger which kept her from playing the piano for a day or two. Sometimes I used to think it was a ploy to get out of practicing.

Jean and Gaines were good students at school. In those times, you went to school until you had passed your High School Entrance Exams or until age 14, whichever came first. In a one-room school with a good teacher, it was common to write these exams when you were 12 years old. They both wanted to go on to high school. Mother dreamed that her children would have a good education, but Dad didn't see the need of anything beyond the elementary level. Jean stayed home for a year, and then was allowed to go to high school for one year. There were no buses for transportation and cars still had limited use. She walked 2 miles to catch a ride with Mr. Washburn, the town clerk and Notary Public for the town of Comber. This was through rain, wind, snow, winter cold, as well as the nice weather. She left home at seven in the morning and returned at six in the evening. Add to that her farm chores and homework. She did not go on to school.

Gaines, who wanted to be a RCMP officer, would need 2 years at high school. When he saw the fight at home to get Jean to school, and the sacrifices she had made to get there, he gave in and went to work on the farm. Although he was a good farmer, his heart was never in it.

Gaines loved to hunt and fish. In the spring when the pike came up into the big ditch that ran across the road from the house he would feign being sick so he could stay home from school. Mother's remedy for a sick stomach was castor oil. He would take it without a fight, crawl back into bed until 9 o'clock, then get up and go fishing for the rest of the day (much of it with his pants down!)). We would have a good feed of fish that night for supper. When he got older, he would fish off the pier in Wheatley for pickerel. A special treat was to be invited for supper. No one cooked fish like he did.

You never knew what Gaines would bring home from a tramp with the gun. Whatever it was, we ate it—rabbit, turtle, squirrel, muskrat, and raccoon. Thank goodness he didn't like snakes! Jack Rabbits had been imported from Britain. The first one he shot and brought home was a novelty. Mother cooked it as she would have cooked a cotton tail. That was a mistake. It was the only time I ever saw her throw out something, pan and all. The stench was terrible. We never did eat Jack Rabbit. He went hunting deer in Northern Ontario a few times. Once he brought home a black bear which we ate. I don't remember the taste of the meat, but the hide was tanned and made into a rug which was the centre piece in the parlour for many years.

Isn't it funny how things work out. When Gaines was about 40 years old, the Raceway opened in Windsor. He got a job as a security guard, complete with badge and uniform. He was finally in his element.

There had been a bold armoured car robbery somewhere between the track and the bank. Gaines was working in the money room—that was a locked, guarded room where the money from the bets was counted and prepared for transport to the bank. A couple of days after the robbery, when he came to work in the money room, he found a bag that hadn't been completely emptied under a pile of other empty sacks. He called the office and light-heartedly chided them for being so careless after the robbery. A month or so later, he was sent to the office to pick up an envelope in the boss's top right-hand desk drawer. Imagine his surprise when he found, on the top of the pile, an 8x10 glossy photograph of himself and a complete account of all his movements both on and off the track since the robbery. He laughed and said it was a good thing he didn't have any money to throw around. He was removed from the list of suspects. (The robbery was never solved. Of the $2.5 million dollars stolen, less than $10,000 was recovered.) From then on, his promotions continued, until, by the time he was ready to retire, he was second in command in the security team.

I had never been to a horse race with betting and all, so just before he retired, I asked him to take us (Mac and me) to the track. That was like being royalty. When we approached the track, he directed us down the road to the stables. At the barred gate, he stepped out of the car and waved to the guard on duty.

"Good evening, Mr. Willan. Brought your family to the races?"

Magically, the gate swung open and we drove through.

"Turn right, here," Gaines said.

There was an empty parking space marked—MR. WILLAN. As we walked through the stables, grooms and owners called out,

"Good evening, Mr. Willan. Brought your family to the races?"

When we walked up to the ticket window to get our tickets into the grandstand, the girl behind the wicket said,

"Good evening, Mr. Willan. Brought your family to the races? How many seats do you need?"

I couldn't believe it. Here we were, sitting in some of the best seats in the viewing area at the raceway with MR. WILLAN, who obviously was somebody you treated with great respect. Our way had been made clear and it hadn't cost us a penny. If I remember correctly, I spent $20 betting—$2 on each of the 10 races, (last of the big-time spenders). I didn't win anything but I felt obligated to leave some money there in appreciation for the red carpet treatment. If you believe that, let me tell you about a bridge I have for sale.

EDWIN

F EW FAMILIES ARE GIVEN THE privilege of having an Edwin in their lives. It was at his death October 20, 1998, that we realized the blessings and the lessons of his life.

Who was Edwin? He was born March 14, 1922. When he was about 20 months old, an epidemic of Whooping Cough swept through the community. This was before a vaccine had been developed to protect children from this terrible disease. Many babies died. Edwin was stricken and lay desperately ill for days. He lived. Years later, when the medical technology became available, doctors found that the disease had interrupted the electrical impulses of the brain so that what Edwin thought and what he said were not necessarily connected.

Edwin was a particularly bright little boy. Before the illness, he talked in full sentences, could remember minute details, and sang words and music to hymns and children's ditties. When he recovered, he suffered with Grand-Mal Epilepsy, and had lost all his memory, how to walk and talk. For a period of time, he was deaf. One day he was sitting on the lane when an engine back-fired near him. He grabbed his ears and screamed. His hearing was restored! Though all this, Edwin did not forget how to carry a tune. He could still sing!

Back then, children like Edwin were often considered a disgrace to a family and placed in institutions. Mother and Dad would hear nothing of this. Edwin was their son, a gift from God, and theirs to love and care for. Years later when I heard someone refer to him as handicapped, I was really insulted. In our family, Edwin was Edwin, our brother. There was never a need to make excuses or explanations for him. He was never hidden away or ignored. He was accepted fully as a special member of the family.

Edwin was simply Edwin. To know the meaning of unconditional love was the first blessing Edwin's life gave our family.

Because what Edwin thought and what he said did not necessarily match, his actions and words had to be interpreted like a giant jig-saw puzzle. Edwin liked to go shopping, seldom asking for anything. Once, when he was staying with Jean at Christmas time, they went shopping in North Bay. Edwin kept saying, "Buy that box of chocolates, Jean Sova." So she did. When they got home, he kept insisting that she wrap up the chocolates. Finally she asked him why she had to wrap them. His reply, "You can't give them to Mother if they're not wrapped." It was always a challenge to figure out what Edwin was trying to tell us.

So much of who he was became statements for meaning in our own lives.

Time: Edwin always wore a watch that must keep time, even though he could not tell time. Sunday was the only day of the week with meaning, for that was the day we went to church. Years were governed solely by the seasons as they naturally came and went. Time was ordered, but not controlling. What a lesson to apply to today's stress and demands on our time.

Money: Edwin always carried a wallet, and that wallet must have money in it, even though he couldn't count money, earn it, or spend it. When he died, in his wallet, he had an old two dollar bill that Rosalind had given him many years before. He taught us that money is a necessary requirement for living, but money is not the measure of who we are.

Order: Edwin's life ran smoothly as long as there was order in what he was expected to do. If plans had to be changed, it disrupted his whole day, and he found it difficult to accept and accommodate the change. I had to smile when I visited him in the home in Chatham. On the corkboard beside the door in his room was a list of how to prepare Edwin for bed. Each step was numbered. The final notation read: If you do not deviate from the order of this list, you will have no trouble with Edwin. In Edwin's way, he seemed to realize that to live within the order of the universe was the answer to stability and peace in life.

Work: Edwin's satisfaction in work was a job well done. He learned to do any task where the skills were repeated exactly the same each time. He could put the feed into the cattle if the hay were measured out. He cleaned the stables, hoed the fields (he hated weeds with a passion and could identify them from the crop), husked corn, and mowed the lawn. Because of the epilepsy, he was never allowed to run machinery. Whatever he did, had to be done to perfection. Not a straw could be out of place in the stable. Not an Elephant Ear weed could remain in the field. Not one blade of grass could stand above the others on the lawn.

There was a Black Walnut tree in the front yard. During the summer, the tent caterpillars often built their tents in the tree. Dad would prepare a torch and burn them out. One summer, there was a particularly bad infestation. Dad kept putting off burning them out. One day, Mother and Dad went to town. Edwin refused to go. Since they planned to be away for only a short time, they felt Edwin would be fine left alone. When they returned, the very valuable walnut tree lay on the ground, neatly cut into fire wood, and the caterpillars tramped into the gravel on the lane. Problem solved!

Bud Coffee owned the land across the road on the left-hand corner. The field was planted with soy beans. Several patches of Elephant Ear had not been cultivated out. These really bothered Edwin—so—on another day when he was left at home alone for a short time, he climbed the fence and hoed out every weed. Mother and Dad were upset, but Bud thought it a good joke.

Another time, when Dad was away on jury duty, the barnyard fence gave way so that the cattle could not be kept in. Edwin had no idea how to measure boards, but he repaired the gate. He cut no boards, using them the length he found them. He ended up with a skewed gate about five feet high to close the gap in a three foot fence. But hey, it kept the cattle in.

Edwin disliked skunks. One day while hoeing in the corn field, he came across a nest of mother and babies. Well, skunks had no place in his field, so he killed them all with the hoe, but not before they had liberally sprayed him and Tippy, the dog. The spray was so direct and so strong, that it made him very sick to his stomach. His clothes had to be buried, and he and Tippy washed down with tomato juice. Edwin gave skunks a wide berth after that!

Neatness: Edwin was meticulously neat. He would spend whatever time was required to fold his clothes and put them exactly in the same place in the drawer after they had been laundered. When he undressed for bed, his trousers were folded on the crease and hung over the back of the chair. His shirt hung perfectly over the pants. His shoes were placed beside the chair with the socks laid on top. He got into bed, pulled the covers up neatly, smoothed out any wrinkles, and folded his arms over the folded back quilt. He slept without moving all night. In the morning, he would smooth out the covers again. You would never know anyone had slept in the bed.

Edwin never had to search for any lost article. He followed the old adage, 'a place for everything, and everything in it's place'. One seldom ever picked up after Edwin. If we could just learn this, how it would simplify much of our daily frustrations.

Beauty: Edwin loved flowers and colour, even though he could not distinguish one from the other. He would bring Mother handfuls of May flowers or orange lilies that grew wild on the ditch bank. A beautiful sunset or clouds drifting across a blue sky never went unnoticed. "That's pretty" was a high compliment from Edwin, and an indication of his awe of nature's magnificence. One late summer day, Jean, Rosalind and I were on our way to Chatham to visit Edwin. The orange lilies on the ditch bank were in full bloom. We stopped the car, waded through the weeds and tall grass, and picked an armful to take with us. When he saw them, he just grinned, but as I kissed him good-bye, he looked at the bouquet and said, "Those sure are pretty flowers." We knew he had said, "Thank you."

Speech: Edwin could not talk plainly following his illness, and with the miss-firing of thought processes in his brain, it was difficult for him to communicate with the family. I was five years younger than Edwin. Mother would sit me on a corner of a blanket while Edwin played on the other corner. As a baby, I somehow learned to communicate with him in his language. Then I would translate what he said into family English. As we grew older and his language skills improved, there was no need to continue with the translation. We learned to understand him, although people who didn't know him had trouble doing so.

Music: Edwin's ear for music was the only memory left after his illness. He was unable to repeat the words, but could always carry the tune. During this time of growing up, Edwin taught me to carry a tune long before I can remember. Thanks to him, I grew up with a talent for music. Edwin's love for music never left him. He had a collection of records and a record player. He couldn't read the jackets, but somehow, he knew every record by name and who the performer was. He spent hours in his room playing his favourites. He was years ahead of the studies that show how music can reach the mind and calm the troubled breast.

Sense of Humour: It was rather unique how Edwin could, at appropriate times, come through with a wry sense of humour that seemed, somehow, to by-pass the miss-firing of his thought processes.

Dad fell in the barn breaking both knee caps. Edwin ran to the house to get Mother. "Maw," he said, "get out here. Your old man's down and can't get up." Weeks later, when Dad was home from the hospital, Edwin was helping him put on his socks one morning. With a grin he asked, "Now, old man, which foot does this sock go on?"

Peter Breen, a young neighbour lad, worked for Dad during the summer. One day, when Edwin was pestering Mother to do something right then, she turned to him and said, "Oh, for Pete's sake, Ed." He grinned and answered, "Pete ain't here though."

When Rosalind was dating Harold, Harold went to Mexico with a group of friends. When he returned, Edwin met him at the door with, "It's a good thing you're home. She had to go out with that other guy." (Rosalind and Harold must have straightened that out. They have been married for more than forty years.)

Jean and Edwin were on the bus coming to South River. Jean drew Edwin's attention to cows that had got into a field of corn. With that grin that could break through in an instant communication, he replied, "We don't have to chase them out, do we?"

Edwin had his favourite people, their titles usually preceded by 'old'. He liked his neighbours Old Lew Forrest and Old Bud Coffee because they always had a cheery 'hello' for him and usually a little humour when they addressed him. Of course, Old Mac Drummond was special, as was Jean Sova. Edwin seldom used the first name alone. He never called me 'Ruth'.

When I visited him in the Home in Chatham, I would ask, "Do you know who I am, Ed?" He would grin and ask, "Where's Old Mac Drummond?" I've never really tried to analyze why he always associated me with Mac. Rosalind's friend, Dianne Bedenham, always caught Edwin's eye. She wore her long, silky, blonde hair in a page boy style which he liked.

And, of course, Edwin really enjoyed all family get-togethers with the Aunts and Uncles. He would turn up his nose and tell you smoking was a dirty habit. Likewise, he would emphatically state that he didn't drink that stuff—liquor. More good advice!

Frustration: The inner turmoil brought on by Edwin's frustrations must have been totally consuming. These were exhibited in bouts of determination and anger. His inability to communicate and to rationalize change brought on fits of temper that were not within his power to control. There were times when he had to be physically restrained to keep him from harming himself or others. These were difficult for Dad and Mother to deal with and required a lot of their energy.

Although the number of outbursts decreased as he got older, the severity of the eruption did not. After Dad died, it became apparent that he could easily overpower Mother when his temper went out of control. Finally, when Mother wasn't well enough to stay in her home, the house was sold and she went to live in Thamesview Lodge, the County Home in Chatham. We found a place for Edwin in a Resident Home in Blenheim. This was a very difficult transition for him to make. From then on, the violent outbreaks disappeared. He would shrug in resignation or grumble to himself. When the home in Blenheim closed, Edwin, too, moved to Thamesview Lodge.

It was at this time, bowel cancer and leukemia were diagnosed. These were terrible times for Edwin and very difficult for us because no explanations could help him understand why he had so much pain and why he was so ill. Thankfully, the medical team agreed that he should have no invasive procedures, but rather be given whatever pain medication was required to ease his suffering. At the last, the bowel cancer went into remission, so the pain was gone. Thankfully, there is no pain with leukemia, just a slow decline in energy and the ability to stay mobile.

When he died, Jean, Rosalind, Bill, and I were with him. His eyes told us that he knew we were there. All the inner frustration which had consumed him for seventy-six years was finally gone. When I held his hand and assured him that Mother and Dad were coming to meet him, he was at peace at last.

These fleeting moments of insight into Edwin's mind and the impact they made on our lives will always be treasured.

MY CHILDHOOD

E DWIN WAS FIVE WHEN I was born. Because he took constant supervision, I was left to my own resources much of the time. I was hyperactive, loud and talkative until I was about 14. It was then that I realized that my actions were a negative attempt to get attention. My obnoxious behaviour was keeping me from having any real friends. I made a conscientious effort to take some of the harshness out of the tone of my voice, (there was still plenty of volume left!), and to think before I opened my mouth to speak. Your tongue can be a wicked tool, you know. Hopefully, I am still a work in progress, and God hasn't finished helping me correct that yet.

My negative behaviour made me a target for the frustrations Jean and Gaines felt in helping to care for Edwin. You couldn't take it out on him, but I was fair game. Jean was responsible for keeping my hair curled for special occasions. I couldn't sit still, so a handful of hair pulled to make me take notice worked well. Gaines had pet names for me which he could spit out like a terrible taste: Pot-licker, and Panty waist. If he couldn't provoke me to tears with words, he wasn't beyond a sharp pinch or accidental kick in the shins.

I, therefore, spent a lot of time out of sight, playing alone, in the corn crib, or in the chips from the wood pile. We had a white cat (named Whitie) who was my friend and playmate. His one blue eye and one green eye made him a misfit, which is what I often felt about myself. He would tolerate anything. I would dress him in doll clothes and push him around the yard or house in an old doll carriage. He was a much appreciated friend who never scratched or talked back.

And I climbed! I had no fear of heights so there wasn't a bird nest in the roof of the barn that I couldn't reach. Trees were wonderful places to sit. But my favourite perch from which to spy on the countryside was the platform at the top of the windmill, about 30' off the ground. What a view you could get from there! However, it did leave you exposed, and more than once Mother came running to the bottom of the derrick carefully calling me down, with a warning to keep my feet on the ground.

In the fall of the year, Mother went to the field with Dad to husk corn. The corn had been cut earlier and stood in shocks. Later, these would be torn apart, one at a time, the corn husked out, put in a pile, and the fodder retied and again shocked. At the close of the day, the corn was picked up in bushel baskets, dumped into the wagon, taken to the barn and stored in the corn crib to dry. It was used for winter feed for the animals. What was left in the spring would be sold. The fodder would be drawn into the barn also for winter feed. Labour intensive? You can say that again!

It was usually cold and damp by the time the farmer got around to husking. I would be dressed up in Edwin's old overalls, (permitted only in the field. Little girls did not wear pants) and left to play on a blanket at one end of the field. When that became boring, I would tramp the field with Mother and Dad. When a shock was torn down for husking, the mice that lived under it would scamper. I would look for the babies in the nest, tuck them into my pockets, and take them to the barn for the cats. No, that really wasn't cruel. Mice were a problem that had to be kept under control. No one seemed to consider the disease they may have passed on to me. When I wanted to help, Dad made me a little husking peg like his. But that was work and soon grew tiresome. A nice day spent in the field was fun, but cold, wet weather was not. To this day, I hate being cold. The following is an assignment I wrote when I took a writing course. It describes what it was like to come home from school on a bleak November day to a dark, cold house.

Depression

As I trudged home from school, the November day had grown grey and gloomy with the promise of early darkness. I pulled my skimpy, worn jacket tightly across my chest to gain some protection from the damp, chilling fingers that poked through the flimsy material. In my mind I could hear my Grandfather say, "It's a lazy wind, child—too lazy to go around so it goes through."

Stones from the gravel road had worked their way through the holes in the soles of my ill-fitting shoes. As I took the short-cut across the orchard, the wetness from the long grass added further chill and discomfort to my protesting feet.

In the orchard, a few contrary, wizened apples held stubbornly to the bare branches. From the ground beneath, the putrid smell of damp,rotting leaves and decaying fruit accosted my senses. An abandoned Robin's nest in the top of a pear tree had little hope of enduring harsh winter winds and driving snow. Only the protesting wind grumbled from the lonely branches.

Shivering, I broke through the edge of the orchard and opened the squeaky gate into the expansive house-yard. Two spreading maple trees had scattered their soggy autumn leaves across the lengthening grass in an attempt to compensate for the loss of colour in the bare shrubbery along the lane. Only a clump of persistent bronze chrysanthemums still bloomed in the withered flower beds beside the house.

The aging, two-story house was silhouetted against the darkening sky. At one corner, white mortar, used to repair the brick work, gave the impression of stacked building blocks. The gingerbread trim around the gables and the long, wide verandas on the front and side were in need of paint. The darkened windows made the house look deserted, almost haunted.

I crossed the yard to the side veranda and pulled open the screen door, its square patches sewn on with black thread. I shouldered open the scarred kitchen door and stepped onto a braided, oval mat. It was encrusted with dried clay which had come in on the heavy work boots during the day. Mud was tracked across the bare, wood floor once bleached white from repeated scrubbings with lye soap and ashes. The air was stagnant—heavy with the greasy, stale odour of fried eggs.

Five chairs, their brown enamel chipped, were pushed back from the square table left messy with the remnants of the noon meal. Dirty dishes were stacked in a battered dish pan on one corner. The sooty chimney on the oil lamp beside it gave no welcome from the middle of this disorder. At the lone window behind the table, curtains of unbleached cotton hung, limply defeated by summer's humidity.

The old, black, cook stove, cracked and dusted with cold ashes,stood shivering against the adjacent wall. Beside the stove, from the empty wood box, a lone cricket chirped its swan song. With a sigh of resignation, I crossed the neglected room to the stairway door. I would change my school clothes and join my parents in the barn where they were milking cows. It would be warm there.

. . . .

I hated walking to school, especially during the winter. Children didn't have the winter clothing taken for granted today. Little girls wore only dresses, usually mid-calf in length. Long underwear and long stockings held up by garters was all the protection you had for your legs. On your feet, you wore high-topped leather shoes (winter boots either hadn't been invented, or were too expensive.). The snow filled the gap between your leg and the shoe. Frost bite and chill blains were quite common. If you got too wet getting to school, you had to sit in misery until you dried beside the stove. If the day was not too stormy, you dressed up to play in the snow again at recess and/or noon hour. Then you came in and got dried out again before you had to start for home.

When I was about 8 or 9, snow pants were designed. These were made from heavy, woollen, melton cloth—very coarse and very scratchy. It meant you didn't have to wear long underwear—but that left leg exposed above the stockings. As the bare skin rubbed against the rough wool, chafing made it very uncomfortable to walk. Mother made me long bloomers to wear under the snow pants. It was so nice to have a creative mother!

One seldom got a ride to school, except, on Fridays. If you were ready in time, you could hitch a ride with Ham Hooper. Ham Hooper wore an old, black, felt hat and an old, black, long coat. Yes, he did indeed remind one of Oliver's Fagan, except this one was a fish peddler. He travelled his route in a horse and buggy loaded with fresh fish packed in ice. And yes, he smelled very fishy. But in the spring of the year, when your bare feet were still tender, it was an option.

The roads were not ploughed for winter use of the family car. In fact, the car often stayed in the garage for most of the winter and on into spring until the roads dried up enough to travel on. Winter travel was mostly with team and sleigh or horse and cutter. We had both.

With more automobiles in the country, there was a need to improve the roads. In the spring of the year, before it got dry enough for the farmers to work the land, the township would hired them to draw gravel to grade the roads. Dad had two teams and wagons—Gaines drove one—that they took to the pits. This provided a bit of cash income for a family. For drainage, deep ditches were dug on either side of the road. These too, were done with man power, horse power, and a strong back. No one heard about engineers for the job. If the water drained as it was supposed to, you had done a good job. If it didn't, you had to do it over again, simple as that. Since you only got paid once, you were sure that it was done well the first time.

One-room Country School

Strangfield School, SS#12, on the corner of the 11th concession and Country Road 37 in Tilbury West Township was built as a one-room school house in 1914 and operated until 1960 when consolidated schools were built and students were bussed to school. I am the little rag-a-muffin, second row, second from the right.

I started to school when I was six years old. At that time, children started after Easter in Primer Class. This was pre kindergarten days. I went to S.S.No 12, Tilbury West, commonly called Strangfield. It was, of course, a one-room country school of about 30 students with Miss Seck (Lily May) the teacher. I loved school from the beginning, mainly, I think, because I adored Miss Seck. She ran the school with strict but loving discipline with respect. A student *'wouldn't say shit if his mouth was full of it.* (Now there's another of Grandma Dean's expressions. You were, of course, expected to use it with discretion.) My first text book was the THE ONTARIO READERS PRIMER which was used in schools from1920 to1937. It's cost price was 4 cents. The first story was in long hand, not printing, and was titled *The Little Red hen.* This little story is still a classic. It goes:

The Little Red Hen

The Little Red Hen found some wheat.
She called the cat. She called the dog. She called the pig.
"Who will help me plant the wheat?"
"Not I", said the cat.
"Not I", said the dog.
"Not I", said the pig.
"Then I will plant the wheat", said the little Red Hen.
And she did.
The wheat grew up.
The Little Red Hen said: "Who will help me cut the wheat?"
"Not I", said the cat.
"Not I", said the dog.
"Not I", said the pig.
"Then I will cut the wheat", said the Little Red Hen.
And she did.
The Little Red Hen said: "Who will help me grind the wheat?"
"Not I", said the cat.
"Not I", said the dog.
"Not I", said the pig.
"Then I will grind the wheat", said the Little Red Hen.
And she did.
The Little Red Hen said: "Who will help me bake the bread?"
"Not I", said the cat.

"Not I", said the dog.
"Not I", said the pig.
"Then I will bake the bread", said the Little Red Hen.
And she did.
The Little Red Hen said: "Who will help me eat the bread?"
"I will", said the cat.
"I will", said the dog.
"I will", said the pig.
The Little Red Hen said,
"You would not plant the wheat.
"You would not "cut the wheat.
"You would not grind the wheat.
"You would not bake the bread.
"You shall not eat the bread.
"My chicks and I shall eat the bread.
And "they did.

Hand writing was an important subject because it was the common form of communication. Remember that typewriters were only found in offices. It was important that hand writing be clear and legible. The form for making each letter was carefully taught and practiced. Individuality was discouraged. It was therefore usual that one person's hand writing would be similar to another's. A page of well written notes, properly punctuated, without ink blots, spelling mistakes, or erasures was a matter of pride. Until Grade 4, you wrote with pencil. Then you graduated to a straight pen and an ink well. I got my first fountain pen in Grade 8. This was a pen with an inside tube, cartridge, that allowed you to write several pages before it required refilling. What a treat today to have ball points! Printing was not taught until grade 4 or 5. Then it was usually introduced as an art lesson, and was used for map work or labelling diagrams.

Sometime between my leaving the Elementary School in 1939 and returning to teach in 1945, this order was reversed. Little students learned to make letters with sticks and balls that had to stand straight and sit within the lines. Writing was not introduced until Grade 3. Was that an improvement? The legibility of hand writing has deteriorated. My assessment—with today's computers and spell checks which speed up written communication, perhaps beautiful hand writing in now an art and not a necessity.

Learning to read was difficult for me. Reading was taught with a 'huff-and-puff' phonetic approach. It made no sense to me. The words on the page had no connection.

Because I could memorize quickly, I could bluff my way through if I heard someone read the passage before me. I can understand the methods non-readers use to get by. This, of course, also made me very poor in producing written answers in Literature and a poor speller. I suppose today, I would have been classified as dyslexic. Thank goodness for teachers who only saw a bright-eyed little girl who had a desire and determination to learn and go to school. My ability to read improved when I was introduced to syllabication. No more laborious huffing and puffing. Thoughts could travel in context across the page. It was a whole new world. I never became a fast reader. Part of that may be the intensity required to read, or it may be the beauty of imagery I found in a page of a well written article or book. There is an advantage in being a slow reader. I seldom have to read a page or book twice. When I was studying and teaching, I could open a book to the page giving the information I was looking for. I still enjoy re-reading a paragraph that has been beautifully written, just to savour the feel of the words or the imagery projected. I suppose that's the same feeling that some people get from viewing great art.

English grammar was taught separately. I could write a near perfect paper in grammar. That saved me many times, and brought my composition marks up to reasonable levels. I didn't seem to grasp how to put a good composition together. My spelling was not good, so I would look for simple words rather than run the disgrace of losing marks for spelling. It was not until I took university English courses years later, that Mrs. Erickson, a fellow teacher, taught me how to put some meat on the bones of ideas. Thanks to her, I learned how to put together an 80% essay. My ability in Grammar was automatic, which not only helped in writing, but was also an excellent background when I took French and Latin in High School.

From the beginning, I was good in Math, perhaps because mastery of addition and multiplication facts was considered so important for everyday existence. My Dad hadn't gone beyond Grade 4 at school, but he was good, and fast at 'figures' both with pencil and mentally. Spitting out the facts was often a game at home in the evenings. Mental arithmetic was a challenge that everyone was expected to master. This meant coming up with the right answer without using a pencil. Short cuts and quick methods of calculation were taught and stressed. You never wasted time and paper if you could do a calculation mentally. Besides, Math always made sense to me—it was so true—without change or exceptions. When you were right, you were right! For four years at high school, I tutored a fellow student, Audrey Fenner in math. When she passed her Grade 12 math course I was as thrilled as she was. She went on to become a registered nurse.

I was also good at Geography. It was not difficult to make good marks here. Now History was another story! I found the events interesting, but dates were hard to remember. I had a high school teacher, Mr. Scratch, who helped me concoct all kinds of little memory joggers to connect the right date with the right event.

In the summer of 1935, we got electricity. The lines had gone passed the house for several years. Dad had agreed to pay service charges to get the line built, but didn't have the money to get power connected until then. What a change! No more lamps to fill with oil or chimneys to clean before you could light the lamp. To save cost, a single bulb in a ceiling fixture was all we had with a minimum of wall plugs.

Gaines brought home our first radio, a second hand Victrola with the logo—His Master's Voice—a little dog sitting in front of a bell shaped amplifier, his head cocked to one side. Late Saturday night he would tune into the Grand Ole Opry from Nashville, and early Sunday mornings we would listen to gospel music from Pleasant Valley in the hills of Tennessee. There were programs you just didn't miss: Amos and Andy, George Burns and Gracie Allen, Jack Benny and Mary Livingston put on comedy; The Green Horrnet, The Lone Ranger, The Shadow were mysteries; the big bands live in concert, Jimmy Dorsey, Guy Lombardo, Benny Goodman; the popular singers, Bing Crosby, Perry Como, Frank Sinatra, The Andrew Sisters. I heard the original broadcast of Orson Well's *War of the Worlds*. This caused a great amount of anxiety among people who didn't realize it was a radio play. Some folks took it so seriously that they fled their homes. A few even committed suicide. How's that for power of the media!

And then of course, there were the ball games. Mother followed the Detroit Tigers and didn't want to miss one play-by-play account. Hank Greenburg, the first baseman and home run hitter, was her star on the diamond. She would turn the radio up to full volume so that she could hear the game from anywhere in the house—or yard. On Saturday night, there was something wrong if you missed Hockey Night in Canada with

Foster Hewitt and the Maple Leafs. You wouldn't be caught dead rooting for the Detroit Red Wings. I think it was the American announcer who turned us off them.

We saved money to buy a used electric iron. The old flat irons that had to be heated on the stove found a spot on a shelf in the pantry. Next came a used washing machine. No more standing with your hand on the lever pulling back and forth, back and forth to agitate the clothes in the tub until they were clean. These were followed in a couple of years with a used refrigerator. Dad quit putting up ice in the ice house. Wow! We had it made!

When I was eight, Jean married Harold Sova, Aug. 31, 1935. This made me the oldest helper Mother had in the house. From that day on, I got up at 7o'clock every morning to set the table and to make the oatmeal for breakfast when Mother, Dad, Edwin Gaines, and usually a hired man, came from the barn chores. We ate oatmeal every morning, winter and summer. The July morning I was married was already hot and humid at 8 o'clock when I dished up the oatmeal. I laughed and said to Dad, "Now, you enjoy that oatmeal because it is the last pot I will cook for the rest of my life." Well, I lied. I did make oatmeal after that, but I never ate it.

After Jean was married, my carefree days were limited. It was now up to me be more helpful in the house. I was extremely small for my age. I had to stand on a chair to wash the dishes in the dishpan set upon the table. I was too small to do heavy cleaning, but not to wash windows. From early spring to late summer, windows were washed, both outside and inside, with Bon Ami. Bon Ami came in cake form. You rubbed a damp rag over the cake and rubbed that on the window. It took a few minutes to dry. Then you polished the glass with a clean cloth. It was hard to get off all the white film. If you missed a spot, you had to go back and rub some more. Inside . . . . outside . . . . inside . . . . outside, until it met Mother's approval. But, oh, the house looked so much brighter with clean windows. Although I don't go at them today with that kind of passion, I still smile when my windows are gleaming.

On June 13, 1937, I got up to find a baby sister in bed with Mother. In those days, older children were not prepared for new additions to the family. Never-the-less, I was thrilled. Here was a living doll to take the place of the white cat in the doll buggy. However, it was a bad summer. The mid-wife who came to help when Rosalind was born came from a home where everyone was sick. In three days, Mother took very ill. The doctor didn't know what was wrong until I came home from school with a high fever. Old Doctor Emerson spied me on the couch, took one look in my throat and said, "Thank goodness, You have Scarlet Fever. Now I can help your Mother."

Scarlet Fever was a dangerous disease. When it was diagnosed, a red card which screamed quarantine was tacked on the side of the house beside the door. This meant that no one could come in and no one from the house, except Dad, the bread winner, was allowed to leave the farm. Jean was there when the doctor made the diagnosis. He gave her a serum so she wouldn't catch it. As it turned out, she was highly allergic to the serum and was as sick as if she had had the Fever. I think that Aunt Effie, who had had scarlet fever when she was a girl, came down to look after Mother. I don't remember because I was tucked away into the front bedroom and woke up 10 days later. Just as I was beginning to move around again, Edwin came down with it so we were quarantined another 6 weeks. It was mid August before we could come and go freely.

There were still the threshing bees to look after. When the men came to our house to thresh the wheat, we were still under quarantine. The table had to be set outside under the trees. There was Mother, who had been desperately ill, with a very cross and fussy new baby, and a 10-year old girl who had also been very ill, expected to prepare food for a gang of 25 to 30 men. It was summer, the weather was very hot, and so was the wood stove that we cooked on. I remember her making lemon pies. She has whipped the meringue for the top and put them in the oven to brown. They burned. She scraped off the burnt egg white, beat up more, and put them into the oven again. They burned. Yes, she scraped them off again, and again whipped up more meringue. Then I was put on a chair in front of the oven door and warned to keep an eye on those pies! Three times is out, they say. We had pies for the men. Then there were the dishes to do. With no one to help it was 4 o'clock before we got the dishes done.

While we were still under quarantine, Miss Seck, my teacher, brought me a large basket of fruit all wrapped up in cellophane. As a child, I treasured this as the most thoughtful, wonderful gift I had ever received.

On October 12, 1937, when I was 10, Gaines married Jean Knister. This gave me both a sister and a sister-in-law named Jean. I think Edwin may have been the one who started adding the last name, so they became Jean Sova and Jean Willan in our conversations. I had my first ready-made dress for the wedding. I remember it well. It was pink taffeta, smocked across the bodice with embroidery cotton. I felt like a princess! I may even have sat still with my feet on the ground for a few minutes. (That would have been a real trick)

At the height of the depression in 1933, Dad had bought the Everett Tilson farm which was next to ours and ran to the corner of the Gracie Side Road. There was so much farm land out of production that the government begged him to buy it. No one had money so they offered the 100 acres to him for $3,000 with nothing down and no principal payment for 3 years. The interest at 1 1/2% ($45) was all he had to pay for each of those first 3 years. This farm was deeded to Gaines and Jean who took over the payments. They built a new house and raised six children there: Donald Robert (married Geraldine Hickson), Shirley Anne (Married Larry Belanger), Donna Marie (married Kenneth Hartley), Linda Anne (married Gordon Ciliska, then Donald Clark), Leonard Gaines (married Trudy Lansue), Robert Earl (married Janis Bailey). Leonard and Trudy own the farm today.

I was not a strong child physically. Any amount of over exertion or too much excitement would give me terrible head aches and a sick stomach which would last for anywhere from 12 to 36 hours. I was very small and underweight for my age. Because of the history of epilepsy in the family—doctors, at that time, thought it was inherited, and that I was a perfect candidate. The treatment was to keep me quiet—ha, ha—and to let up on expectations of what I could do. This meant that I missed a lot of school. The year that I took Grade 7 & 8 together, I was sick all of December. The doctor thought that if I had my tonsils out, I would thrive better. That happened in January. It seemed to take me a long time to get better. I went back to school early in February, and promptly came down with Chicken Pox—another two weeks absent. (Many years later, the doctors discovered I have a Rheumatic heart—a condition left by Rheumatic Fever, so that is probably what I had at that time.)

Anyway, I completed Grade 7 & 8 in one year. To prepare for the High School Entrance Exams, from Easter on, we went to school an hour early every morning to study for the exams which were set by the Ontario Ministry of Education. We had to go to the high school in Comber to write: English Literature, English Composition and Grammar, Spelling, and Mathematics. These were 3 hour exams, one each day. I managed to write them all without getting sick and passed with 69%.

Educators today look at the results of those examinations and are striving to get similar results. They aren't doing their homework. After I became a teacher and learned about the Bell Curve, I did some research. In 1939, the year I wrote those exams, the average mark for Ontario Students was 43. Now, you couldn't fail 57% of the population! The marks were put on a curve to raise the 43 to 60 and the other marks adjusted to fit. When I taught in Wheatley I had an inspector who showed me how to set an exam that would give results on a Bell curve. His method was: two questions (twenty marks) that all students could answer correctly, six (sixty marks) that most students could do well with, and two (twenty marks) that the best students would find challenging. If your class results were poor, then you hadn't done a good job of teaching or your test was either poorly constructed or vague in what you wanted in the answers. With practise, and sometimes re-teaching, my student's results would fit the Bell Curve without adjustment.

HIGH SCHOOL

So now I'm 12 years old. I have passed my High School Entrance Exams and the law is I don't have to go to school any more. Oh, how I wanted to go!

Fate, luck, determination on Mother's part, the fact that I was small for my age and not strong, a combination perhaps, got me to Comber Continuation School.

Mother desperately wanted to go to school and because she hadn't been given the opportunity, she so wanted it for her children. Dad and Grandma Dean, on the other hand felt it was a waste of time and money to educate a girl who would just get married anyway. I guess they felt it didn't take brains to run a house and raise children. I suppose that was because the 'man' of the house controlled the money. Wives were given a few dollars to run the house and expected to give over all other money management to the husband.

Here was where fate and luck come in. Mother had inherited four to five thousand dollars from the Mellish estate, which Dad considered to be as much his as hers. Imagine the determination it must have taken for Mother to say NO. Dad wanted to buy a new threshing machine and tractor so that he could do custom threshing to make extra money. This was a beautiful piece of equipment, all stainless steel—it wouldn't rust, you know—and a great big, powerful Graham Bradley tractor with tip-toe wheels that could work all day without stopping or breaking down. Mother's inheritance would allow him to buy the outfit and pay cash. That was a big deal when you had just fought your way through the depression. A bargain was struck the last week in August. Dad got his threshing machine and tractor and I got to go to school.

There were no school busses then. Six families set up probably the first car pool to get their children to school. Yes, a driver and six students with books in one car was a bit cramped but we piled in anyway, seat belts unheard of. This worked for grades 9 & 10. Then there were only 3 of us continuing to car-pool. For Grade 12, I took a job with a family to help with the meals and to baby sit their three children after school hours. I put in some long days, starting at 6:30 in the morning and finishing at 9 o'clock at night. Then I went at my homework. I wasn't strong enough to put in these hours and came down sick in January. I also had the mumps at that time. Dad relented, brought me home, and allowed me to drive the car to school each day for the rest of the year.

Poor health dogged me throughout high school. I seldom wrote a full set of exams. I would be ill before they were finished and I would have to pick up a letter from our family Doctor Emerson to excuse me. It was so common that he would simply take Mother's word that I couldn't attend school and leave the note in an envelope on a table in his office for me to pick up. I had barely passed Grade 11 and had decided not to go back. I hadn't failed anything, but my average dropped from 69% to 55%. I was pretty discouraged. My friends were out working and making money. I got a job picking tomatoes that summer. That had to be the dirtiest, hardest way to make a few pennies that there could be. There are 60 pounds (about 13 kilograms) in a bushel of tomatoes. Tomatoes were picked in half-bushel baskets, but when they were full, they weighed 45-50 pounds. The pay was 8 cents a basket. You worked all day with your butt turned up to the sun—hot, dirty, stinking—with your back aching until it became numb. You had to work hard to pick 100 baskets a day—I never made it—for $8.00. In September, I dressed up and went to the tomato field instead of going to school. At 3 o'clock the light bulb came on! What was I doing here! The next morning, I went back to school.

The year I was 16, and in Grade 12, I grew! Until then, I had been the smallest kid in the whole high school. I wore a size 8 child's dress. Mother always made my dresses with at least an 8" hem so they could be let down, but often the dress was worn out without touching the hem line. In less than a year, I grew 8 or 9 inches to the height I am today—5'4". That's still not tall but at the time, it made a big statement. After this growth spurt my health improved somewhat.

What did I study in high school? The curriculum was set. There was no choice. Basic were: English, French, Mathematics, History, Geography,

Science, Health and Phys. Ed twice a week. There wasn't a gymnasium so the Phys Ed classes were held during the fall and spring when the weather permitted. The emphasis was on field sports; long jump, high jump, track events, plus basketball. There was an outside basketball court and a cinder track. Because I was so small, I was outclassed in all events except running. I could run! I was seldom beaten on the track.

In Grade 10, I chose Latin in place of secretarial courses. Everyone had one year of Bookkeeping. At Comber, there were 3 teachers. One of them, Mr. Scratch, was also the Principal. In Grade 9, the teachers came to your classroom. There was one Grade 9 class with about 30 students. The majority of kids only completed Grade 10. As the grade levels increased, the class sizes became smaller. The students did the walking. There were 10 of us left in Grade 12.

The courses of study were pretty elementary. The first two years of science were farm oriented with the study of the breeds of cattle, horses, pigs, chickens, and methods of farming which included crop rotation, and the various varieties of corn, oats, wheat, and barley. Hybrid and genetically altered seeds hadn't been thought of then.

In Grade 11, you studied Physics. I remember well coming to the chapter on the atom. The teacher said, "What we know about the atom is hypothetical, and some fool thinks it can be split. If that happens we'll all be blown to pieces. We'll go on to the next chapter." It was 1942. Within 3 years the atom bomb was dropped on Hiroshima! The chemistry course in Grade 12 was also very elementary. We had to memorize the valences and do basic experiments. Compared to what students study today, I learned very little in the field of chemistry.

There were two math courses, Algebra and Geometry. These were taught to a greater depth than the science but still not as intense as today's math which combines the two with trigonometry.

History was a must for all 5 years. Areas of study included ancient, medieval, and modern, with civics stressed. These were the years when Canada was at war, so each lesson began with an update of current war developments followed with discussion. It was necessary to read the newspapers and listen to the radio nightly to keep up with events. We certainly knew where we came from and where we were going. Our knowledge of history was far beyond the understanding of most students now.

In Comber, the French course was taught in English. Written French was stressed with vocabulary and grammar. We practiced translation from

French to English and English to French. We seldom spoke the language. When I went to Wheatley for Grade 13, the teacher, Mrs. Staddon, had studied in Quebec and taught French in French. I was lost until Christmas. Today I would have been put out of the class, but she had the patience of Job. She refused to break into English for me, and kept repeating her question in French. By June I could answer in French, although I'm sure my accent was poor to say the least. To this day, I can still read French enough to get the gist of it, but no way would I attempt to speak it.

I took Latin for three years. Like French, it was taught through translation. Latin was a practical course because it gave an excellent background for derivation of English words and the basics of grammar.

For Grade 13, I transferred to Wheatley Continuation School and stayed with Grandma Dean and Uncle Garret. There were four classrooms and four teachers so I could get the nine credits required for Normal School (Teachers' College today) in one year. The credits were: English Literature, English Composition and Grammar, French, Algebra, Geometry, Trigonometry, Biology, Zoology, and History. Passing Ministry of Education Departmental Exams qualified students to go on to university or Normal School.

There were just three of us in Grade 13—Olive Pinch, John Chute and me. It was a very interesting year. Miss O'Ryan, who taught English and History was a very young, very clever, red-headed Irish girl not much older than we were. We loved and admired her, but, good heavens, she smoked! Her landlady found out and turned her out on the street, bag and baggage, in stormy weather, the day before Christmas Holidays. It took her hours to get home to Windsor. She died of pneumonia! We were shocked when we returned to school in January.

There was a shortage of teachers. It was six weeks before Mrs. McQuarrie came out of retirement to take over the class. Then, at Easter, Miss Williamson who taught Trigonometry ran away with a married man who lead the Baptist Church choir. Dear, dear, the gossip was knee deep. No one was found to replace her, so John, Olive, and I went into class every day as if we had a teacher, and with the help of the Principal when we ran into trouble, completed and studied the material together in preparation for the Departmentals. With the effort we put into it, we probably knew the work better than if we had had a teacher.

Upon graduation, John joined the Navy, Olive worked for the druggist in town, and I went to London to Normal School.

These were my room mates when I went to Normal School in London, Ontario, 1944-45.

Standing: L.R. Elizabeth Reed, Mary Ferguson, Martha Rumley and Ruth Willan (me)

Notice that we all had biblical first names. Because we usually travelled together, we were often called "The Angels from Duchess Street".

NORMAL SCHOOL

L ONDON NORMAL SCHOOL SERVED ALL of southern Ontario for teacher training. I had really wanted to be a nurse, but Mother insisted that I be a teacher. She felt that I was not strong enough to handle the work load required of nurse's training. She was right, no doubt. Nurses-in-training at that time worked six hours in the hospital wards, and then six hours in class—a 12 hour day. Besides, it had been her dream to be a teacher. She had sacrificed so much to get me where I was, that I didn't put up an argument.

I boarded with Mrs. McGregor at 123 Duchess Avenue, in London. She had two bedrooms which she rented out to four girls at $10 a week. I shared a room (and bed) with Mary Ferguson. Martha Rumley and Joan Edmonds shared the other room. Joan was a bit on the wild side. We let her in the door after curfew more than once. After Christmas, she changed her age on her birth certificate and joined the Women's Air Force, (WAF'S). We lost track of her after that. Elizabeth Reid moved into the house to share the room with Martha. Notice our first names—Mary, Elizabeth, Martha, and Ruth. Biblical women? Why, of course. (You'll forgive that stretch of the imagination, I hope.)

Mrs. MacGregor was a widow. Mr. Leason (I think he may have been a 'Home Boy' from England) had been the hired hand when the MacGregors owned a farm. He had no family and was a little slow. He had a room in the basement and was her go-for. He had no hair, not even eyebrows, the result of having typhoid fever when he was young. He wore an ill fitting red wig. We felt sorry for Mr. Leason, not because of his ridiculous wig, but because Mrs. MacGregor treated him as a servant, and didn't let him forget that he had a home through her generosity.

We were looked after very well by Mrs. MacGregor and Leason. She was a good cook and prepared balanced meals. Well, pretty much balanced. She had a peach tree in the back yard. We ate peaches until we all had diarrhoea and had to refuse dessert.

We were given teaching numbers at the school, arranged alphabetically and divided into four classes by those numbers. All except for the young men, that is. Since there were only seven of them, they were put together in A, the first group. With Willan, my maiden name, I was #107 in Form 4. Wilson and Young followed me. Of the 109 who started, 98 graduated.

The professors at the school were a joke. Dr. Mark, the principal, was at least 75. He was congenial and could be talked into letting us run the extra curricular programmes we wanted. The youngest, Mr. Roberts, who taught math and school management was at least 60. He was forever talking about us getting a job and buying a fur coat. Mr. McEackren, the English prof wore thick glasses and was never sure who was in class. You had to sign in and if you were absent, you got someone to sign for you. I don't think he ever marked a paper. We never got anything returned. As long as you turned something in, you got 75%. You made sure you never got caught alone in the lab with Dr. Hofferd, the Science teacher. (He was at least 70, the dirty old man!) The shop teacher was jolly and made his classes fun and practical. Miss Ryan, the Home Economics teacher, made you think of a prison guard. She was tall, thin, and looked at you down a long, pointed nose. Now, come to think of it, she reminded you of a witch. She was also in charge of deportment. Right! Don't get caught in a hotel, let alone a bar, or out after curfew. Don't be seen or caught in the wrong place at the wrong time. Always look and behave like a teacher no matter where you were. The first time I went out to a school to teach, I was failed on my lesson because my hair was too long and I didn't look like a teacher. I was ordered to have it cut. Mentally, I fumed. My hair had grown for five years. It was well down my back, thick and heavy. So every time after that when I went to a school, I braided my hair and pinned the braids across the back of my neck, put on my high heels, my one plain suit, and pretended I was in command.

My long, blond hair was both a boon and a curse. I went to school with a budget of $2 per week for spending money. It meant you looked for creative ways to provide entertainment. Well, you could walk rather than take the bus. To afford a movie once a week, I braided my hair with ribbons tied at the ends. Then Mary and I would go to the show before the prices changed at 6 o'clock, on an adult and a child's ticket. By splitting the difference, we could both go for 50 cents. I could roller skate on a child's ticket for 25 cents. The only problem was, with my hair in braids and ribbons, I couldn't get anyone over 16 to skate with me. Darn! Not quite true. I did meet Dan Malloney, age 18, a wonderful tap dancer. I went to a couple of shows put on for the service men and women with him where he was a featured entertainer. That was a bit of a thrill—like going with a rock star. He was an Irish Catholic, and much too intense for me, so that didn't last long.

The water in London was very hard. Detergent shampoos hadn't been developed. It was next to impossible to wash my hair and get all the soap rinsed out. The residue darkened the natural blond colour. At Easter, I gave up, had my hair cut short and had a poodle cut perm. It was a bit of a shock but it made a hit with Miss Ryan!

My time at Normal School would have been a complete loss if it hadn't been for some excellent critic teachers who were exceptional at their profession. These were the teachers who opened their classrooms to student teachers twice a week. For the first visit, you watched her. Then you were given an assignment to teach the next day when you came back. This was how you learned to apply the theory of teaching and how to make it all work for each student in the class. The belief was that every child could be taught. It was up to you to unlock his learning patterns so that he could succeed. Whatever success I had as a teacher I attribute to those critic teachers!

THE SECOND WORLD WAR: 1939-1945

W ORLD WAR II BROKE OUT September 2, 1939, so I was a teenager attending high school and Normal School under the dark cloud of war. Almost immediately, the country was introduced to rationing. Sugar and fats (butter, lard and shortening) were needed to make gunpowder and ammunition. Coffee and tea had to be imported so they were on the list. Meat was needed to feed the service men and gasoline to drive trucks, tanks and planes for the Canadian Forces. These items were rationed. Coupons were issued to each member of a household which limited the amount you could purchase each month. Living on a farm made rationing less of a hardship, since we produced our own meat, butter and lard. Sometimes the unused coupons could be traded for sugar coupons. Gasoline to run farm machinery was not rationed, but it was dyed purple. There was a hefty fine if you filled the tank of your car with it.

Children were encouraged to buy Savings Stamps (25 cents a week) and adults to buy War Bonds to support the war effort. Income Tax was introduced to pay down the cost of the war. This was supposed to be removed when the debt was paid off. Now, isn't that a laugh! We're still paying.

I wasn't allowed to date until the beginning of my Grade 12 year. Dating, too, was defined by the war. With the rationing of gasoline, few people had fuel to drive very far. This may have been the beginning of the idea to car pool. Several kids (maybe three boys and five girls) climbed into a car, sometimes two deep in the back seat, to go to a movie or dance. It was a great time to learn how to grow up since hardly anyone went steady. You could have a lot of fun in the group without having the pressure of a one-on-one relationship. There was always a shortage of young men. Some of them had 'roving hands' which had to be held all night to keep them under control. There was, however, safety in numbers. You learned how to ward off unwanted advances and excuses, especially lines like, "I'm going off to war. I may not come home. I love you. Won't you have my baby?" Yes, there were girls who fell for it, and you felt sorry for them. Papa may have come home, but not to them! I guess some things never change.

Anyway, besides the movies and dances, we created a lot of our own good times with house parties year around. We played a kind of tag called *Two Deep* on the lawn in the summer, and in the winter, we went ice skating on Two Creeks in Wheatley. I always went, even though skating was torture to my feet. Sitting around the big campfire with my friends was worth it.

I had a few not so steady boyfriends who remained just friends who were boys. In the spring of 1944, a public school chum whom I hadn't seen for five years showed up on my doorstep in an Air Force uniform. Handsome? Yes, I thought so! The crush I'd had on him at 11 years old was soon rekindled. When Max left for overseas that fall, I had promised to be his steady girl. (He didn't give me a ring, but he did give me an expensive Bulova watch, which, by the way, kept perfect time until the day I married someone else. Then it stopped, never to run again. For old time's sake, I still have it in the drawer.) It was rather a nice arrangement. I wrote him a couple of letters a week, still had fun with the gang, but didn't have to worry about one-on-one dating. Does that make me sound shallow or just immature? Let's say immature, OK? Besides, school, my horse, and chores kept me pretty busy.

No one knew how far the war would spread—maybe even to Canada. We had courses on how to recognize our planes from German planes by the silhouette against the sky. We were taught where to take shelter in case of an air raid, and at school, we practised marching in columns. Everyone became fiercely patriotic Canadians.

The young men began to show up in uniform. Each year in May, senior students would disappear from class as they were granted their year and joined one of the services. It was not long before those terrible telegrams began to arrive—killed in action, or missing. Memorial services with only an 8x11 coloured photo and a single basket of flowers were a stark reminder of our loss by the conflict in Europe. As the war dragged on, these were the boys you wrote to, sent pictures and parcels to, and wept for when they were killed. Vern Elliott, who sat behind me for four years in school joined the Air Force and was trained as a tail gunner. The life expectancy of a gunner in battle was 3 minutes. He was listed missing in action, presumed dead in the skies over African. John Chute, my fellow student in Grade 13, was lost at sea.

All conversation stopped when the news came on the radio. Wall maps kept track of countries that fell under Nazi domination. First, Hitler invaded the Balkan countries (Austria, Hungary, Yugoslavia, and Czechoslovakia).These countries appealed to the League of Nations, (The United Nations today). The leaders said, "Tut, tut, naughty boy. Don't do that again." Then Hitler grinned and invaded Poland. At that time, I can remember hearing Hitler speak in a loud, German rant. Even though you could not understand what he was saying, the ominous power of it chilled your senses. 'Heil Hitler' was his battle cry.

That was enough. The Britain declared war. Neville Chamberlain was Prime Minister. He reminded you of Charlie Champlain, except Neville carried an umbrella in place of a cane. Benito Mussolini, the dictator of Italy and leader of the Fascist power, joined with Germany. We listened while the Scandinavian countries and the Netherlands were over run. At the same time, lands in Africa were falling under Italian Fascist military power.

Winston Churchill became Prime Minister of Britain. To hear the command in Churchill's voice in an evening newscast was inspiring. Soon France fell to the invaders. There seemed to be no stopping Hitler's mighty war machines. Then, only the little island of Britain stood alone. We were glued to the radio. Our forces were trapped between the invading Nazis and the sea. Like a miracle, the winds went down, the waters calmed, and dense fog covered the whole area. The troops were evacuated by small boats, from Dunkirk in France, across the English Channel, to safety on the White Cliffs of Dover. This brave story can be found in many books and was even made into a feature movie, Mrs. Miniver.

The German Luftwaffe (Air Force) was very advanced in capabilities and over powering in numbers. England, which was quite unprepared for war, had only a few planes and anti-aircraft guns to defend themselves. Germany bombed England without mercy, hoping that Britain would give up. This time was called 'The Battle of Britain'. Great tributes were made to the people who withstood the bombings with courage and determination. Songs were written : *The King Is Still In London,* and a spoof, *We'll Heil, Heil, Right In the Fuhrer's Face.* Princess Elizabeth, (Queen Elizabeth today), joined the WAC's, (Women's Army Corps). She took mechanic training and drove an army truck.

England and her Commonwealth, (Canada, Australia, New Zealand, etc.) stood alone until Japan bombed Pearl Harbour on Dec. 7, 1941. This brought United States into the war. Hirohito, the Emperor of Japan, became allied with Hitler and Mussolini.

It took 3 more years to build the strength to free Europe. The beginning of the end came when Hitler decided to invade Russian. If he had studied history he would have known that was a bad move. A Russian winter will defeat any army, and he ran out of fuel for his planes and tanks. A massive move was made to attack Hitler and Mussolini on four fronts: European invasion, African counter attacks, Russian front, and the Pacific. Finally, the end came in May 8, 1945, when the Nazi forces surrendered, followed almost immediately by the Fascist Powers. With efforts then concentrated in the West, and the invention of the Atom Bomb, Japan followed in defeat in August, 1945.

There, that's my history lesson. I suppose I felt it necessary to describe some events in detail because that is what we lived under for 6 years. Every history lesson started with an update and commentary of the action and current fronts. Many of the details are still very real to me. I know exactly what I was doing when the counter invasion forces were landed at Dieppe. The horses had got out the night before. Dad and I found them near Tilbury. We saddled Nancy and I drove the rest home. At nearly every laneway, people I didn't even know would run out to tell me how the invasion was going. The experience of living it can never be completely captured in a history book.

On the home front, Canada had no army when war was declared, so when young men signed up by the thousands, many with no more than a grade 8 education, there was a need to find out who could be trained for what. This was the beginning of I.Q. and aptitude test development on a wide scale. If you scored high on the test, then you were taught the basic educational skills required to do the job you had an aptitude for. Farm boys who made their living milking cows might become crack fighter pilots. Army and Air Force Bases sprang up over night. The training was intense, sometimes no more than 6 months before shipping out to England. As the skies in Britain became dominated more and more by German planes, young men were brought to Canada for training at our bases. They came from Britain, Australia, and from European countries where they had escaped and had joined the Allied forces. Many Canadian homes 'adopted' these men in uniform when they had leave for a week end.

With so many young men joining the forces, there was a shortage of labour everywhere. Girls with Grade 11 education were hired to work as tellers in banks—a first—and married women were allowed to continue teaching. In the factories converted to produce war materials—guns, planes, ships, guns, tanks, shells, bombs, and torpedoes,—the work force trained women welders, riveters, assembly line workers, truck drivers, etc. The factories ran 24 hours a day, seven days a week. The work week was 48 hours. Women were paid $10.00 a week—that's about 21 cents an hour.

Women were freed from being 'the little woman'. For the first time, it was possible for them to make their own money and enjoy the independence that brought. It was acceptable to leave your children with Grandma, Auntie, or the neighbour next door, so that you could work and contribute to the war effort. When the war finally ended and the veterans returned home, there was a problem. Were these women content to be shoved back into the kitchen? I guess not! Although the Feminine Revolution is attributed to the 60's, the seeds were sown in 1945 by women who wanted the equality that came with the ability to be productive outside the home. It was and is a long struggle that continues yet today.

The war years also gave birth to the 'efficiency experts'. Many studies were done to combine jobs and to save motion while you were doing them. In other words, how to do more in less time. Every task was analysed for every movement so you could work harder and accomplish more for the war effort. Yes, we fell for it, until it began to border on the ridiculous. A popular song came out at the time to poke fun at the whole idea. I wish I could remember the name and the words, but it told what to do with your right hand while you did something else with your left, while you used your right foot on one pedal and your left foot did something else. Your head was used to push buttons. Then, they tied a broom on behind so you could clean up after yourself.

Another up-date. Today there are still studies to see how we can do more in less time, but we now call it multi-tasking. The results haven't changed. We still have the same body parts to put to work, except now they say we can read, while we talk, while we type, all different subjects of course, while we are driving the car down a 4-lane highway. When expectations become ridiculous, collapse is sure to follow no matter what you call it. The latest studies show that multi-tasking increases stress related illness, reduces productivity, deteriorates the quality of work, and increases the number of accidents.

In May 8, VE Day, 1945, victory was declared in Europe. I was just finishing up my studies at Normal School. Immediately, when the news was broadcast, everything stopped to celebrate. The student body headed for downtown London en masse. Stores closed, schools were let out, factories blew their whistles and turned out into the streets. The streets were filled with celebrating souls hugging, and slapping each other on the back. Literally we danced in the streets, and celebrated without violence or destruction of property. After 5 years, we were about to return to peace. The first soldiers began to return in August.

Your Granddad Mac, a dispatch rider during WWII, was in Celle, Germany at the close of the war. He took a photographer to document the conditions in Belsen Concentration Camp. The photographer took this picture on Mac on his motorcycle. June 1945

LAC DRUMMOND M, R105402

THIS WAS YOUR GRANDFATHER'S RANK and serial number when he was an enlisted member of Canada's Air Force during World War ll. It was the fall of 1940. Mac was 20 years old and apparently was not 'shaping up' to suit his father. So his Dad gave him $50, took him to the end of the road and said, "Son, I don't want to see you until spring."

With all the bravado of a young man ready to conquer the world, he hitch-hiked to Toronto and got a job with Loblaw's Groceteria, unloading boxcars for 18 cents an hour. Yes, that was poor pay even in those days. After you paid for a room and your meals, there wasn't much left. In his rather rash way, Mac wrote in large letters on a black board, 'Great Gross of Arse Holes'. Can you believe he signed his name? You bet he was called down to the office. Only Mac could get away with that and end up with a raise—25 cents an hour!

In the spring, May 30, 1941, he was going to work on the streetcar when he met a man in Air Force Blue. "Where can I get one of those," he asked, and was directed to the nearest enlistment office. He got off at the next stop, caught a bus going the other way, and by the end of the day, he was an enlisted member of the RCAF.

He did not qualify to be trained for air crew. He was sent to St. Hubert, Quebec and trained as a security guard. He was posted to Rockcliff, just outside of Ottawa, where he served his shift guarding the Parliament Buildings as one of his duties.

He was in Rockcliff when the movie, "Captain of the Clouds" was made, telling the story of Canadian World War l hero, Billy Bishop. James Cagney starred in that film. If you should happen to find this old movie, look closely and don't blink. You will see Mac as one of Billy Bishop's Honour Guards.

Guard duty in Canada could become a bit tedious. In typical Mac fashion, he and a fellow guard, Dan McCarthy, decided to liven things up a little. This was the plan—From his guard corner, Mac would shout, "Halt, who goes there," then fire off a volley of shots. Leaving enough time for a intruder to move from one corner of the base to the other, McCarthy was to repeat the order and shots. However, McCarthy didn't wait. Almost immediately, shots rang out from his corner. Called up on the carpet, both stuck to their stories. The episode remained unsolved.

However, years later, when Mac and I attended a performance of 'Private Turvy's War' at The Confederation Theatre in Charlottetown, PEI, this bit of Canadiana was re-enacted on the stage. We, of course, were the only two people in the audience who knew the inside story. We laughed until we were in tears.

In August, 1941, Mac was sent overseas on the *Louis Pasteur*, a tug of a ship that brought German prisoners to POW camps in Canada, and returned to England with Canadian soldiers. The ship was filthy dirty, alive with rats and bugs. The food was not fit to eat. On the second day out, when a rat floated on the top of the stew, his appetite preferred chocolate bars for the rest of the trip. Progress was slow because ships travelled in convoys, dodging German submarines. It took 11 days to cross the Atlantic, finally landing in Glasgow, Scotland.

From Glasgow, the troops went by rail to Bournemouth, England. When they were marched from the station to their barracks, people lined the streets. One English woman was heard to shout, "Here come the Canadians. Look, they're white!" In her colonial mind, she thought Canadians were Indians.

Mac spent some time at Croydon, on the southern outskirts of London, and then was moved to Gilford, a base closer to the English Channel.

At Gilford, Mac's restless nature caught up to him again. Guard duty—well, he'd been there, done that. Coming back from the mess hall, he saw an officer's motorcycle parked beside the building. He 'borrowed' it and took a little ride. When Mac brought the bike back, he bluffed the officer into thinking he knew how to ride. "Well," the officer said, "we need Dispatch Riders. Why don't you go down to headquarters and apply for a transfer?" If it was routine and boredom he wanted to escape, and new territory to explore, he found it! He was assigned to 143 Wing as a Dispatch Rider.

His first bike was an old Norton, 500 c.c. He says he had to kick it a lot, but coming from a farm, he had a pretty good background in mechanics so was able to keep it running well. His next bike was a Matchless, a better machine for cross-country trips. That was replaced with an Enfield, 500 c.c., equipped with a sidecar in which he often carried officers. He rode this bike a lot until he scared the #@*! out of an office by raising the sidecar to go around a telephone pole. Just before the invasion of France, he was issued a new Harley 45. It was his pride and joy. The Harley was not a good cross-country bike, but it was the best for convoy duty. This was the bike he rode until the war ended.

A Dispatch Rider did many things. As the name suggests, he carried dispatches (messages) from base to base, and later, under combat, from the front lines back to the officers in charge. He also did convoy duty—that is—he was responsible for moving 50 to 100 or more trucks, tanks, and equipment from point A to B, making sure all stayed together. He had a map to follow, but sometimes it was not accurate. This demanded long hours, dedication and often the worse of conditions from the weather and the terrain. Mac took great pride in getting his convoys through without mishap.

Sitting around in England waiting for the invasion of Europe was not a dull time. Mac's favourite place to go was Canada House, just across from Nelson's Statue in 'down town' London. This was the meeting place for Canadian soldiers. If you wanted to get in touch with someone, you left your name and location on the 'board'. In 1990, when we visited England, it troubled him to find the building in disrepair; the guard wore a turban; the guide knew nothing about Canada; the Art Exhibit in the basement was American, not Canadian. Many other Canadians must have made the same complaint. Since then, Canada House has been given a 'face-lift'.

Of course, there were always dances to go to. He says he would look around for the best dancer and get her to teach him different steps. (Now there's a line to help you pick up a girl friend.) He got to be a good dancer! It took me a long time to learn to follow his lead.

It should not surprise you to hear that cribbage, poker and dice—craps—was also a common pastime, or that sometimes you win, and sometimes you lose. He and a buddy did not have enough money to go into London on leave. They pooled their cash and played craps, winner take all, to see who would go. The buddy went to London for a week, Mac caught a train to a farm in Wales to help milk about 40 cows.

This was a very old farm. The house roof was thatch. The farmer's wife cooked in an iron pot which swung in and out over the fireplace. Food was basic. Sometimes it was wild rabbit stew which was hunted between milkings. Milking was done by hand from 3 to 8 in the morning and again from 3 to 8 in the afternoon. The stables were cleaned using a dump cart pulled by a Welsh pony. In the evenings, they would walk down to the neighbour-hood pub to join the other farmers for a pint of bitters and a game of darts. Mac was taken to a horse sale and was impressed by the quality of the horses.

Mac spent nearly three years in England, waiting for the Allied Forces to gather for the invasion of France—D-Day, June 6, 1944. Sixteen days after D-Day, Mac landed at Bayeux on a big, barge type, landing craft that was built to carry trucks, tanks and supplies needed for the front lines. The craft pulled up to shore as close as possible. Then it dropped down the high front which acted as a ramp for unloading. Every motor was running. His bike was carried on the back of an officer's jeep. His was the first off. As soon as they reached solid beach, he jumped down, unloaded the bike and began gathering up the vehicles for his convoy to move them to the airdrome. Fighting was intense both from the air and with ground shelling. The airdrome, about 10 kilometres inland, was a collection of tents laid out in a farmer's field. Wire mesh was laid down to serve as runways.

Living in tents did not give much protection from shelling and bombs. A lot of time was spent in ditches and under bridges until the attack was over. Keeping clean was a challenge. Each soldier had to do his own washing. Bed bugs, head lice, and scabies made themselves at home on men sleeping on the ground. Mac spent five days in hospital with scabies. After that he washed his woollen blankets every week in gasoline to kill any unwanted bed mates. Disease was spread from unsanitary conditions and the poor health of the people who survived the German occupation. Needles and vaccinations were common to protect the soldiers from typhoid and tuberculosis in particular. In spite of this, Mac came home with TB scars on his lungs.

The lines moved back and forth, kilometre by kilometre. Coming back from the front, Mac got caught behind the lines of a German spearhead. He hid his bike in a ditch beside the road where German tanks were moving in. He spent about 36 hours hidden there until the Germans were driven back and he could return to camp.

Slowly the front moved forward east to Tille and Caen. The British fell back at Caen and the city had to be retaken by the Canadians. The death and destruction was terrible. Mac still can't talk about it. It haunts his nightmares to this day.

Heavy casualty to German tanks and planes, plus the pressure from the Russian front, began to tell on the German defence. By October, the lines moved forward more quickly. By spring, Mac had ridden dispatch through France, Holland, Belgium, and Denmark, as each country was freed. Eleven Dispatch Riders had come to France from 143 Wing. By the end of the war, only he and one other were still alive. Besides dodging bullets, there were land mines and piano wire stretched between trees at neck level. The worst that Mac suffered was three broken ribs when his bike hit a shell hole, flipped and came down on him. He was able to right it and continue on his way.

While he was still in France, Mac spent several days with George Broomfield, a Canadian war artist, who took pictures of the battlefields, later to paint the scenes into oils. He gave Mac copies of the photos. George Broomfield became a highly acclaimed artist for his work. Many of his paintings hang in the War Museum on Ottawa. Mac still has the photos from which they were painted.

Because Mac was lent to the British Army for about three months, and to The Americans for a while, he didn't meet many of the 'boys from home'. He ran into Morley Shilson, who was a Military Policeman, in Eindhoven, Holland. His meeting with Ron Geddes, a friend from Coatsworth, is typical of some of the unbelievable stories that were told during the War.

Ron Geddes was an ace Spitfire pilot. He flew from the Gilford Base in England where Mac was also stationed. Before he took off each time, Ron would give Mac his wallet and papers, saying, "If I don't come back, you know what to do with them", meaning, send them home to my folks. The ritual continued until June 4. Mac sat counting the returning planes. Ron's was missing. Another pilot said he saw the plane go down in flames but Ron had bailed out.

Mac couldn't bring himself to write to Ron's parents. He wrapped up the wallet and papers and tucked them into the bottom of his kit bag as he packed for the invasion. Now move ahead 67 days to an airdrome somewhere in France. Mac had just returned from a run and was checking his bike when he saw a dishevelled, bearded, dirty man walking down the road toward camp. Thinking this was another Frenchman looking for something to eat, he didn't pay much attention until the fellow came up to him. It was Ron Geddes! A French farmer had hidden him out in a barn. The Germans were headquartered in the space below. The farmer smuggled raw potatoes and carrots into Ron to keep him alive. Ron could barely speak. He was sent home on leave for three months, then returned for another tour of duty.

Another freak encounter—we were standing in line waiting to get into a United Church Fowl Supper in South River in 1965. As usual, Mac and Elgin Schneider were kibitzing good naturedly when Mac said, "Don't mess with LAC Drummond M, R105402. The Anglican Church Minister behind them said, "That sounds like an Air force number to me." They began talking and found that they had both been based with 143 Wing at Gilford and had landed at Bayeux together. They began to 'remember when' when Mac said, "Do you remember the jeep full of officers that hit the tank carrier and were all killed?"

"Remember?" he replied. "I was returning from leave and had hitched a ride back to camp. I was in the cab of the carrier."

"Well," Mac added. "I was going on leave and I had hitched a ride into town with the officers. I was thrown clear and suffered only a couple of broken ribs."

Fifty years after the fact, they realized they had been in the same accident.

Even though it was war, discipline was strict. For not cleaning his room properly, Mac got 3 weeks kitchen duty. When the hint of a grin crossed his face, that was increased to 6 weeks. Soldiers were still expected to be properly dressed in full uniform when they were on leave. On leave in Holland, he was walking down the street without his tie. He was picked up by an MP and taken before the officer in charge. He was sentenced to 3 days pack drill carrying 70 pounds on his back.

Army food! That's not recalled with any relish! Mess hall was aptly named. In Britain, the main meat was mutton. To this day, he refuses to eat anything that comes from a woolly beast. The Americans ate well as he learned when he was on loan to them. He didn't miss the opportunity to stop for a meal if he was close to an American camp. Because he was never sure where he would be at meal time, he always carried hard tack and bully beef in his saddle bags. Hard tack was a hard biscuit, filled with nutrition and vitamins, that you could dip into tea or suck on if there was no liquid to help soften it. Bully beef was canned corned beef. He must have had to eat a lot of it. It was years before I was allowed to have a can in the house.

Letters and parcels from home could always make your day. As long as he was in service, every month, Loblaw's sent him a package of food, cigarettes and candy. The Sally Ann (Salvation Army) had socks, mitts, and scarves to hand out when you needed them.

When Germany fell and the war ended, Mac was stationed in Germany, at Celle, midway between Hamburg and Hanover. He doesn't like to remember a lot about the clean up that followed the peace. He was with the first crew sent in to clean up Belsen Concentration Camp. The smell, the corpses, the walking skeletons—atrocities unbelievable to any imagination. Don't ever let anybody tell you that concentration camps didn't exist, and that it was only allied propaganda. That would be a great slap in the face to soldiers who fought the war and helped clean it up afterward. If you really want to study this part of history, see the film Nuremberg. The pictures and detail are gruesome and true!

It's now late July, 1945. Mac has been moved to Flensburg, just south of Norway's border. He has returned from a convoy mission and is asleep in his bunk. Another D.R. shakes him awake, and tells him he has his repatriation notice. Since Mac won't believe him, he runs to the office, pulls the notice off the board, runs it back to barracks and waves it in his face. Yes! he's going home as soon as he can clear the base!

Repat. papers only gave him permission to go home, not a nicely prepared ticket. He had to get there on his own. It took him 3 days by train to get back to a French port. Bridges were still out. You rode as far as you could, carried your bags across the gulf, and caught the next train. This was repeated several times before he reached the coast of France. Next he had to find a boat to cross the Channel, and finally one to Canada. On the ship that brought him home, he met—guess who—Ron Geddes! They disembarked at Halifax and caught the first train to Tilbury. They flipped a coin to see who would call home for someone to meet them. Ron called his dad who dropped Mac off at the Drummond laneway about 7 o'clock in the morning. Imagine the shock and the reunion! Just the day before his Mother had received a letter from him written in Flensburg.

HOW I MET YOUR GRANDFATHER

O.K. It's now August 4th, 1945. The War is over, and I have
graduated from Normal School. Jean and Harold had bought the
Churchill General Store and Feed Mill in Staples. The store was in half
of the building with living quarters occupying the other half. There was a
bell over the store door to let you know when a customer came in. I was
staying with Jean and Harold, helping with painting and other clean-up
chores.

Such excitement when Harold came in from opening the Mill. Mac
Drummond, the first soldier to return was home from the War! He had
walked into his parent's house that morning. Why his Mother had received
a letter from him written somewhere in Germany just yesterday. He was
with his brother Ray, who had come for grain for his cattle and meat for
the threshing bee at his house that day. Hmm. Mac Drummond? I could
vaguely remember hearing his name as one of the first in the area to join
the Royal Canadian Air Force.

Harold went back out to the mill. Jean and I were getting breakfast
ready. The bell rang over the store door. A customer! Jean asked me to
wait on him while she finished cooking the eggs. Guess who? It was Mac
Drummond. He asked for a pack of cigarettes. I waited on him . . . (he
hates me to say this . . . and I have been waiting on him every since.)

It was the last Saturday in August before Mac 'came to call'. For some
reason, I was home alone and had just brought the cows up to the barn
ready for Dad and Mother to do the milking. My horse, Nancy, had been
sold. My current horse was a bay gelding called Rocky. As usual, the tom
boy in me had not bothered to pull on a pair of slacks or shoes. I had
climbed up straddle his back in an old cotton print dress. I brought the
cattle into the barnyard and jumped down to open the gate to let Rocky

and me through. The mud oozed up between my toes. Well, that was better than having to clean it off your shoes! I closed the gate behind me and almost bumped into Mac. He wanted to go dancing with me? I guess I must have cleaned up pretty well. He seemed to approve when I came down the stairs 30 minutes later. At least he was still there.

You don't know what romance is until you have danced to the big band sound. Can you get the picture? You're at the lake shore, the stars over head, with the soft summer air caressing your hair, and the moon is playing on the ripples of the water. In the park, there is a band shell large enough to hold a 25-30 piece band complete with trumpets, trombones, French horns, clarinets, flutes and a piccolo or two, a piano, a tuba, and oh, yes, drums and a conductor. An amplifier is only used to pick up the voice of the band vocalist as she/he croons the words of *Moonlight Becomes You, Moon Over Miami*, or *Star Dust*. Now that's BIG BAND.

The roped off terrazzo floor was smooth as glass. For 10 cents, you entered the dance area and the band played 3 numbers, about 15 minutes of music. The dance floor would then be emptied, and refilled—for 10 cents a couple. When you tired of that band in that spot, you drove further along the lakeshore until you came to the next town, the next band shell, the next band, but hey, the same moon. Who said you can't believe in fairy tales? We had them live.

There were any number of local bands that made good music, but several became famous. Guy Lombardo and His Royal Canadians from London, Ontario, played for many years at the Waldorf-Astoria Hotel in New York City. If you hadn't made plans for Saturday night, you could hear the broadcast live on the radio. The Dorsey Brothers, Jimmy and Tommy, started out as one band, then split into two. Wayne King was known as the waltz king.

The world was weary after the war and ready to embrace anything new and up beat. Some of the popular songs were played with a jazz tempo. These caught on quickly. Bands such as Benny Goodman who played the clarinet, Gene Krupa with drums, and Stan Kenton on the vibraphone became the rage.

This music required a different dance step, and the Jitterbug was born. I never learned how to Jitterbug. My feet moved to a constant one, two three, four. Mac was the dancer. He would double the time in mid-step or syncopate the rhythm to fit his mood. It took concentration to follow him. I must have been a slow learner—it took me about three years.

Dress was also affected. There was no more need to limit the amount of material in your clothing. The really 'with it' young men wore Zoot Suits. These were suits sewn with very wide padded shoulders, a long coat, and tight trouser cuffs. A large brimmed hat with a chiffon band, and a long chain dangling from the belt. completed the look. Girls wore poodle skirts with at least one but sometimes two, very full, heavily starched, crinolines beneath to make the skirt stand out and sway when you danced. Yes, the crinolines were very picky, but pride feels no pain, you know. Sometimes skirts were made in full circles. Of course, everything required ironing. That could take hours. Add to this bobby socks and saddle shoes if you really wanted to be in style.

Lead singers often split with the bands to become solo artists. Popular names were Bing Crosby, Nat King Cole, Frank Sinatra, Perry Como, Dean Martin, Eddie Fischer, and Van Johnson. Some of the female stars were Peggy Lee, Rosemary Clooney, Sarah Vaugh, Jo Stafford, and Ella Fitzgerald. Also in demand were trios and quartets such as The Andrew Sisters and The Ink Spots. Music was put out on records (they were 45 rpm's) which could be played on a portable player. These were pretty crude and bulky compared to your CD players. Many of these artists moved into the motion pictures, and were stars in the extravaganzas of the new movie musicals.

It took a few months before Mac and I became a couple. You see, I had this problem—a steady boy friend named Max, in uniform, overseas. So . . . just before Christmas, (how heartless) Max got a 'Dear John' letter. Yes, my dears, that was very cruel and unpatriotic of me, but—c'est la vie.

I was also very busy teaching in my first school at S.S.# 5. Mersea Township, a one-roomed school, for $1,300 per year. That figure is correct. I didn't miss any zeros. It also happened that all the little Drummonds attended that school—that is Ray and Leola's children: Kaye, Madeline, Villa, Merle, Yonne, and Vida Joy (Alvin and Ruby's daughter). (Joan was too young to go to school). Yonne and Shirley Scratch were my Grade 1 class. Such bright, sweet little girls, so anxious to learn. Phonics had been thrown out by that time. Children learned to read by sight. That worked well until they had a vocabulary of 150 words or so. Then they became very frustrated. They wanted to read and they had no skills for unlocking new words. I did the unthinkable. I introduced them to phonics as initial and final consonants, along with a few vowel combination sounds as they needed them. Now those two girls were off to the races! By Christmas, they could read almost anything you put in front of them. When the inspector came to the school in February, he couldn't believe their skills. I pulled my phonic cards out of the drawer and explained how I combined them with sight words. He took my method to other schools. I wasn't very smart. I should have published a book. Someone else put it all together and made a fortune.

I had five students in Grade 8 that year: Kaye Drummond, Mary Dundas, Gerald Armstrong, Shirley Whittal, and Madeline Drummond who had completed grades 7 and 8 in one year. These kids were required to write and pass the High School Entrance Exams in English Literature, Composition and Grammar, Spelling, and Mathematics before they could go on to secondary school. From Easter until exam dates, we came to school an hour earlier in the morning and reviewed and drilled until they were ready to write. We worked hard—they all passed!

July 18, 1946. Our wedding photo. Your Grandparents.
Weren't we young!

The great romance had grown and blossomed. We introduced Mac's best friend, Morley Shilson, when he returned from overseas, to my best friend, Marie Whittal, and we became a four-some. Our wedding was planned for July 18, 1946, at 3 pm, in Windfall United Church. Morley and Marie were our best man and maid of honour. Jane Lattam was bridesmaid and Rosalind was our junior bridesmaid. My two cousins, Wilbur Tetzlaff and Bill McIntosh were ushers. My good friend, Margaret Walker, played the wedding music. Erla Hill sang *I love You Truly* and *Wait and See.*

They tell me weddings are supposed to be hectic. If that is true, ours was a big success. To begin with, the day was already hot and humid by 8 o'clock in the morning. I got out the iron to do whatever pressing had to be done before the day got any hotter. I went to get Dad's pants for his new suit—no pants! The suit had been bought two months before with the pants left at the tailor's to be hemmed. No one had remember to pick them up. Dad walking me down the aisle in his underwear was not in the plans. What to do? I called Harold who was going to Leamington to do his banking. Would he pick up Dad's pants? No problem . . . . except the tailor wouldn't release them without the ticket. This is where you swear under your breath. It was now 11:30. The stores all closed at noon on Thursday. I jumped into the car, raced to town with the ticket and got my toe in the door just before it was locked for the day . . . Phew.

I delayed dressing myself because of the heat—it was about 85' by 2 o'clock. My long dress was made of white satin with lace trim. The neck line was heart shaped, the sleeves were long and finished in a point over my hands. Do you feel warm already? When I finally pulled it over my head, you could see my body shadow through the material. That wouldn't be a problem today, but it was a no-no then. Quickly Mother fashioned a half slip to remedy the problem. Right, one more layer of cloth to keep me warm. But, we did make it to the church on time!

Mac tells me it was also hectic on his side. Suits were still difficult to buy. He and Morley had ordered theirs from a store in Chatham three months before. Mac went to pick his up a week before the wedding. Neither suit was in, but there was a ready made one in the right colour, and in his size. So he bought it. Morley went to Chatham the morning of the wedding to pick his up. It hadn't come in, but Mac's had. The two men were the same size, so Morley took the suit. As I said, it was Thursday and stores closed Thursday afternoons. The pants needed to be hemmed.

The tailor had left for the day. Morley found him downtown in a pub, and persuaded him to come back to the shop and hem the pants. Morley put on the suit at the tailor's, arriving at the church, just in time.

The reception for the immediate families, (34 guests) was supposed to be held on the front lawn, but it was still too hot, so tables were set up inside for the adults, and on the front veranda for the children. I don't remember what was served, except it was a cold meal. I do remember giggling to myself when we changed and drove away. Someone else had to do all those dishes!

Our honeymoon, was next to a disaster! We drove all night to get to Vida and Harold's house in Troy, Ohio. Why? You'll have to ask your Grandfather. The weather remained very hot. I was expected to cook our meals—really??! Money was tight, We came home three days later.

The large, white house on the Drummond farm was divided into living quarters for us—a kitchen, living room and bedroom. Pa and Grandma took the front part. Mac was going to take over the farm from his dad. I was going back to teach at S.S. #5 in September.

So here I am with a new husband, a new name, and a whole new extended family to adjust to.

DRUMMOND FAMILY TREE

James Walter (Joe) Drummond	Married Dec 23, 1903	Arvilla Jane Tuffin
Born: Apr 17, 1876 Died: May 19, 1961		Died: July 3, 1989 Born: May 20, 1887

Walter Ray
(Leola Collard)
Children:
1) Kaye Walter
Married
Kathleen Dawson
Joan
David
Tom
Lisa
2) Madeline Leola
Married Jack Mills
Mary Ann
Judy
Douglas
Joe
3) Villa May
Married
Bob Richmond
Ronald
Louann
Nancy
5) Elsie Yonne
Married
Jerry Liddle
John
Linda
Robert
Mary Jane
6) Joan
Married
Lynn Wright
Bill

Alvin Kenneth
(Ruby Collard)
Children:
1) Vida Joy
Married
Oville Kimball
Bonny
Richard
Darlene
2) Susan Alzora
Married Tom Reid
Christopher
Janet

Vida Marie
(Harold Lattam)
Children:
1) Jane Marie
Married
John Fennie
Walter
Gary
Scott
Dirk
2) Mac Arthur
Married Martha Weisner
Amanda

Mac (Ruth Willan)

see Your Family Tree

Seated: Arvilla and James Walter (Joe) Drummond, your great grandparents. Standing: L.R. Alvin, Vida, Ray, Mac (your Granddad) Circa 1948

THE DRUMMOND CLAN

WALTER JAMES (JOE) Drummond and Arvilla Jane Tuffin were married Dec. 23rd, 1903. Joe Drummond was affectionately call Pa by his grandchildren. He was a quiet man with little room for nonsense, yet he enjoyed his family completely. He was a good farmer and highly respected by the community. He and Grandma were the anchor for the Drummond and Tuffin families. When someone needed a hand, they were there. Children were sent to spend the summer with Uncle Joe and Aunt Arvilla. Grandma would sew for them so that they had new clothes for school in the fall. When Uncle Roland returned from World War 1, he was very ill, having been gassed by the Germans. Pa and Grandma looked after him until he died 3 or 4 years later. Uncle Glen returned from WW1 with a British bride, Aunt Gertie. They made their home with Pa and Grandma for almost a year until they could become established on their own. Pa didn't feel he was giving a hand out, but rather a leg up.

The grandchildren were special to Pa. He could relax with them more than he could with his children. He enjoyed listening to them and sharing in their fun and activities. When Erla was just toddling, she followed him around the field by the house where he was building a fence. She chattered incessantly. I think he didn't understand a word she said, but he would answer and talk away to her as if she were a grown up.

Pa lived to be 85 years old. He was one of the few people I knew who grew old gracefully. He enjoyed watching baseball and hockey games. His chair was pulled up close to the television. The volume was on high. He disliked the Detroit Red Wings with a passion. The announcer said, "Geordie Howe has the puck! He shoots! I don't know what kept it out of the net!" To this Pa exclaimed, "The goal post, you darn fool!"

Pa remained interested in what people were doing, how the crops were going in, and the price of wheat and corn. He died May 19, 1962. His body wore out but his mind remained sharp until the moment he died.

Grandma Drummond had a great sense of humour. A water pail sat on a shelf just inside the kitchen door. It was a common prank to throw a dipper full through the screen at an unsuspecting member of the family as they came to the door. One day, by mistake, Grandma threw a dipper full of water on Pa. Oooops . . . . he was not impressed.

She was a wonderful cook. She seldom measured anything, but her cakes and cookies would melt in your mouth. Her pie crusts were always flaky, and she always seemed to have pie, cake and cookies for every meal. Well, now, I could do okay with meat and potatoes, but don't ask me to bake. The wood stove was either too hot or not hot enough. My chocolate cakes turned into sad brownies or dried tooth breakers. So I made a deal with Grandma. If she would bake for me, I would clean for her. It was an agreeable arrangement for both of us.

And, of course, Grandma was the ideal babysitter. Her grandchildren adored her. (maybe because she always had cookies in the jar). On our first anniversary, we didn't have any money to celebrate. She came in with a $5 bill and offered to keep Erla while we went out to dinner. Yes, at that time, you could have a nice dinner and go to the show for $5. I will always treasure that memory.

By the time she was 80, Grandma was developing Alzheimer's. She was not safe to be in her own home. Leola looked after her as long as she could. We tried to keep her with us, but she wouldn't stay. We had to make the hard decision to have her live in the Sun Parlour Home in Leamington where she would get round the clock care. Within 10 years, her mind was completely lost both to us and to her. She died in her 102nd year, July 3rd, 1989.

MAC'S BROTHERS AND SISTER

WALTER RAY DRUMMOND WAS THE oldest of the family, born June 8, 1905. He was married to Leola Irene (Collard) They had 6 children: Kaye, Madeline, Villa, Merle, Yonne and Joan. Right, all of these but Joan were students in my first school. Because Ray and Leola lived on a small farm almost next door to the Drummond farm, these kids were very close to us. They worshipped their Uncle Mac. Erla, Debby and Jill grew up almost like their little sisters.

One had to admire Ray and Leola raising this large family during the depression. It had to take a lot of sacrifice and desperate budgeting. To their credit, all 6 children graduated from high school—a real change of thinking for the times.

Ray and Leola had been married more than 60 years when Leola passed away July 12, 1997. Ray continued to live in his little apartment in the Manor until he died March 25, 2000, just short of his 95th birthday.

Alvin Kenneth Drummond was born October 29, 1908. He was married to Ruby Alzora Collard). Right. Brothers married sisters. Alvin and Ruby had one daughter, Vida Joy, who was also a student in my first school. Susan Alzora was born much later, Oct. 7, 1955. Alvin was the quiet, steady, foundation for the family. He never seemed to worry about the weather or the price of grain. He could settle down arguments and hard feelings with a few words of wisdom. He worked hard, but never owned land. He and Ruby share cropped a number of farms, finally working for Burns Coulter on a sand farm near Leamington. A sand farm meant spending long hours on your hands and knees weeding carrots, onions, spinach, which were grown for the Heinz factory. During the summer of '54 he had two serious accidents. After the first one, he had a large tumour removed from his spine. In the fall, when they were digging potatoes, he got caught in the power take off of the tractor. He fought madly to keep from being pulled into the machine. When he finally broke loose, he had only his shirt and his shoes left on his body. The rest of his clothing had been eaten up in the power take off. The backs of his legs were worn raw exposing the cords and muscles.

Shortly after his recovery, Ruby became ill. Finally a smart doctor tested her for pregnancy. The test was positive. Alvin's nerves were already taunt. He felt that he was too old to be a dad again. He already had a granddaughter (Vida's Bonnie) 2 years old. This was so unlike him. He loved children. The family doctor finally convinced him to see a psychiatrist who wanted to admit him to hospital. Alvin convinced the doctor to let him go home for the week-end. On Friday, March 17, 1955, he committed suicide. We were all shocked and stunned. Autopsies were seldom done in those days. I have wished so many times that we had thought of asking for one. It seemed to me later, that his problems all started with that first accident and the damage to his nerves. It would have meant so much to all of us to have a reason. Unanswered questions—the haunting aftermath of suicide.

Alvin had no will. Ruby was left without a home, expecting a baby. The government stepped in, evaluated everything she owned. She was allowed one-third, Vida Joy one third, and one-third was put away for the unborn baby. To get money to help raise the baby, Ruby had to apply every six months from a trustee in Ottawa. Vida was not yet 21, so her one-third was also put in trust. As soon as she reached 21, she turned her share over to her Mother. The lesson here—don't die without a will!

In January, 1956, Ruby and Susan came to live with us. We paid her a small wage, one that we could afford, but certainly much less than she deserved. She helped raise Erla, Debby, Jill and Will. She was a stabilizing member of the household. No matter what went wrong, she could handle it with her calm efficiency. When we decided to move to South River, she chose to stay in Wheatley. She got a job at Woolworth's store in Leamington. She worked there until she was pensioned at 65. Susan grew up to be a lovely young women. Today, Ruby still lives in her little house in Wheatley.

The lone girl in the family was Vida Marie Drummond born November 8, 1911. She married Harold Lattam June 21, 1930. They had Jane Marie and Mac Arthur. Harold was a sausage maker by trade. He worked for a number of meat packers and made a good living. When we were married, he worked in Troy, Ohio. From there he moved for a short time to Port Huron, Michigan, and finally to Garner, North Carolina. He developed the first cheese dog, (a wiener with cheese in the meat), which was a big hit in the south. The company refused to give him a patent and fired him. He had a job immediately in Charleston, but before they could get moved, he died suddenly of a heart attack May 10, 1957.

Vida and Harold came home often, not seeming to mind the long trip. Vida always brought something for the kids. She brought Erla the first disposable diapers. Oooh, they were a far cry from today's diapers, but they were sure great to carry when you went away from home. We visited them about once every 3 years or so. One time, Alvin, Ruby, Grandma, Mac and I went down. What a great trip that was. Another time we drove Ray's car with Ray, Leola, and Ruby as passengers. We laughed all the way there and back. Vida loved a good time.

After Harold died, Vida got a job as bookkeeper in a men's clothing store in Raleigh, North Carolina. Jane was a registered nurse, and was married to John Fennie. Mac Arthur was just 14. He went on to graduate as a textile engineer from the university in Raleigh. Vida retired from her job when she was 70. She lived very well alone until she lost both Jane and John within 3 years. Like her mother, Alzheimer's set in. She grew too weak and forgetful to stay alone. For a time, she lived in a nursing home in Greensboro. She died August 11, 2001.

Of course, in an extended family, there were the aunts and uncles to meet. Pa didn't drive the car, so Mac and I took him and Grandma wherever they were invited to visit. There was a big family on Pa's side, but they kept in closer touch with Aunt Fanny Reed, Aunt Jenny Brown, and Uncle Bob Drummond. Mac and I were good friends with some of the cousins, especially Benson Reed, (Aunt Fanny's son), Harold and Mabel Drummond, (Uncle Bob's son),and Ivan and Winnifred Drummond, (Uncle Archie's son). On Grandma's side, her brothers, Uncle Glen and Aunt Gertie Tuffin, Uncle George and Aunt Annie Tuffin, and their families were well known. Your parent will remember these uncles because they often visited with us in South River. Uncle Glen was known for his jokes. He not only liked to tell jokes, he like to play practical jokes on people.

YOUR FAMILY TREE

Grandfather	Married:	Grandmother
Mac Drummond	July 18, 1946	Ruth Irene Willan
Born: Sept 22, 1920		Born: Feb 4, 1927

Erla Marie	Deborah Ruth	Roxanna Jill	Mac Willan	Paula Jane Michelle
Born: June 28, 1947	Born: Mar 14, 1950	Born: Oct 28, 1951	Born: April 15, 1958	Born: June 5, 1963
			Died: Feb 7, 2004	
Married Aug 11, 1969	Married Sept 19, 1970	Married July 9, 1974	Married Aug 2, 1980	Married May 16, 1987
Dale Tebby	Phillip Aubin	Ian Campbell	Louise Snider	Paul Vella
Born: Aug 4, 1947	Born: Oct 6, 1948	Born: July 13, 1950	Born: Jan 21, 1958	
Divorced				Divorced

Married Feb 21, 1981
Ron Pacaud
Born: Feb 13, 1948

Deborah Ruth — Children:
1) Benjamin Gerald
Born: May 2, 1973
Married Andrea Scherban

Divorced

Married June 20, 2008
Judith Wilson
Children:
Cadence Brooke
Born: July 28, 2009

2) Justin Phillip
Born: Jan 17, 1975
Married July 28, 2001
Dana Piper
Born: Apr 2, 1976
Children:
Rowan Benjamin
Born: Feb 19, 2003
Keaton Piper
Born: Apr 21, 2005

3) Xavier
Stillborn: Dec 15, 1983

Divorced

Significant Other
Jesse James
Born: Feb 24, 1941

Erla Marie — Children:
1) Troy Ivan
Born July 23, 1981

Divorced

Significant Other
Kim Stewart
Born: June 20, 1955

Roxanna Jill — Children:
1) Elizabeth Kathleen
Born: June 18, 1982

Divorced

Significant Other
Wayne Fuga
Born: Feb 6, 1959

Mac Willan — Children:
1) Deborah Ann
Born: June 9, 1984
Married: July 9, 2005
Darren Graves
Born: Oct 21, 1978
Children:
Kaylee Marie
Born: May 11, 2007
Abigail Maddie
Born: Mar 28, 2010

2) Katie Louise
Born: May 16, 1986
Significant Other
Mason Mack
Children:
Jacob Kenneth
Willan Mack-Drummond
Born: June 9, 2005

Divorced

Married May 2, 1992
Jane Webster
Born: March 22, 1958

Children:
3) Sarah Jane Ruth
Born: Dec 12, 1993

4) Valerie Grace
Born: May 13, 1998

Paula Jane Michelle:
Married Sept 10, 1997
Pierre (Pete) Ferreira
Born: Feb 9, 1966

Children:
1) Gloriana Irene
Born: Feb 28, 1998

2) Antonio (Tony) Mac
Born: Apr 9, 2000

HOME FROM THE HONEYMOON

I WELL REMEMBER THE FIRST morning we got up in our part of the house at Drummond's. It was 10 to 6. Mac said, "It's time that I held down my share and took some of the work load off Dad's shoulders. After all, he is 70 years old." Later when he came into the house for breakfast, he was laughing. He had beaten his Dad to the barn and Pa was mad. You see Pa believed he had to turn the sun on each morning. The next morning, Mac again went to the barn at 6 o'clock. But when he came in for breakfast, he was mad. Pa was in the barn by quarter to six. Mac fumed, "If he thinks I'm getting up at 5 o'clock just to beat him to the barn, he's crazy!"

The Drummonds grew tomatoes for the Heinz factory in Leamington. So, I went to the tomato field with the rest of the pickers. Grandma's job was in the house where she baby sat and got the meals for the gang. She could make her voice heard anywhere on the 84 acres. The first day I was picking, I heard her call and figured I'd come as soon as I had filled the basket I was working on. When I looked up, the others were almost to the house. I was told that if you didn't come when she called, she would clear off the table and you could go hungry. From that day on, I had no problem leaving a basket half full when I heard her call.

The first years of our marriage were rather rocky. A soldier newly returned from war had a lot of problems to deal with. I will try to explain what I can understand about returning to civilian life after spending 4 1/2 years carrying a gun and fearing for your life.

Mac had terrible night mares, as often as two or three a month. He would flail, mumble, and come up fighting when he had one. You did not waken him abruptly from a sleep, for he might come up with fists flying, ready to defend himself.

He talked very little about his experiences, preferring to forget what he had seen and been through and to get on with his life. If would be nice if bad memories could be dealt with that easily. The inner turmoil broke through with restlessness and the inability to stick to a job.

Add to that the fact that I was pregnant by Christmas. Married teachers were allowed to teach but pregnant ones were not. We lost the independence that an extra pay check provided.

Erla Marie, born June 28, 1947, weighed in at 8 lbs. 1 oz. (The gossips were disappointed. We had been married 11 months and 11 days.) She was a pink and white picture. She was born with fuzz for hair. I bought Nestle's Baby Curl, dipped my fingers into the solution, and made little spit curls all over her head. At one year, she had enough hair to put a curl down the middle of her head. I dressed her like a doll, changing her clothes at least three times a day. Her Grandma Drummond would come home from town with enough material to make matching dress and panties. She had panties, hair ribbons and stockings to match every dress. I spent a lot of time washing and ironing.

Erla walked at 10 months old. By the time she was a year, she was running. and climbing. There was nothing that she couldn't reach. She would pull out the drawers of the cupboards or chests and walk up them like stair steps. She was also a determined toddler. 'No' was a fighting word. Everyone said, "Don't put things up out of her way. Teach her to leave them alone." By the time she learned that, there wasn't much left to break.

Erla adored Pa, who returned the devotion. He put up a fence around the field near the house. She toddled along beside him, jabbering in baby talk. He appeared to be listening, would take her hand and move on to the next fence post.

The economy had not yet recovered from war production. Jobs were not plentiful. Farmers were still not paid adequately for the food they produced. The farm simply did not make enough money for two families. In September, Mac got a job managing a 200 acre farm just east of Wheatley. There was a Japanese family who had been relocated from British Columbia, and a German family moved from New Brunswick. Mac had been hired as the boss. There was a large herd of cattle to be milked, and pigs and chickens to tend. Needless to say, these two families didn't get along at all. Not only did they fight, threatening to kill each other, but they were also robbing the owner blind.

We had been there three weeks and I still wasn't completely unpacked because I went back to Drummond's to help pick tomatoes nearly every day. Mac came in and said, "Pack up. We're moving! I just finished fighting one war. I'm not going to fight another!" We rented a small four room house owned by Harvey Wilkinson just outside of Leamington. Mac got a job with Philpott's Bakery in Leamington. He baked pies, cakes and cookies. You could live on the pay if you budgeted carefully. This job lasted until Mac got a carbuncle on his arm from eating too much sugar. I guess he sampled his work too much.

We moved back to the farm into the front part of the house this time. Mac helped Pa with the farming and worked at Nelson's Wood Products in Wheatley where he operated a large band saw. He bought a second-hand motorcycle to ride to work. Madeline rode behind him to attend Grade 9 at Wheatley Continuation School. For Grade 10, the high school in Leamington had been expanded and busses were put on to take the students from Mersea Township to attend high school there.

But I'm getting off the track. You could see Mac getting restless, and it would be no surprise when he said he had quit his job. Fortunately, by now, jobs were more plentiful. From Nelson's, he went to work for the Co-Op in Comber, first driving truck, then working in the hardware. We were able to save up enough money to have our own home. Now, this was a big investment. We bought a vacant, old house on a farm about 2 miles down the road for—get this—$400.00. We hired the Shad Brothers from North Buxton to move it to the farm across the lane from the big house. That cost us $76.00. We spent another $200.00 on a foundation and on the inside to make it quite liveable. Don't knock it! It was warm, comfortable, and we owned it without a mortgage. Know what? There are still people living in that house today.

On March 14, 1950, Deborah Ruth, weighing 8 lbs. 2 oz. was born. How could we be so lucky to get two beautiful little girls! I wanted to call her Nola Irene, but the rest of the family thought that a terrible name. Friends of ours, who had two boys, suggested Deborah Ruth. I think that was a good choice.

Debby was the typical second child. She could wrap anyone around her little finger with a smile. She was born with a full head of hair which she never lost. By six months, it had turned very blonde, and by 8 months it was long enough to braid. I called her 'my little papoose' until one day, she put her arm around my neck, looked into my face and asked, "Is I you're little poopass?"

Two little girls to sew for and dress like dolls! However, I soon learned that a little girl could wear the same dress all day. By now, we could afford a refrigerator, with small, built-in freezer. Why do I remember this? Well, at that time, cotton had to be starched, dried, dampened, rolled up, and then ironed. In hot weather, if you left it too long, the material would mould, leaving it stained. What does this have to do with a refrigerator? If you didn't get the day's ironing done, you rolled the rest up in a towel and put it in the freezer!

As was accepted in those days, the man of the family made the decisions. In the spring, 1951, it was no surprise to find that Pa, Ray and Mac decided to change properties. Pa bought our little house, Ray bought the home farm, and Mac bought Ray's 42 acres. We all packed up our things and moved the same day. What a hoot! It was common to open a box and find Grandma's or Leola's things, so boxes were shipped back and forth until everything got straightened out.

To get money for our share of the land switch, we borrowed money from The Veteran's Land Act which had been set up by the government to help returned veterans get established after the war. Several good things came from this. For one thing, my name was put on the land title. Recognizing that a wife was a co-owner of property was a real step forward for women. We (I should say I) had to keep books of how much money was earned, and where it was spent. This was a good habit to establish and helped tremendously in planning for payments and getting ahead.

Our third little doll weighing 8 lbs. 3 oz. arrived October 28, 1951. I had picked the name Roxanna Jill and I wasn't prepared to argue about it, so I sent in the registration card before I left the hospital. When folks began to make other suggestions it was too late. The name fit the family, as did this beautiful, little blondie.

The farm house was cold, drafty and hard to heat. There was no way to keep Jill warm in a crib that winter, so by midnight, when she was wet and hungry, I'd pull her into bed with me and kept her snug until morning. Mac worked the 4 to midnight shift at the Ford factory in Windsor. Without a car or a telephone, the evening chores to do, and three little ones with runny noses, it was a long winter!

When Jill was about 20 months old all three girls came down with Whooping Cough the same day. Although they had had the serum, they took it very hard. Because of Edwin, Whooping Cough was dreaded. This disease causes phlegm to build up in the throat and lungs. The child coughs to get rid of it, giving a deep intake of breath that sounds like a whoop. Jill, being so young, whopped until she couldn't catch her breath. I ran to the telephone, and called the doctor. Luckily, in those days, you could get the doctor at 9 o'clock at night. He said to get some whiskey down her throat. We didn't have anything alcoholic in the house. Kaye happened to be there, said his dad had a new bottle, jumped in the car, and was back in no time. We managed to get a bit down Jill. Then her dad picked her up by the heels, and while he held her upside down, I put my fingers into her throat. That loosened the phlegm. She brought up more than I could hold in my hands. Then she went into a comma. Again, I called the doctor who said he would call the druggist to go down to the drug store (it's now 11 o'clock at night) and Mac could slip into town to pick up a prescription. There were 5 doses in each prescription. It took three before Jill was herself again.

It would be simple if Whooping Cough lasted a couple of weeks and you would get better. The girls whooped all winter. Coughing would start about 2:30 every night. We would both run upstairs. One would get Erla out of bed, onto her knees in front of a pail. Then we would tend to Debby and Jill until the coughing stopped, usually after they had lost their supper.

By spring, Erla was healthy again. Infection had settled into Debby and Jill's tonsils. It was early summer before they were well enough to have their tonsils removed. Debby picked up quickly after that and was healthy to start to school. It took Jill six months or so more before she had fought off the infection.

At one time or another, they had all of the communicable childhood diseases. Whooping Cough had to be the worst. Chicken Pox and Measles came and went. Erla, however, didn't build up an immunity to Measles. In total, by the time she was 16, she had them five times.

But life was good. The girls grew. I found that they could live in jeans and slacks during the day. The fussy dresses were kept for Sundays and parties. It wasn't long until Jill was the same height as Debby. I dressed the two of them alike. Since they were both blondes, they were often taken for twins. This changed when Debby started to school and insisted on her individuality.

Two's company and three's a crowd is the old adage. It was often true with three little girls. Erla and Debby would play together and exclude

Jill. In an attempt to be noticed and included, Jill would take away a toy and run with it. When everything was gone, Debby just sat, looking sad, in the middle of the floor. Jill stopped in front of her, bent down, looked into her face, and asked, "What's the matter Debby?"

Debby replied, "Poor Debby. Debby has nothing to play with." Right! She soon had all the toys back, and more! Come to think of it, Debby may still use this tactic.

Jill was slow to say words. She jabbered incessantly but we couldn't tell what she was saying. She was two years old when she got up one morning and there she was, talking plainly in sentences. I read to the girls every night from books on Erla's level, so this is the vocabulary that was normal for Jill. Sometimes other kids got lost in her conversation because she used words they didn't understand. Debby would translate.

It came time for Erla to go to school. She had to walk back through Ciliska's lane to the next concession, turn right, and walk another half mile to S.S.#5 Mersea school. (Yes, that's the one I first taught in.) We walked the trip a couple of times before September to be sure she knew the way. On that first day of school, she insisted that she could do it by herself. Off she went, waving happily as she disappeared from my sight. Oh, she did fine! It was her mother that had to call Ciliska's about 20 minutes later to be sure she had come through and turned the right way.

Erla and Debby played school every night. Jill was left out because 'she was too little'. Does that sound familiar? I tore the sheets from the calendar and gave Jill a pencil. The back of the sheets were not written on. What would she write? Of course, she traced the writing that shone through. In no time at all, she could write her numbers from 1 to 31—all backwards! When I realized what had happened, I took time to correct it, but you know how hard it is to unlearn something. Jill tells me, occasionally when she is in a hurry, she reverts to backward numbers if she isn't careful.

Mac made the girls a king-sized teeter-totter. It had a long plank which was very springy. They would get on one end and he would bounce them from the other end. They called it a bucking bronco. It scared me then and seems even more dangerous now! They soon learned how to position themselves to compensate for the difference in weight so that they could teeter by themselves.

Erla got a new sled for Christmas. In Essex County the only hill you can find is on the side of a ditch bank. Patiently, they waited for snow. Erla had the first trip down. Well, it was her sled. She found herself at the bottom of the ditch in slushy water. "Get off," everybody hollered. "No," she answered, as she bravely sat on the sled as it slowly sunk. "I don't want to lose my sled." Really, there was little chance. The water was only six or eight inches deep.

Cowboys and Indians was a popular game, complete with cowboy shirts. chaps, boots, and toy guns. Jill was a wild horse. They caught her and tied her up to the door knob with a rope around her neck. She panicked pulling the rope tight. Luckily, I was right there to set her free. The girls got another lecture on playing safely!

B-I-N-G-O

W E GOT A PUPPY WHEN we lived on the farm. Bingo was half
English setter and half black Labrador Retriever. He was named
'Bingo' after a very smart dog in the comics. Mac brought him home in
January with the declaration, "This is to be my hunting dog. I don't want
him spoiled by living in the house."—Sure!-

After three or four days, I asked him how his puppy was doing.
"Not too well," he said. "He doesn't seem to be eating and he's not very
playful."

The next morning, after Mac went to work, I went to the barn and
brought Bingo to the house for the day, warning the girls, "Don't tell your
Dad."

After three or four more days, I again asked Mac how the puppy was
doing. "Great," he answered. "His appetite has improved and he's so glad
to see me . . ." There must have been a hint of a grin on my face. "You've
brought him to the house, haven't you", he accused. From then on, he
compromised. Bingo came to the house each morning, but he still had to
sleep in the barn at night.

Bingo lived up to his name. He learned quickly. He could do almost
anything but talk. When he was still a puppy, Mac ran over him with the
trailer. We took him to the vet who said he was only bruised. However,
there must have been something broken. After he healed, he walked with
a cane leg. That didn't slow him up as a hunting dog. Nothing got away
from him. It didn't matter who shot the bird, he brought it back to Mac.

Bingo was also a wonderful pet for the girls. It wasn't long before
he slept in the house on their beds. He moved to Wheatley with us and
became a favourite at Gulliver's Garage. He walked to work with Mac each
morning and rode around in the wrecker all day. He came home covered

with grease at night. Mac decided he had to sleep outside on the porch. Bingo caught pneumonia. Mac relented after he paid for the penicillin to make him better.

Grant Watson, the mechanic, used to take Bingo home for lunch to play with his little boys. When we decided to move to South River, it didn't seem fair to coop a hunting dog up in an apartment. Grant needed no coaxing. He gave Bingo a good home. For a few years, Mac returned to Wheatley to hunt pheasants, and Bingo continued to be a top hunting dog. But the last time he went, he found Bingo on a rug by the furnace. He was now about 10 years old and suffering from Leukemia. He remembered Mac, crawled painfully into his lap and licked his face. Tears flowed. Bingo died a few weeks later.

BACK TO THE FARM

I N THE SUMMER, 1955, OUR tomato crop was destroyed by cut worms. Tomatoes were a 'cash crop', that meant that farmers depended on the money—ready cash—from tomatoes to get the extra things you wanted. We decided that I should go back to teaching. Teachers were scarce. The pay had risen considerably to $2,300 per year. That was more than 3 tomato crops! Besides, one more year of teaching would give me a permanent teacher's certificate, and you never knew when that might come in handy. It was the end of June. I called the Public School Inspector to see what was available. Within four hours, I had four trustees from Hillman School, S.S.#10 Mersea at my door. This was a two-room school. They were looking for a senior room teacher who would also be principal.

It looked good to me. I took it. It wasn't until I found the Inspector waiting for me the first day of school, that I got the low down. The kids at Hillman had run out five teachers in four years!

Joan Brooks, a Grade 12 graduate with a 6-week summer course, was the junior room teacher. Joan was fantastic, with an innate sense for teaching. She and I became friends instantly. We had those kids whipped (no, we didn't use the strap) into shape in no time.

We had wonderful support from the inspector. He was at the school every day the first week, and twice a week for the first month.

The school board was also great. One morning in mid September, when I drove up about 8:20, there sat Mr. Derksen, chairman of the board, waiting for me. I thought, "Oh, my goodness, what have I done now?"

He got into my car and asked, "How are my children behaving in school?'

There were four Derksen children, two in Junior room and two in mine. All of them were well behaved and eager to learn.

"Mr. Derksen," I replied, "if all the students were as well mannered and easy to teach as yours, there would be no problem."

"That's what I wanted to know," he reassured me. "We send them to school to learn. If there is a discipline problem, please let us know and we will deal with it at home."

Then there were the VonZittwitz and the Taggarts. These families lived side by side. Two boys from each family fought like you wouldn't believe. They had to be separated on the playground. It was the spring when they arrived at school one morning, scratched and bleeding. At that time, a teacher was responsible for students from the time they left home until they arrived back after school. (Kind of a crazy regulation) I wrote a note and sent them home for fighting. The VonZittwitz boys returned almost immediately, with a note from their mother which said, "I send my children to school for you to teach. You have my permission to use whatever discipline is required to do this."

For the rest of the year, the four boys were confined to the classroom all day, given separate 10 minute washroom breaks at recess and lunch. On alternate weeks, the VonZittwitz boys left school first, the Taggarts were dismissed 20 minutes later. The next week this was reversed. Things were cool. When the boys returned the following September, the first question I got was, "Mrs. Drummond, what happens if we fight this year?'

"Do you remember last year?" I asked. "The same applies this year."

Those four boys became good friends. There was no more trouble from them.

Rudy VonZittwitz came into my Grade 5 that September. Somewhere, he had missed learning his addition and multiplication facts. In desperation, I decided to keep him after school to master these. Oops, that was a Friday—not too bright! But I had learned that you couldn't change your mind or back down from the VonZittwitz boys, So stay he must. I looked out the window and who should be waiting for him but his Father. Mr. VonZittwitz was rather intimidating. He had been a Luftwaffe (the German Air Force) Pilot for the Nazi's in the Second World War. When he came to the school, he didn't knock, but 'goose stepped' (that was the term given to the way the Germans marched) across the room. That day, gratefully, he waited the half hour in the car while Rudy and I worked on addition facts. One Monday morning, Rudy came into class and said, "Boy, was Dad ever mad on Friday night."

I didn't know if I should ask why, but I did. Rudy explained, "Yeah, Dad said it was about time someone made me learn to add. He was at me all week end. He wouldn't let me count on my fingers. He made me put my hands behind my back. But, do you know something? I can count on my fingers just as fast behind my back as I can in front."

There were some memorable students at Hillman. Jakie Wilms, an exceedingly bright young man, knew how bright he was. His arrogance sometimes bordered on making him impossible. His test results were so letter perfect that I thought he must have copied the answers from the text. I watched carefully. He hadn't copied. So we played a little game. He would lose a mark for a blot on the paper, or for not leaving a line after a title, or some other really insignificant little thing. With his good natured grin, he said,

"One day I'll turn in a perfect paper where you'll give me 100%." At the close of Grade 8 this happened. Jakie quickly wrote his final Math paper, and asked for more foolscap (the regulation paper for examinations). He carefully copied the complete answer sheets. They were like a work of art. Jakie got his 100%. I lost track of him until years later when I learned he had a large Real Estate business around Niagara Falls.

I taught at Hillman for two years before I took a school closer to home. In my best memory of schools, Hillman is near the top.

Mac was the first, the original, 'stay-at-home-father'. He looked after Debby and Jill—Erla was in school—did the farm work and looked after the house. It wasn't long until he had found every corner had to be cleaned. He was quick to remind you to take off your shoes at the door. He had just scrubbed the floor!

The biggest chore was the washing. We still didn't have water on tap, so we brought in the big copper boiler, placed it on the back of the stove, filled it with water pumped from the cistern, built up the fire about 3 o'clock in the middle of the night and started to wash by six. I would go off to school at 8 o'clock, and Mac would hang out the clothes when it got day light. This worked fine, until one morning, as he was hanging out 28 pairs of women's underwear, a neighbour went by on the road. The neighbour thought this a big joke, and used it at Mac's expense whenever he got the chance. From then on, I had to hang out the 28 pair of women's pants before I went to school.

This worked well as long as there was plenty of outside work to do to balance the house chores. We had saved enough money to put in a bath room and a pressure system providing running water. We drew the water from the cistern, so the supply was limited. We bought water by the truck load, 1000 gallons, $20.00 a load, and dumped it into the cistern. You had to be very careful how you used it to make it last a month.

When winter settled in, Mac was fit to be tied. By Christmas we needed a saviour. She showed up—Aunt Ruby! In January, 1956, she and Susan, who wasn't quite three months old, came to live with us.

Debby started to school in the fall, walking through Ciliska's lane with Erla. The first morning her expectant face suddenly turned to tears. "What's the matter, Sweetie?" I asked. "I thought you were excited about going to school."

"They won't want me at school," she sobbed. "I can't do anything. I don't know how to read or print words." It took some reassurance to convince her that it was O.K The teacher would help her. Debby found school to her liking. She was always a good student.

It was the spring of 1957, here we go again! Mac was restless. It was time to move. Forty-two acres of land was not enough to farm profitably. Morley Thompson owned the forty-two acres on one side, and Ciliska's owned forty-two acres on the other side. Neither one was interested in selling. Morley wanted to buy. The deal was made.

We bought a big, old, house on Erie Street South, in Wheatley, almost across from Grandma Dean. We moved after Easter. Ruby and Susan moved with us.

Mac, at this time, was working for Olmstead's Fishery as their chief maintenance man. Young Leonard Olmstead came up with an idea to bread, cook, package, freeze fish. He was given $5,000 to build his invention. Mac was sent to work with him. First, they built a giant mix master to stir up the batter for the fish. Then they constructed a conveyor belt on which the breaded fish were placed. This ran through an oven which sprayed the fish with oil as the fillets were cooked with infra-red light. The fish came out the other side, cooked and cooled. They were packaged and sent to the freezer. The big day came to show off this innovative idea. All the big wigs were there. The motor was started on the conveyor belt. The breaded fish entered the oven—and—the whole thing burned up.

The Olmstead's were folks of few words. Dad Leonard asked, "Do you know what went wrong?"

Son Leonard replied, "I think so."

Dad L., "If you built another, would it work?"

Son L., "I think so."

Dad L., "Here's another cheque for $5,000"

So Mac and Leonard Jr. took the bugs out of the oven until it worked like a charm. Olmstead's put the first pre-cooked frozen fish on the market. Leonard Jr., some years later, sold his patent for a rumoured $5,000,000.

The girls transferred into Wheatley Public School. Jill started to kindergarten, a big step for a five year old who still needed an afternoon nap. She went all day until 2:30 each afternoon. As soon as she got home she fell asleep for a couple of hours. Kindergarten was a mystery to her, as was Grade One. The balls and sticks had no meaning. She was put at the bottom of the class with the little yellow birds. Just after Thanksgiving, everything fell into place. By Christmas, she was reading with the top group. She became an avid reader. In high school, she was one of very few students to write a perfect I.Q. (intelligence quotient) test, which means that her I.Q. is at least 135. Later, she recorded the highest score in reading speed and comprehension at Canadore College, a score that remained unchallenged for many years.

I was hired by the Wheatley board in September to teach Grade 6. This was the first that I had taught a single grade. What a snap to have the time to do all the subject applications that handling all eight grades didn't provide!

This only lasted until Christmas. Mac and Ruth were expecting another bundle of joy. I left the class at the end of December. Mac Willan Drummond was born April 15, 1958. He was a handsome, big boy, 9 lbs. 10 oz., a real butter ball, with a lot of blonde hair like his sisters. By six months, he had a brush cut. From the beginning he was happy to be cuddled, especially by his Dad. It took the two of them a while to adjust to going to bed to sleep after 11 o'clock.

Teachers were still scarce. In September Debby's Grade 4 class didn't have a teacher. The board almost begged me to come back to work. It was Debby's class. What could I do? I went back to teaching. Will settled in nicely with Aunt Ruby.

This was a challenging class. Nine of them had been accelerated in Grade 3 and had completed the Grade 4 curriculum. Debby was one of those. Ten had not completed Grade 3 work. A new inspector did not agree with acceleration or with failure. I looked at those 30 dear little faces. Thank goodness for my one-room classroom experience. The nine at the top learned to research and present topics. They could read any map placed in front of them, They rhymed off all the counties in Ontario, and could point each out blindfolded. They sight read music and could sing it in three part harmony. Those who had come into the class behind were motivated to learn. By June, every student in the class tested ready for Grade 5 work. Yes, I'm bragging. I was some proud of those kids!

The next year, I was promoted to vice-principal (no extra money, just the honour of the position) and given a Grade 7 of very bright kids to teach. Erla was in this class. These students had missed phonics in Grade 1. They read well enough but couldn't spell to save their souls. I went to the Grade 1 teacher and got all the phonics material. Then I boiled it down and gave the class an intensive 2-week course. Next, I got a class set of dictionaries and taught them how to find correct spellings. They were encouraged to use the dictionary for every subject, except spelling, of course. Gary Coulter put up his hand and asked how to spell 'neither'. I replied, "Gary, use your dictionary."

"But Mrs. Drummond, how can I find it, if I don't know how to spell it?" We had a little more work to do.

The inspector felt that I was marking this class too high. I insisted that they were an above average class, so he gave them an I.Q. test. When he returned with the results, he said I was marking them pretty hard. No one tested below 107, which is high average.

I introduced this class to poetry which delighted them immensely. They were soon reciting their favourites and writing their own. One day I happened to write H2O, the chemical formula for water, on the blackboard. From that day onward, bright-eyed David, in the front seat, became very interested in science. Years later, he became a chemical engineer.

Erla had a hard time that year. Because the class learned so well, she and Gary usually ended up at the bottom—with averages of 68% or better. It was necessary to continually remind them that these were good marks. Gary had a crush on Erla. He sent her 15 valentine cards.

The girls not only enjoyed school in Wheatley, but also the number of kids on the block to play with. Our house sat on a double lot, the back half left vacant. It was a perfect place for baseball, tag, football. As a result, we usually had at least 8 or 10 kids around. I didn't mind because it meant that I knew where my children were.

Some of the boys were bigger and older. They liked to tackle and wrestle. I felt this was not an appropriate activity for my girls. I called them into the house and laid down the law! Out they went to play. Lo, and behold! They were at it again! I called them in and sat them on chairs while I finished the baking. They wiggled and squirmed. Finally, Jill spoke up.

"Mom, are you going to spank us?"

"I don't know," I said. "I haven't decided yet. Why?"

"Please," she begged, "when you do decide, can I have mine first so I can go back out to play?"

How could you spank after that? The girls went out to play. The law was laid down to the boys!

One day, Jill came racing home at noon, ran into the house, grabbed up her skipping rope, darted out the drive to hide behind a big maple tree at the sidewalk. She moved around the tree to stay hidden until one of the older boys, who had been teasing her, walked past. She jumped out behind him, grabbed him by the belt, and began to beat him with her skipping rope. He was so startled that he took off running. She held on tight, pulled along with giant steps. Every time her feet touched the ground, she hit him again. She returned grinning. That young fellow gave her a wide berth after that.

One day, I was late coming home from school. The bigger boys realized this and began to harass the girls, who took refuge in the house. When they pushed open the back door, Erla was ready with a heavy iron frying pan which she applied to the young man's head—boing! That was that. No more bothering the Drummond girls!

Poor Jill! The rule was, that if you got a strapping at school, you got another when you got home. Jill was in a Grade 3 advanced class. This meant that she was in the top learning group and the teacher was to enrich their curriculum. This was rather a lazy teacher who insisted that these kids simply did more of the same work. So instead of doing 75 math problems, they were expected to do 100 in the same period of time. Jill disgraced the group by having 5 wrong. The teacher strapped her. Although I was teaching in the school, no one told me. The mean older sisters knew, though. They blackmailed Jill for several weeks, getting all sorts of favours for their silence. One day, Mac came home for lunch with some insignificant piece of information, and said to Jill, "What's this I heard about you at school?' Jill broke into tears and the whole story came out. Sometimes rules have to be broken. The teacher and I had a little chat.

Erla and Debby participated in public speaking, each winning the sectional divisions and going on to the county competitions. Erla's speech was entitled *The St. Lawrence Seaway*, complete with diagrams and maps.

Debby spoke on *My Favourite Teacher*. They did well, earning honourable mention at that level. Jill competed in public speaking in high school and won the Legion Trophy.

Mac had developed arthritis in his hands from working in the cold water at Olmsteads. Oh, yes, he changed jobs. He invested money in Gulliver Motors and worked as a grease monkey in the garage. It didn't take long before he realized he wasn't going to make money on this investment. One August morning as he was walking to work, he stopped to talk to Bill McVittie, who was washing the windows of his 5/$1.00 store. Mac respected Bill as a good business man.

"Where can I go to start a good business of my own?" he asked Bill.

"Mildred (his wife) and I just came back from our cottage at Eagle Lake, South River," Bill said. "That town really needs a good 5/$1.00 store. There's a big empty building right on main street that would be a great location."

"Ruth and I are going on a holiday next week," Mac reasoned. "Where in the world is South River? Maybe we could take a look."

And we did! Oh, My! We arrived about 7 o'clock on a Saturday night. Until this time, I had very little experience with the 'north'. I don't know what I expected, but this wasn't it! South River looked like a town out of an 1880 western movie. The middle of the street had been paved, once. The shoulders were not. Some of the sidewalks were board. Yes, they were. The insulation hung from the electric wires that lined the streets. The street lamps must have had 25 watt bulbs in them. The store fronts were unpainted, The town was deserted.

Even the 1957 Chevy station wagon we were driving had a problem going this far away from home. For the last 10 miles, we nursed a fuel pump that was ready to quit any time. We found a garage open with a young fellow who only served gas. He knew nothing about motors.

"Well," Mac said, "if you will give me permission to run this car into the garage and show me where the tools are, I can fix it myself."

The young man called Orv York, the owner, who came down and got Mac the tools and parts he needed. By this time a bed looked good. We spent our first night in South River with Jean and Wally Tough who owned the Almaguin Motel, one of the few modern businesses in the area.

The next day, we looked up Jack Currie whom Bill McVittie knew well and had given us a letter of introduction. Jack was an interesting man who had lived in the area most of his life. He spent several hours showing us around. He pointed out the empty McGirr store which stood on the corner of Ottawa and Toronto streets, downtown South River. Wow! We decided to think about it over night before going any farther with this idea. We spent another night at the Almaguin Motel. After breakfast, Mac asked, "Well, do we call the McGirr's or do we get out of town?" That was an easy decision. "Let's get out of town. How far is it to Ottawa?"

Back in Wheatley, things settled back into routine, except that now, Mac had this idea about owning a store in South River. Every time things slowed up at the garage, he would wonder, "Is that building still for sale in South River?" By February, he couldn't stand it any longer. It was apparent that Mac was about to change jobs—again.

I had read in the paper that northern Ontario had a record amount of snowfall. "Let's stop this foolishness right now," I thought. "If he sees that country buried in snow, that will put an end to this pipe dream once and for all." (It's a shame my knowledge did not include putting up with swarms of black flies that came every June. I would have been more careful about gambling that he would change his mind!) So bravely, I said, "Why don't you take a drive up there to see for yourself?" And he did! He put a $1,000 bond which we had just finished paying for into his pocket, and on Sunday morning he took off for the great white north. He returned four days later. He had bought this big, empty building with living quarters above the empty store space, for $18,000! He came home by Orangeville, and stopped in to see the fellows at Merchant Supply who agreed to supply him with stock. On the 14th of March, he packed up the car and left to open a 5/$1.00 store in South River! Well, yes, it did take the wind out of my sails for a while, but it was all part of the fun of the roller coaster ride when you were married to Mac Drummond.

Mac lived in the apartment over the store with the McDermotts and Mrs. McGirr, who had reserved living space until their cottage was ready on the 28th of June. He was surprised to learn, after the snow melted, that there were three steps up into the store. He worked like mad to shape up the store ready to open. This was a big, old empty space that had not been open for business for some time. Everything had to be built—the counters and shelves. He remodelled a lot of what he could find, beg and borrow. That's Mac. He's always been creative in recycling.

It took a lot of letters back and forth to keep him encouraged to follow his dream.

After all, we had jumped in with both feet. It meant—sink or swim. Mac, who wasn't much at writing, got pretty good at it. I could even read most of what he wrote.

Merchants' Supply Company admired his spunk, I think. They made regular visits to give him ideas and encouragement. He had only $5,000 for stock, which was lost in the big space of the store. So there were a lot of big pictures, one row deep on the top shelves.

Jean Sova, Ruby and I drove up to South River the night before, to be there for the opening, Friday, April 28th. We stayed at Wally and Jean's Motel, and arrived at the store about 7:45 a.m. the next morning. Already there was a line up waiting for the doors to open at 9. I went upstairs to talk to Mac. I found him sitting on the edge of the bed, in his underwear, looking pretty down.

"Oh, Ruth," he said, "what have I done? We have all our money sunk in this thing, and nobody will come. I've put the last $50.00 into the till to make change."

When I convinced him to look out the window at the line up, he wasn't long getting dressed!

The opening was a big success. That night, before we went to bed, Mac sat counting the money. He couldn't believe it! The next morning when I woke up, he was still counting the money.

When we closed Saturday night, he was in a panic again. He had sold out more than half his stock. "What will I do on Monday?" he lamented. "I have nothing left to sell." Merchant Supply was a step ahead of him. They had already phoned in an order which would arrive on Tuesday.

Back in Wheatley, there I was, a single mom with a full time job, four children to look after, and a house to sell. Ruby did not want to move north with us. In May, she bought a little house and got a job working at the new Woolworth Store in Leamington. Will missed his Dad, Aunt Ruby and Susan. His cruel old mother took him across the street, around the block and left him with this stranger all day. He was not a happy camper! He started to scream "Ma, Ma," like a lost little calf, the minute he hit the sidewalk.

I was going to be methodical in my packing. Every night I did loads of washing, packed the clean, folded items into big boxes, and carefully marked the contents. I was doing very well, until Dad, who was going to move us in his big, farm truck, showed up to say he and Mother planned to go west to the Calgary Stampede. They would be out to pick up the first load of furniture on the 15th! It's a good thing to be young. The first load pulled out as scheduled. The kids and I moved in with Dad and Mother. Will was no happier. This time it was Mother who tried to calm him all day. After school, I returned to the old house to clean it up, making it respectable for sale. I used a lot of soap, water and wax. That house shone and smelled so clean that it sold two weeks after we left town. We had bought it for $5,000 and sold it for $7,000. We thought that was a good profit in those days.

On the 29th of June, I packed up the green station wagon with the four kids and the rest of our belongings. There was barely enough room to get everything in. About 8 o'clock, I bravely waved good bye to Mom and Dad and headed North. It was at least an 8 hour drive.

SOUTH RIVER—HERE WE COME!

WHAT CAN I SAY? GET ready for a cultural shock. Our new home was a large building on the corner of Ottawa and Toronto Streets. Toronto Street was part of Highway 11 before the by-pass was built. It ran through a pretty valley with two bridges that spanned South River. Whitehead's Hydro Power Plant produced electricity from water behind a dam in the river, through flumes that ran from the dam, under the bridges, and down to the power plant 100 feet below. There was not much traffic on the street anymore because Highway 11 now by-passed the town, so this was a good place to play and ride a bike. The kids soon named it 'the dam road'. This took some explanation when strangers came to town.

The store was bricked on the two sides facing the streets and covered with insul-brick on the other sides. Insul-brick was a cheap material used to up-grade the outside of old buildings. It was a combination material made from tar and red sand patterned to look like brick. As an insulation, it was a good product. However, it was highly flammable. When it caught fire, very little could be saved. It soon was replaced by a better, safer product.

The whole first floor was now THE SOUTH RIVER 5/1.00 STORE. On the main street, two offices had been attached—Johnson's Insurance and Kincaid's Barber Shop, from whom we collected rent.

The only entrance to the upstairs apartment was through the store. This was no problem as long as the store was open. However, after hours, it meant that someone had to come all the way from upstairs, through the store, to open the door. It was not unusual to throw stones at a window to get someone's attention. A door bell would have been a good idea, but that would have cost money which we didn't have.

A long flight of stairs led to the upstairs living quarters. The space was large, occupying about 2/3rds of the total floor space of the second floor of the building. The apartment was nicely laid out, with three bedrooms, kitchen, living room, dining room and bath room. There were lots of windows to give good lighting. It definitely had possibilities.

I had moved into a lot of places, but nothing that needed the work that this required. There were good hardwood floors in the living room, dining room and kitchen. They all needed refinishing. The bedrooms had only sub-flooring. All the walls were painted a sick yellow-green colour. The top sashes of the windows had lost their blocks and some had slipped so much that you could run your hand into the space. That wasn't a problem during the summer, but I wasn't looking forward to that much fresh air come winter.

Ah, the kitchen! There was a sink, but no taps. Water had to be drawn from the bathroom. There was no hot water. The source of electricity was expensive and unreliable. An electric clock wouldn't keep time. One turned on the hot water tank to heat water for a bath on Saturday morning. By evening, the water seldom got beyond lukewarm. Mrs. McGirr had left her old kitchen stove until we could get our propane one hooked up. This old stove burned wood. The oven door was held shut with a broom stick If you stamped your foot, the broom stick prop fell out and the oven door dropped with a thump. Cupboard space was limited.

Where to start? Definitely, the whole place needed a thorough cleaning and paint. Without money to redecorate, we had a problem. In the back room of the store, I found cans of the first cold water paint that had come on the market. Let me tell you about that cold water paint—It dried with a flat finish so rough that you wore out a cloth when it needed to be wiped down or washed. However, it was paint. There was enough to do one bedroom pink, one blue and one green, but not enough of any one colour to paint the other rooms. So I took all the paint that was left, mixed it together, and got a satisfactory grey that went on the living room and dinning room which were like one room divided by a wide archway.

We put the mattresses on the floor in the living room and started one room at a time, bedrooms first. I bought rugs which were cheaper than linoleum, from the catalogue, to cover the floors. As each room was finished, we moved in the furniture and unpacked what was needed for that room.

I tried to lay out a schedule to have the whole thing completed by September when I had to go back to school. So much for the best laid plans of mice and men. We had company! It seemed everybody we knew in Wheatley was curious to see where we had moved. People would 'drop in' about 4 or 5 o'clock in the afternoon. They didn't call ahead, bring any food or bedding. They expected to stay with us and be shown around. One group would leave and someone else would show up before I even got the bedding washed.

Was I stressed? You bet! After the first two weeks I set the agenda.

"Good to see you, folks. You are the answer to my prayers. We are painting this bedroom today. Would you like to use the brush or the roller?" Everyone seemed genuinely pleased to be part of the action.

Oh, yes, the windows! Mrs. Bud Bagley worked for Mac in the store. Her husband, Art, had a very bad heart and was unable to work, but he understood the challenge I had and came to help. He showed me how to shove the top window sashes into place and anchor them with blocks to keep them from slipping. He made frames which we covered with plastic to hook onto the outside. These acted as storm windows for about four years until we could afford to replace them.

By school time, every room, except the kitchen, was painted, and everything unpacked. Ahhhhhhh.

The girls had little place to play. Most of the kids were at the lake with their parents. As usual, they made their own fun. They played ball in the back yard. We hadn't been in town a week until they hit a ball through Mrs. Smeltzer's window. That irate lady marched into the store complaining about the hoodlums who broke her window. Mac had to soothe her complaints, promise her it would not happen again, and paid for a new window. Happily, the girls' reputations were not seriously damaged among the other town's folk.

The back yard was a disgraceful place filled with broken bottles, and weeds featuring thistles. Disregarding rules, Mac brought in a bull dozer in the middle of the night to dig a huge hole. This was cribbed with railroad ties, the septic system drained into it, and the hole covered with planks and layers of black tar paper. That was then covered with good top soil. The crime was never detected. The back yard was now covered with grass and flower beds.

It was the first day of school for the girls in a new community. There was a common put-down among kids at that time—'You're ugly and your mother dresses you funny.' I'm afraid I hadn't heard it. I dressed the girls in their fussy dresses, complete with ruffles and crinolines. I thought they looked adorable. They broke into tears. "Nobody dresses like this in South

River," they objected. They went to their Dad for reinforcements. It was one of the few times he went against my judgement. Out numbered, the kids pulled on their jeans and happily went off to school.

Jean and Harold, Dee Ann and Barbara visited that summer. They had always dreamed of living in the north. They made a deal for a garage, and a house to rent, but they couldn't get into the house until the middle of October. So that the girls could start school in September, they moved in with us for six weeks. That put 10 people together in the apartment, but it worked out well for everyone. The five girls got along well and Jean took care of Will, who by this time had settled back into the agreeable little guy he was before we had moved.

Manitoulin Transport delivered stock to the store. On the way home from North Bay, we had passed such a truck. The girls were curious to know if it would be coming to the store. As soon as we got home, they rushed to the empty storage space above the back of the store to watch for it. There was a door there which was often kept open to allow for ventilation. As Debby stood in the doorway, the wind caught the door, slamming it shut, and pitching her out, to fall about 20 feet to the ground below. Erla and Jill came screaming for me. I found Debby in a small square of cement, surrounded by piles of brick and chunks of stove wood. Without doubt, she had a broken arm. Her ankle was beginning to swell already, and she was still a little stunned.

At the hospital, her arm was set and put in a cast. Her ankle was badly sprained, but not broken. They kept her overnight to be sure there was no concussion. As she was lamenting about her broken arm, I said to her, "Honey, you are so lucky. With all the junk below that door, you could have been hurt much worse."

"No, I couldn't," she argued. "All the way down I thought about how I was going to land."

It took a while before we finally had our living quarters the way we wanted them. Very soon after we came to town, South River broke the contact with Whitehead's Power Contract. Ontario Hydro took over, and we had lots of cheap power. We had the kitchen cupboards rebuilt, taps on the sink, and hot water! We took space from the empty storage room behind the apartment, converting it into a laundry room and a bedroom for Will. We added an entry from the back yard with stairs to the apartment so that we didn't have to come through the store.

By an act of fate, we got the bathroom remodelled. About noon, one day, the toilet drain in the apartment sprung a leak and dripped through the ceiling onto the counter below in the store. We were the only store anywhere that had genuine toilet water on the toilet goods counter. Of course, that meant that the bathroom had to be completely re-plumbed that afternoon. The old fixtures were thrown out and replaced by cupboards with a built in sink. Isn't it wonderful how every cloud has a silver lining.

Mac sold bedding plants in the spring. When he had boxes that were wind burned, or dried out, he would give them to me to plant in the flower beds. The barber, Fred Kincaid, was considered to be the best gardener in town. He always had the first, the biggest and the best blooms. He would walk along the flower beds each morning before opening his shop and remind me that he would have blooms before I did. While I was unpacking, I came across a bunch of old plastic flowers. After dark, I stuck these into the flower beds among the greenery, and waited to see Fred's face the next morning. It was priceless. Fred took a double take and marched upstairs into the kitchen to tell me I was cheating! It became a joke with us, but that summer, I got the first bouquet of gladioli from Fred's garden.

Also, within that period, Mrs. Johnson, who owned a house across the street, decided to sell her home. She came to Mac to see if he would build her an apartment in the empty, back storage area over the store.

"Alma," he said, "I don't have the money to do that."

"I do," she said. "How much do you think it would take? I will lend you the money and take it out in rent."

How could you lose? I drew up the plans for a two bedroom apartment with a living room, dining area, kitchen, bath and laundry room which, if I remember correctly, was built for about $5,000. Alma and her 16-year old daughter, Donna, moved in. They were terrific neighbours and friends.

Across the street from the store sat a very dilapidated old building referred to as 'The Checker's Inn'. When the Dionne Quints were born in Calendar in 1934, tourists travelled miles to see them. The Checkers was considered to be *THE* place to stop for a meal, and even had rooms above where you could stay overnight. By 1950, when the Quints moved to Montreal, the tourist traffic had stopped. For more than 10 years, 'The Checker's' had deteriorated to a vacant building with windows broken out and covered with rusty sheets of tin. There was a big hole in the roof. We looked out at this eye sore from our bedroom and living room windows.

Then it came up for tax sale, i.e. the taxes on the property hadn't been paid for more than five years, so the town was allowed to put it up for sale. We borrowed $1,000 from the bank to put in a bid. The council called about 10 o'clock at night to tell us we had bought it. Early the next morning I was awakened by the sound of pounding from across the street. I jumped up to look out the window. There I saw Mac atop the Checkers mending the hole in the roof. I opened the window and yelled,

"Mac Drummond, what are you doing on that roof?"

"It's supposed to rain today, and I don't want water to run down into the building," he yelled back.

"What's the big hurry to fix it? That roof has been leaking for years," I reminded him.

"I didn't own it then," he replied.

Well, we went to the bank and borrowed another $10,000. With a new roof, windows, brick siding, furnace, and newly designed interior, we turned it into a great dentist's office with two bachelor apartments above. Durwin Chamberlaine, newly graduated from Loma Linda Dental College, and his wife, Sharon, rented the office and one of the upstairs apartments.

The office was to be ready the first of September. Durwin breezed into town around the 1st of August wanting to know when he could move in. There was still a lot of work to do. John Brott was laying brick.

"I laid brick to put myself through dental school," Durwin said.

"Did you?" Mac answered. "Well, if you want into this office by the first of September, you'd better get your trowel and get to work."

At that, Durwin disappeared, returning half an hour later dressed in jeans and carrying his trowel. Could he lay brick! He just about buried poor John, who had a hard time keeping out of his way. Then Durwin helped finish the inside by helping to lay the carpets in the office, up the stairs, and in the apartments.

The first time I sat in Durwin's dental chair for a check up, I reminded him that he used to be my bricklayer.

Mac got a new nick-name—"The Chancellor of the Ex-checker's", and some called South River, "Mac's/Maeck's Corners'. Gordon Maeck had a barber shop and pool hall on one corner, Lorne Maeck owned a service station on one corner, and Mac owned the buildings on the other two corners.

There was an old storage building behind the store. The town was looking for office space. The bank wouldn't lend us any more money without jeopardizing the limit we had to buy stock for the store. I had just started teaching in Powassan, so I went to the Bank of Nova Scotia to borrow money in my name to renovate the building. At that time, it was unheard of to lend a married woman money without her husband's signature. I persuaded the banker to do just that on the strength of my teaching contract. This meant that I had established my own credit rating independent from my husband, very unorthodox for 1962.

So, anyway, I borrowed $5,000 to turn this old building into three office spaces. One rented immediately. For a while, the other two stood vacant. Then Sy Yoshida came to teach at Powassan. No one would rent him an apartment in North Bay. He was living out of a suitcase and sleeping at the school. We turned the two back offices into an apartment in a period of two weeks. Again, we were connected to the right people. Sy had experience as a carpenter before he became a teacher. He took over, turning the space into comfortable living quarters in no time. Sy was also an amateur photographer. He took a lot of pictures of Will and Paula playing in the back yard. Sy became a good friend who often, at Will's request, came to dinner.

South River was good to us. The store prospered. Several very good women worked for Mac. Bud Bagley was there from the start and helped while the store was being set up. She and Mac argued back and forth good naturedly. After I arrived, I went down to help one day when Bud was off. Of course, I was green about the stock. A customer lost patience with me, and scolded, "Where is Mrs. Drummond? She knows what I'm talking about!" When I explained to her that I was Mrs, Drummond, she wouldn't believe me. "You can't be," she said. "The way they argue, they have to be married."

Mrs. Folliott kept a watchful eye out for shop lifters. A few weeks before Christmas, she recognized a woman who had been in that morning, It was now nearly supper time and she was back. She noticed her tucking a string of pearls into the front of her coat. When she brought a few items to the till, the pearls were not among them.

"Is that all?" she asked the customer.

"Yes, that's all for today," was the reply.

"Wouldn't you like to pay for these?" Mrs. Folliott asked as she grasped the lapel of the woman's coat and pulled it open. To her surprise, several articles tumbled out on the counter. The police were called. After searching the woman's house, they found nearly $200 of stolen goods. The woman was banned from the store for a year.

Jill Tiernay and Elsie Proudfoot also worked in the store. Mac was sick one summer. With the capable help of these women, Debby, just 17, stepped in and ran the store for three weeks.

Customers came from Powassan, Port Loring, and Burk's Falls to shop. Mothers loved him because he could take any child and amuse him/her while Mom shopped in peace. He would break up any set and sell just the part that a customer wanted. What happened to the rest of the set? Often, it came upstairs for our use. We never lacked for water pitchers, plates or silver ware. Of course, none of it matched.

Debby had a friend, Laura Temple, who was always bragging about the expensive china and silver that they had. Debby got a little tired of this. One day Laura asked her what she used at home.

"We only eat from Swinnerton's", Debby answered with great pride. Laura was quite perplexed. She hadn't heard of that china. She never found out that Swinnerton's was the trade name for the cheap china Mac sold in the store.

The biggest joke was the day Mac brought me a pair of denim shorts. "Some fat old lady tried these on and broke the zipper," he said. "I thought maybe you could fix them for yourself"

I took one look at those shorts. They were size 44. I wore a size 10. There was enough material to go around me twice. I don't know who finally wore them. I didn't.

Mac would sell anything. Another friend of Debby's, Patty Elliott, left her bicycle at the store. When she came back two days later to pick it up, Mac had sold it. Oops! His face was a bit red when he had to buy it back.

My figure skates hung in the basement the winter I was pregnant for Paula. The next winter I went to get them to go skating with the girls. And there they were, both of them, gone! Mac had sold them. A bit irate, I asked him why. "You were pregnant," he said. "You weren't wearing them." My goodness! Paula was our fifth baby. Did he think I was going to be pregnant the rest of my life! By the way, he didn't replace the skates, nor did I get the money out of the pair he sold.

Mac was always looking for ways to increase sales. He was the first to bring in Santa Claus for two evenings before Christmas. Lloyd Gough, the local photographer took pictures of each little dear with the grand old man. The third year, Santa showed up drunk.—Oops—end of that promotion!

Most of the men folk worked in North Bay, so when there was an emergency, people called Mac, because he was always available. The new minister, Miss Huntley, asked him, "How come you always get here before I do?"

Mr. & Mrs Duff lived in the big white house behind the store. They were a dear old couple. Mr. Duff had had a stroke years before. He was left very teetery on his feet and his speech was affected. It was hard to understand what he said. Whenever the old man fell, or got into difficulty, Mrs. Duff called Mac.

There was a troublesome kid name Ricky Fraser who live around the corner. He stole Debby's rabbit out of its hutch in our back yard. She marched down to his home and got it back. Ricky broke some windows out of Mr. Duff's garage. The old fellow waited in hiding and caught the young culprit. He grabbed him by the collar, lifted him off the ground with the side of his foot, and said very clearly, "Bad young Bugger!" He repeated these moves all the way through our back yard, finally depositing the bewildered kid on the front sidewalk. Ricky might have been a bad kid, but he was not stupid. He gave the Duff property and our back yard a wide berth after that.

PAULA—OUR NORTHERN BABY

PAULA JANE MICHELLE WAS BORN June 5, 1963. Because she was three weeks premature, she weighed in at 6 lbs, 2 ozs. That was small for a Drummond baby. Erla, who would be 16 on the 28th of the month, could hardly wait to get her home. She grabbed her up and laid her out to change her diaper on the counter top in the bathroom. "Help," she called. She was not prepared to see a baby sister that looked like a little bird just hatched from an egg.

Paula was a tall, thin baby. Her little arms and legs seemed too long for the rest of her body. She didn't feed well and didn't sleep long at a time. She would go to sleep in the car, but wake up the minute you brought her to her crib. So, she got walked, and jiggled, and rocked, and sung to a lot.

We padded her into a Jolly Jumper much younger than recommended. The tips of her little toes could just touched the floor. By three months, with the exercise from the jumper, she was growing and happy. Her little feet and legs grew very strong. When she started to walk, she went on her tip toes. She had a perfect beginning to be a ballet dancer if we had live in the city where she could have taken lessons.

Erla got her driver's license when she was 16. One Saturday morning in October, she dressed her doll sister up in her furry, white, bunting bag to show her off to her friends at the high school. On the way home, she had to stop quickly. This was before car seats were demanded for babies. Paula slipped forward and hit her head on the cigarette lighter. It was a nasty gash that bled profusely all over the white outfit. Erla carried her into the apartment, crying—"Oh, Mother. Look what I've done to our baby!" The Doctor stitched it up nicely. The scar has all but disappeared.

Paula was a little sweetie. Like her sisters and brother, she had lots of blonde hair, which we tied up in pony tails. I dressed her in matching leotards and turtle necks with bright over-jumpers. Also like her sisters, she fought wearing anything with lace and ruffles.

When Paula was 15 months old, I went back to teaching at Powassan. We had a couple of baby sitters before we found Eleanor McIsaac. Eleanor was like a grandmother. Her first job was to take care of Paula. She rocked her, played with her, took her for walks. Eleanor taught her to sing little songs. Favourites were:

> Every time I go to town
> The boys keep kicking my dog around.
> It makes no difference that he's a hound
> You got to stop kicking my dog around.

> -and-

> Once I had a little dog,
> And BINGO was his name, oh
> B-I-N-GO, B-I-N-G-O, B-I-N-G-O,
> And BINGO was his name, OH

As long as Paula had Eleanor, she never minded seeing me go off to school.

These are my children, your mother, father, aunts or uncle.

L.R.: Paula, Deborah, Will, Ruth (Grandma), Mac (Grandpa), Erla and Jill
NOTE WILL IS IN UNIFORM

PETS

-AMOS-

O N A FAMILY TRIP BACK from Orangeville, we passed a kennel selling French Poodles. The girls begged their Dad to stop. There was a six month old puppy that the breeder had bought to improve the blood lines of her puppies. It turned out that his front teeth were not properly aligned, so she was willing to sell him at a reduced price. The girls offered to give up their allowances, and anything else they had to bargain with, if they could have the dog. The girls gave him a French name—Mon Ami.

Amos was truly a family dog. When we travelled, the girls would sneak him into a motel room, and he wouldn't make a sound. He liked to get on the bed with me, a no-no for Mac, so he slept on the mat beside the bed and checked several times a night to be sure I was still there. When Mac got up in the morning to go to the bathroom, Amos would quickly jump up on the bed, and stretch himself out beside me, with his head on the pillow. The instant he heard Mac returning, he would be back on the floor, on the mat, as if he hadn't moved.

One day, when I got home for lunch, Jean was waiting for me.

``Do you know that Amos sits on the kitchen table when you aren't at home?" she said. "When I came in the door, he was sitting square in the middle of the table, watching for you to come down the street. When he saw it was only me, he went back to watching."

Imagine that! Amos wouldn't even sit on the chesterfield without permission, let alone the table. Oh dear, when the cat's away, who knows what goes on?

We wondered how Amos would accept a baby in the house when Paula was born. He sulked for a week or two, then he became her watch

149

dog. He slept under her crib and was never far away from her. When she got big enough to sit on the floor, he sat beside her, carefully sharing her cookies, one nibble at a time. She learned to stand by clutching her fingers in his woolly hair and pulling herself up. When she was ready to walk, Amos took a step, she took a step, Amos took a step.

One thing became quite clear. Amos was not a hunting dog! Early one morning when Mac and Will set out to hunt ducks, they decided to take Amos with them to retrieve the ones that fell in the water. All went well until the first shot was fired. Amos bolted out of the blind and was gone—gone—gone. No amount of calling or whistling could bring him back. They searched and searched—no dog! Bravely, they tried to contrive a tale that I would believe. This had to be a good one since I had told them to leave the dog at home. After much tramping about the bush without seeing any sign of the animal, they headed back to the car. There, waiting patiently beside the driver's door was a very dirty, wet poodle looking for a ride home.

Amos had ear infections which needed a lot of attention. By ten years old, he was night blind and a severe ear infection would have required surgery, leaving him deaf. We couldn't bear to see him suffer. The vet kindly put him to sleep and buried him in a special pet cemetery that he kept for beloved animals.

-MEOW MESSER AND COMPANY-

The girls wanted a cat. Marg and Russ Wood owned the general store and grocery across the street. Debby had poured out her desire for a kitten to Russ. I'm sure he had a chuckle behind the gift of 'a male cat who needed a good home'. I looked at this cat with misgivings, but you know how easy it is to get Mom to give in. Reluctantly, I said it could stay.

Well, this was one stupid animal, far from being house trained. After a couple of days the ultimatum was final—the cat had to go! While the girls were planning how to get rid of the cat, the next morning he turned into a she and gave birth to a batch of 6 kittens in the middle of the kitchen floor while we were getting breakfast. Since she didn't know how to make a proper bed for her babies, the girls found a box, lined it with an old blanket, and safely placed it in the bathroom. The kittens grew until finally, they had their eyes open and were running about the house. Training them to use a litter box was impossible.

The girls named the lot. Mom was called Meow Messer. The babies were named: Poopy George, P. P. Penelope, Crappy Charlie, Smelly Samantha, Diddly David, and Got to Go.

It got to the point that even the girls decided enough was enough! In deep thought and with much consideration, they sat down to find new homes for the seven. Since they felt it was not kind to separate the family, the whole batch would have to go together. But who in their right minds would want one, let alone seven, stupid, dirty cats? They couldn't find a farmer who wanted cats who didn't know how to catch a mouse. In final desperation, they found a large box, put the cat and kittens inside, and persuaded their Dad to take them for a ride. They stopped at the road to East Bay on Eagle Lake, got the box from the back of the car, opened it up, and waved good-bye as Meow Messer and Company. They proudly put their tails over their backs and marched off bravely to apply for residence in a pretty little white cottage at the end of the bay.

And that was that!

-CHA-

Time had passed. Debby still wanted a cat. She persuaded her boy friend, Darrel Wilson, to give her a Siamese kitten for Christmas. It was fine until Debby went to school in Toronto to train as an X-ray technician that September. Siamese cats are well known for chewing wool, a habit that Debby and her friends in the apartment in the city were not willing to tolerate. So the kitten, named Cha (Siamese for cat), came home to chew wool. He played no favourites. Sweaters, socks, anything knitted or wool, he chewed. If you weren't smart enough to put things away, he would find them. Cha would sneak into the store, jump up on the sock counter and chew the elastic tops of the socks. These then would be brought upstairs for Paula to wear. She was six years old and going to school before she found out that other kid's socks did not come with a fringe around the top.

Siamese cats came from Siam where they lived in the monasteries as guard animals. They could jump from the floor to your shoulder with no effort. The minute you came in the door, you better get rid of whatever you had in your arms and be ready to catch the cat! He would put his two front feet around your neck and purr so hard in your ear that he had to stop to catch his breath.

As I mentioned, Cha chewed socks, and sweaters. We had an older model wringer washing machine with a tight fitting lid. It was a constant vigil to remember to tuck your dirty clothes into the washing machine to outsmart the cat. One night, as I was watching the late news before going to bed, Cha marched out proudly carrying a soiled sock in his mouth. I laughed at him as I retrieved the sock and took it to the washer. Back in front of the T.V. I was surprised to see the cat coming from the laundry room with a sock in his mouth. "Well, where did you get that?" I laughed at him as I again took the sock and put it into the washer.

His patience was really tried now. As soon as I put the lid on the washer securely, he was right up there, ready to lift it with his paw. This time, the rubber around the rim of the lid pulled off, letting the lid slip snugly into the rim. He couldn't move it. I laughed at him again, "Too bad, Cha. No sock for you tonight", and went back to watch the last of the news.

Cha came grumbling through the house. I declare, he was swearing at me. I laughed at him again, and he bit my toe. He was a cat with an attitude!

The girls would put their wet clothes from tobogganing into the drier, and dry and exchange three or four outfit's a day. Often, the door was left open. This was a cosy, warm spot for a cat to take a nap. One day, thinking the drier was empty, Erla threw in some cloths, slammed the door and turned on the machine. Wamp! Wamp! Thump and bump! She jumped to open the door, thinking she must have inadvertently thrown in a shoe. Out crawled a very dizzy Cha, quite unharmed. That was either the last time he slept in the drier, or maybe the girls remembered to shut the door.

Cha was a hunter. Mice and birds were not safe in his territory. He brought his catch home live and dropped the day's triumph at my feet. When I didn't show the proper appreciation for his bounty, he was very irate. One day he brought home a beautiful red Pine Grosbeak. The moment he dropped it at my feet, it flew to the top of the curtain rod. He was ready to climb the curtain to retrieve it. We managed to catch it first and released it outside. Cha was mad, insulted, p-d off. He demanded to go outside. He didn't return for hours. By the distension of his stomach, it was plain that he had eaten everything he could catch!

We left the bathroom window open so that Cha could come and go as he pleased over the flat roof of the barber shop and down a pole to the back yard. It was common to see him perched on the very edge of the roof of Mrs. Smeltzer's house next door, picking off sparrows as they went back and forth to their nests under the eaves.

Once, in the middle of the night, there was a terrible fight in the bathroom. Apparently, a big, fat, ugly, tom cat had followed Cha home, onto the roof, and into the house. He was not welcome! Everyone jumped up to see what was the matter. By this time, the intruder had been driven out, but the smell was overwhelming. It took a gallon of Mr. Clean to deodorize the apartment. That ended the open window immigration policy.

One summer, Cha seemed to establish a ritual. About 10:45 p.m., he would go out, to return about half an hour later, stretch out on the living room rug and sleep peacefully all night long.

That same summer, Steve and Anne Allen had bought the Northland Hotel, just three doors down from our store. At the Christmas Lion's Club Party, Steve asked me, "How much do I owe you for the floor show services?"

This, of course, raised a few eye brows.

I was in the dark. "What are you talking about?" I asked.

"Didn't you know?" he answered. "Every night, your cat comes to the window behind the bar, and orders a night cap. The bar tender gives him a saucer of beer, which he daintily laps up, and then goes home to bed. I have patrons who make it a point to be in the bar every night at 11 o'clock just to see your cat."

Cha did his best to use up his nine lives with several close calls. He like to use Carl Maeck's garden for his toilet, a habit that Mr. Maeck didn't appreciate. Cha disappeared for a couple of days. I found him on the doorstep the next morning badly hurt. I wrapped him in a blanket and rushed him to the vet who took one long look and shook his head. "His skull has been fractured," he told me, "and infection has set in. There's not much I can do for him. I'm sorry."

With that, Cha opened his eyes, gave a plaintive meow, and reached up with his paw to pat my cheek.

The vet was touched. "Such a pet," he said. "I will see what I can do. If the infection has spread into his brain, he will develop meningitis and can't be saved. However, we can give him a chance." He explained to me what symptoms would develop if this were the case. He operated, reset the skull bones, stitched up the incision and I brought him home. Cha had also been struck across the back, and although no bones had been broken, his kidneys had been damaged. With a lot of attention and tender loving care, Cha healed without noticeable side effects. He also stayed clear of Carl Maeck's garden!

When we left the store and moved to the farm, Cha was a pretty old cat. He enjoyed being the privileged grand old man among the pets. We had a tabby cat in the barn who brought her kittens to the house every morning to be fed. Then they would curl up in the cool shade under the car for a nap. So when anyone started the car, he/she waited for the mother and children to get out of the way before moving the wheels. One morning, I jumped into the car to run into town for something and waited for the cat and kittens to move. When I saw them safely to the side, I backed up the car. I'll bet you are ahead of me and guessed what happened. Cha, who by this time was quite deaf, had been the last one to realize the motor was running, and was too late to escape the wheels. I ran over him. In tears, I made the final trip to the vet. He was too badly injured to be saved. He was gently put to sleep in my arms and buried in a special place on the farm.

We fostered two puppies for the Lions Club Canine Vision Program. This meant taking the puppy everywhere so he would get used to crowds, noises, etc. This was our first puppy, Barton, in a walk-a-thon to raise money for the Canine Vision Program. When the group moved on, Barton rode in the sidecar of Mac's motorcycle.

LIFE FOR THE KIDS IN SOUTH RIVER

Paula played with Stevie Allen whose parents owned the hotel just three doors down the street. The two of them played on main street either in front of the hotel or the store. We used to call Paula our little gutter baby because they would sit on the sidewalk with their feet in the gutter.

The old men who congregated in Kincaid's Barber shop kept an eye on them. No stranger would have dared to touch those two. Someone always had a candy or gum in his pocket as a treat. What a wonderful time for kids. Little ones today can't be so trusting and allowed to roam so freely, even in a small town.

One summer evening, about 9 o'clock, I had put Paula to bed and was reading Will a story, when the phone rang. "Mrs. Drummond, do you know your baby is sitting on the sidewalk in front to the store?"

"Oh, that can't be Paula," I answered. "She's asleep in her crib."

"I think you should look," she told me.

I went into the bedroom to check. Sure enough, the crib was empty. She had crawled out over the top of the railing. I found my pyjama clad little girl sitting on the steps of the store chatting to all the passers by.

When Will was three years old, he fell down the long flight of stairs from the apartment to the first floor. Luckily, he was well padded with winter clothing, which saved him from bruises and broken bones. However, he knocked out his two top front teeth. The dentist was concerned that the tooth buds for the permanent teeth had not formed sufficiently to come in later. As his mouth grew, he was fitted with a spacer contraption to wear at night. That was fun, trying to keep all that hardware in a child's mouth. He wanted to persevere, but in the middle of the night, he would pull it all out. In spite of all that, his permanent teeth grew in pretty straight.

Life was not easy for Will with three older sisters, who at times, teased and tormented him. It was just after Halloween. I don't know what the details were, but he decided that he had had enough! He packed his bags to go to Wheatley to live with his Granddad Willan. His loving sisters helped him pack. They loaded him down with toys, books, and his big bag of Halloween candy. He tucked his piggy bank under his arm and went down to the store to tell his Dad goodbye.

"I don't want to see you go," Mac said. "I will really miss you, but, I guess a fellow has to do what he has to do."

Will staggered out the door and hauled his burden down the street toward the highway and the bus stop. He met a friend, Mike Cooper, whom he talked into abetting his get-a-way. They were almost to the highway, when the bus went by. Will dropped everything and waved and shouted. Oh, dear, the driver didn't see him and kept right on down the road without stopping. Not to by daunted by that small mishap, Will continued to the bus stop, put down his things, and poured out the contents of the piggy bank for a ticket to Wheatley. Then he sat down to wait for the next bus. I am telling you the truth. His Aunt Jean has this captured on film.

After some time, Mac went to talk to him and convinced him that home wasn't so bad after all. Everything was loaded into the car and put back on the shelves. He never ran away from home again.

THE KIDS AT SCHOOL, WORK AND PLAY

-PAULA-

P AULA LEARNED TO READ BY osmosis. She would spend hours sitting on a high stool in front of the book shelf in the store. She was allowed to look at the books as long as she didn't spoil any of the pages. She seemed to absorb the words in the stories from the pictures on the page. To keep her from losing interest, we enrolled her for two years in a private kindergarten class taught by Mrs. Marion Morris.

When the Allens moved to North Bay, Bill Kehoe, Jerry Harkness, Bruce and Lyle Sohm, Jamie and Eric Payne were added to her list of buddies. Her best girl friends were Kerry Lee Constant and Gail McCaig.

When she started to Grade 1, Paula was reading almost anything she could get her hands on. She was encouraged to read by the teachers until she reached Grade 3 when they would not allow her to read above a Grade 4 level. This was a real hardship for her. For a short time, it almost turned her off school.

Paula has always been a reader. I encouraged her to read whatever she chose. When she was about 10 years old, she brought home *The Exorcist*. This is pretty heavy reading for adults. She read the first few pages and decided not to finish it. I was relieved. It was too scary for me. As a teen-ager, her favourite authors were Stephen King, Tom Robins and Timothy Findlay.

Paula did well at school with every subject except Mathematics. "But honey," I would tell her, "You had nine months of math before you were born. This should be duck soup for you." (I had taught Math in Powassan all the time I was pregnant for her.)

"You know what my problem is," she replied. "Somehow I know what the answer is, but I don't know how I know it." She dropped Math after Grade 10. English was her best subject.

In extra-curricular activities, Paula played basketball until she was in Grade 11. She enjoyed the theatre productions, having the part of Farmer Munchkin in *The Wizard of Oz*. She worked with the production crew and costuming for several later plays.

Paula learned to play the trumpet in her music classes and joined the band. I travelled with the band as the female chaperone. We went to Toronto to compete in the Ontario Music Festival. We had a new, young music teacher who didn't know how to enforce rules when the band travelled. One boy, who thought he was God's gift to women, brought a couple of girls to his room. When curfew came at 11 o'clock, I ordered them out. The teacher was mad at me because I had upset his lead trumpet player. Things went down hill from there. A group of tired, defiant kids played poorly at the competition. Even so, they placed third. Imagine what they could have won if they had been up to playing their best. I left the band as soon as we got back home. Some of the band members made Paula the scapegoat for the fiasco because they were upset with me. It was most unfortunate. She dropped out of the music programme following that.

Paula took swimming lessons earning her bronze level, canoeing, and Life Guard qualifications. She made good use of these by teaching two summers at the Hockey Opportunity Camp on Eagle Lake.

She worked as a waitress at Caswell's Resort evenings and weekends while she was still in high school.

When she came home from college for summer break, Paula was waitress, then chef at Cricket's in South River. She planned the menus and kept the staff working in the dinning room. A kitchen helper was hired to work with her. This girl was rather slow. She had to be told in the finest detail what to do. One day Paula came home laughing. "I really had to catch myself today," she said. "That girl is driving me crazy. She's at my elbow all the time wanting to know what to do next. I finally turned to her with your words—for goodness sake, open your eyes—find a job and do it! Mom, it's frightening to hear yourself talk like your Mother."

The pay was poor, but Paula put so much effort and energy into the job, that she thought she would be rewarded with a nice bonus at the end of the summer. She came home the last day, very upset. I didn't blame her. The owners insulted her with a new pair of shoe laces!

Paula thought she wanted a boy friend, but, like a puppy chasing a car, she didn't know what to do with it when she caught it. She was happier in a group situation than on a one-to-one basis.

When she went out on a date, we would negotiate a curfew which was usually her suggestion. Eleven, or twelve, or one o'clock would strike. Where was Paula? I would be pacing the floor, contemplating getting into the car to look for her. When she walked in several hours late, she would apologise and set her own consequences—two weeks without privileges. Thinking about it now, I believe she may have done this subconsciously, knowing that it would save her from having to deal with a steady boy friend.

In the second semester of Grade 13, Paula became very bored with school. She had only two subjects a day—not a sufficient work load where she had to apply herself. She got a job grooming horses for a man who spent the winter in Florida. When she told me about it, she said, "Mom, please don't think you're a bad Mom, but I can hardly wait to get out of here."

I thought for a minute and replied, "Honey, please don't think that you're a bad daughter, but I can hardly wait for you to go."

So, she prepared to head for Florida. Did I worry? Of course I did, but I felt it important that she try her wings. So, when she wanted me to drive her to Toronto to catch the plane, I advised, "Sweetie, you want to be on your own. The best way to do that is to catch a bus from Sundridge and take it to Toronto."

"How will I get from the bus depot to the airport?" she questioned.

"That seems to be the first decision to make on your own," I replied. "You could take another bus. A taxi might be very expensive."

With something like $150 tucked into her pocket, she took the bus to Toronto. Then she used her head. She called a part-time boy friend who lived near Brampton. He picked her up and drove her to the airport.

She wasn't in Florida long until she realized this was not *the* job of a lifetime! She hadn't enough money left to get home. That idea I didn't like. I asked her where to send money. She said she would find out and call me back. There was nothing for two days. Here we go again—Where's Paula?

She was in Toronto. She had called her friend again. He sent her a ticket to fly home. A friend in need, is a friend indeed, but she didn't return his affection. He wanted to marry her. At eighteen, she knew she was too young to become that old. She returned to Sundridge, reimbursed him for the ticket cost, and applied to Humber College in the Equine Arts Course in September.

At Humber College, Barbara Wilson and Michael Botterman became her best friends. The three of them live together in an apartment. Michael was gay, a perfect room mate for two girls living in Toronto.

I was completing a summer course at University of Toronto when they moved in. They did not have a car, so I picked up what they had left to move. It was after six when we finished. I offered to buy supper, they were to choose the restaurant. We walked down Young Street, turned into a hole in the wall, passed through a wide empty hall, and opened the door to a cosy dining room with lots of atmosphere. When we were finished eating, I noticed the three of them getting rather edgy. Finally, they spoke up. "We forgot to tell you. You know that hallway we walked through to get here. It's a lesbian bar. It will be crowded when we leave. There is no other way out."

"So, what's the problem," I answered. "If we are finished, let's go."

We walked through the bar, threading our way around the women. As we were walking back to the apartment, Barb said, "You're amazing. That didn't faze you at all. My Mother would have had kittens."

"You forget, Barb," I replied. "After 20 years of counselling teenagers, there's not much that I haven't seen or heard."

Paula graduated from Humber College, got a job, was on her own. Yes!

-WILL-

Will developed night mares when he was in Grade 1. After getting up five times one night to calm him down and get him back to sleep, I decided to see the doctor. He was both underweight and under size for his age. He was diagnosed with bad tonsils and adenoids. Dr. Lang assured me that Dr. Hallam at the Burk's Falls Hospital was one of the best surgeons he knew, and that we should take Will there.

Well, no thank you! We nearly lost Debby there when her appendix was overlooked. When they finally operated, the appendix had ruptured. If it hadn't been for penicillin, she would have died. When Paula was born, I was left without a nurse and she arrived with no one in the delivery room to untangle the umbilical cord which was wrapped around her neck. It's only because I have terrific volume that my shouts brought everybody running to get her untangled. Give that hospital another chance? Really!

But Dr. Lang persuaded me. "You can hold him until he goes into the operating room," he assured me. "As soon as he is out of the anaesthetic, you can bring him home. If there are any complications, we will take him to North Bay, and you will already be partly there." There were no complications, thank goodness, but it took Will two weeks to recover before he could go back to school.

We had thought Will would now do better at school However, he continued to struggled with reading but was always good at Math. Because he was the son of a teacher, I think his teachers kind of humoured him along and tended to overlook his reading. He covered his frustrations with a grin.

About this time, the idea of perceptual handicap in children was making news. It was a broad term which identified a weakness in the coordination of eye and hand movement. I read everything I could find. The conclusion seemed to be—Don't make the student feel inadequate or stupid. This is a matter of nerve maturation. Nothing can be done to rush this process. Be patient and careful not to destroy the child's self concept until it corrects itself. For boys, this could be age 20 or more.

For Will, it meant that he constantly upset his milk at a meal, couldn't tell his left hand from his right, fell a lot, and never seemed to know where his hands and feet were. The rule for the rest of the family was—don't criticize. Will learned to jump up from the table to clean up the spill without anything being said. Since he didn't know right from left, we encouraged him to be right handed. He developed the habit of a nervous grin when something happened.

Teachers didn't seem to pick up this problem, or said nothing about it, until Will went to Land of Lakes Senior Public School for Grade 7. I was surprised to get a call from the school saying that Will was causing problems in class. What! Not **My Will?**

The complaint from the teachers was that Will would try to write with either hand. In shops, he tried to hammer or saw with his left hand. He was clumsy, bumping into things and spilling anything that could be upset. When he was chastised, he would just stand and grin, which they took as clowning to disrupt the class. I pointed out Will's inability to tell his right from his left. The grin was an attempt to disguise his embarrassment. The teachers had failed to notice this.

His math marks were good. He was having problems in reading. His eyes would jump to the line above, below, or backward. This meant that he also had trouble with spelling. With his lack of coordination, it was no surprise that his writing was atrocious.

I got books on the same level as they were using in class and started to tutor him at home. His friend, Stewart Towle was having the same problem. For two years the boys sat around the kitchen table where they read, studied spelling, and wrote stories.

By the time Will got into high school, he had mastered reading with the only frustration of being a little slow at it. He had a fantastic memory, remembering almost word for word everything he heard and read. Oh, but his writing! The teachers agreed that I might type up his assignments as long as they were his and not mine. Will's sentence structure and grammar were excellent. He would dictate from his notes and I would type as he read. This gave him a measure of success and developed my typing skills.

Will got along with all of his teachers except Marjorie Brandt who taught business machines. With her pointed nose and sharp chin, she might have been a good choice for a Dickens character. She was a perfectionist who had little tolerance for errors and jammed up machines. Will managed to be proficient at both. Dropping the class was not an option. However, skipping seemed to be a solution. The problem was, at the end of that day, Marjorie asked me if Will was sick. Around the supper table that night I casually asked, "How did your Business Machines class go today, Will?"

"I might have known better," he confessed. "You know I skipped it. Nothing gets past you."

He stuck with the class under duress. I believe his mark was a granted credit.

Most of Will's friends were older than he. If they had something planned that he didn't want to do, he had no problem saying so and coming home to amuse himself. One nice Saturday afternoon, three of his friends decided to hike back to Bacon Lake in the bush east of town. As a family, we had made excursions to this beautiful, untouched, little lake several times. We would hike along the well marked trail, carrying a couple of tea bags and a tin can. We would dip water from the lake, and bring it to a boil over a small fire on the beach, and relish the tea, sipped from a collapsible cup. When Will told me where he was going and with whom, I had no qualms about saying he could go, not until 7 o'clock and he wasn't home for supper. Four very anxious sets of parents were pacing the floor. It would soon be dark! We were waiting for the police to help set up a search party, when the oldest of the boys came running down the railroad, out of breath, and knowing that everyone would be mad that they had been so foolish.

It seems that on the way back from the lake, someone mentioned an old log cabin just off the trail. The boys decided to investigate. They got turned around and couldn't located the trail that would lead them out of the bush. In their confusion, they waded through beaver dams and marshes. Will was so scared he began to cry. "Just shut up and keep walking," he was told.

By a stroke of good luck they came upon the railway tracks. These would lead them back to town! The older boy, whose father was a forest ranger, knew he was in big trouble for straying off the path. He ran home ahead to try and soften the reception.

Everyone was so glad to see them all safe and sound, I don't think a word was said. Those boys were quick learners. It didn't happen again. Will had an interest in playing the trumpet when he was at Land of Lakes. We bought a second-hand instrument and he took lessons from Bob Brandes. I must tell you about Mr. Brandes, for it always makes me think of the movie *The Music Man,*—you know, seventy six trombones lead the big parade. Bob was the first music teacher hired for the music programme at Almaguin Highlands. The problem was, there were no instruments for the students to play. For the first four months, he taught music without even a piano.

By the time Will got to high school, he was good enough to play in the junior band, moving up to third trumpet in the senior band when he was in Grade 11.Jerry Teahan was now the music teacher. He did wonderful things with the band. I travelled with them as the female chaperone. At the same time I had a group of 12 girls who could sing a cappella—without accompaniment. We also had numbers arranged with the band. The girls were good.

Jerry decided that we should go to The National/International Music Festival being held in Toronto. I'm sure he was as green about this competition as I was. Bands came from all over United States, Toronto, Windsor, and Ottawa. This was BIG! Some of the bands from the States had 150 members, including majorettes and colour parties. Wow! Did we feel like the country mice. The band played exceptionally well, getting honourable mention from the judges.

As for my singers, there wasn't a choir there under 50 students, except for our little group of 12. Kindly, a category was made for us.

At the presentation of awards a glowing complement was given for our performance, and a special award was presented to Almaguin.

The shop teachers put up with Will's clumsiness because he understood and could explain the concepts. Mr. Binns, the machine shop teacher, took him under his wing with patience and understanding. Will idolized him. That may be why, years later, he chose to become a machinist.

Will wanted to play basketball but his lack of coordination kept him off the team. When he was in grade 11, Phil Aubin, (his brother-in-law) was the coach. He made Will the manager to look after the uniforms and oranges for the players. In Grade 12, John Smith was the coach. He also made Will manager. This meant that he got to go to all the games and be part of the team.

When Will enlisted in the Armed Forces, he was still plagued with poor coordination. In basic training at Cornwallis, he was about to be denied graduation with the class because he couldn't march. The others found this out and determined that he was not to be left behind. They marched him up and down the barracks, shouting out commands until he improved enough to pass.

Later, when Will as stationed at Petawawa, he was home for Christmas. He walked through the cluttered living room to the stairs, stopped and came back to the kitchen with his perpetual grin. "What are you smiling about?" I asked.

"Mom," he said, "do you know what a thrill it is to know where your hands and feet are every minute" Hallelujah!

And do you know, by the time Will was stationed in London, he made the army basketball team.

Will was the only one who had to put up with his mother as a teacher in high school. He was scheduled into my Grade 9 Math class. I offered to have him moved to another teacher, but he was happy to stay. I taught this class in a portable classroom. I had to come from the second floor of the main building, so I was usually the last one in. I was following Will one day. He didn't know I was there. He opened the door to the classroom and asked loudly, "Is the old lady here yet?"

In an equally loud voice, I answered, "She's right behind you." I don't think I've ever seen a redder face. At no time after that did he refer to me at school, or at home, as 'the old lady'.

Will seldom rode the bus to school, preferring to drive in with me. He was a gentleman, carrying my books to my office. It was common for him to walk with me down the halls if he were near. In his last semester in Grade 12, he would come up behind me and put his arm around my shoulder. One day, a student made fun of him. With his ready smile, he replied, "Don't you wish you had this kind of pull with a teacher?"

The girls began to notice Will in Grade 11. With his good looks, ready smile, and friendliness, he was the 'catch of the school.' in their eyes. In particular, Betty Prior and Wendy Giesler had crushes on him. To this day, when I meet them as grown women, they still ask about him.

The Sadie Hawkin's Dance that year was a boost to Will's ego. A top student in Grade 12 asked him to escort her to the dance. He was excited and smitten. For the rest of the semester, he rushed to meet her coming from class to carry her books. It was a short-lived romance. When she returned to Grade 13 she was too involved with getting good marks to go to university to be bothered with a boy friend. Ah, the heart break of a first romance!

Will finished high school and joined the Canadian Armed Forces. His post secondary education was spent at Cornwallis in Nova Scotia. It was hard for him to be so far away from home. The phone bills were high, but I kept saying they were less than college tuition. We were there for his graduation—a very impressive display of discipline and regimentation. We were so proud of him.

-JILL-

Jill, two years younger than her peers in high school still did very well. Being an avid reader, she excelled in English. She won the Creative Writing Award in Grade 12. When she tried the test for reading and comprehension at Canadore, her score was so high that it wasn't matched for years.

She was interested in sports as well. A growth spurt in Grade 9 made her too uncoordinated to play, so she became manager for the basketball teams and got her qualifications to referee both basketball and volleyball.

Mr. Sheffield, who taught English, got her interested in theatre. In Grade 9 she had a part in *Bobby Socks*. She continued to work with the productions every year. Between Grade 12 and 13, during the Trudeau years, a theatre summer programme was set up across the country. Jill got an audition and made the cast. The production was *Babel*. After rehearsing for three or four weeks, they toured cities in Ontario to the East Coast.

The final performance was held in Ottawa. Mac, Will, Paula and I were there. It was a thrill to see your daughter on the stage.

The cast had a last get-together at a beach. Jill came home with the worst sun burn I have ever seen. She spent a couple of days in the tub, in a lukewarm bath with soda. This did not dampen her enthusiasm for the stage. She enrolled in the Radio/Television course at Cambrian (now Canadore) College following Grade 13. There, her writing talents shone out. The professors did their best to interest her in becoming a reporter. No way! She was more interested in the action behind the camera, running the cameras and control boards. The problem was, that one had to join the union to do this work, and this was a closed shop for men only. She wasn't able to get a job in that field. However, this knowledge was very useful to her later when she worked for a construction company in charge of contracts and over-seeing the work done on the job.

Jill taught herself to be a ventriloquist when she was about 12. Edgar Bergan and Charlie Macarthy were big on the TV. That may have been where she got the idea. To be a ventriloquist, you must have a dummy. These were not to be found in any regular store. I crafted her a large Raggedy Ann doll complete with a hole up the back for her hand, and a space in the head where her fingers could move the lips. She wrote her own scripts and jokes. She got very good at it. Mac, on a buying trip, ran across a salesman who could get him an honest-to-goodness real dummy. Jill was thrilled. She performed before several audiences, and then refused to do it anymore. She tells me now that she would be so sick to her stomach before she went on stage, that she didn't think it was worth it.

When Jill was in Grade 13, the principal, John McDermott, suspended three students for smoking in the washroom and cut off all extra curricular activities for a week. The Grade 13 students thought it was very unfair to punish the whole student body for three students' mistake. They organized a 'sit-in', a very new idea in protests. They had it well planned. Shortly after 1 o'clock, they, and those they could recruit from other classes, walked out of class, and parked themselves on the hall floor outside the principal's office. They had notified the press and the TV station in North Bay. Yes, they made the news!

Poor John McDermott didn't know how to handle the situation. The sit-in lasted a little more than an hour when he negotiated terms with the students. Extra curricular activities were restored and a smoking area was set up outside the school. Bill O'Hallaran was 'Head Boy' at the time. Bill didn't smoke, but argued for the right of those who wished to. Years later, when Bill returned to teach at Almaguin and was vice-principal, it was his task to monitor the smoking area, which by this time, was a problem, that haunted him.

I'm afraid I handled the situation badly. Being a teacher in the school, I was embarrassed to see my daughter among the protesters. I insisted that she apologize to the principal and teacher whose class she had missed. Hopefully, I have lived and learned. Today I would applaud the students for taking a stand against an injustice.

When Jill was just 14, she got her first job pruning Christmas trees for Dr. Copeman who had several plantations from Powassan to Burk's Falls. This was hard work, in the hot, summer sun of July. The kids were picked up in town, climbed aboard a truck, and were transported to the site. This was very early in the morning, if the plantain were far north or south. They weren't paid for the time they were on the road.

Shears were used to shape the trees into a good pyramid shape. You had to wear heavy gloves, jeans, and long sleeves to protect yourself from blisters and sharp needles. The bigger boys pruned with machete knives. They had to wear a steel protection on their legs in case the knife slipped or went wild. The knife pruners got five cents more an hour and worked two weeks longer than the others. Jill persuaded the overseer that she could handle the machete as well as any boy. And she did! A Drummond Kid never quits. She spent two summers pruning trees.

There had to be something that paid better. When she was 16 she got a job as a waitress in the restaurant at Happy Landing. She worked one or two school nights and week ends there until she went to Cambrian College in North Bay. She graduated from the Radio Television Course and headed for Toronto to get a job.

-DEBBY-

Debby had no problems at school. She too was a speed reader with high comprehension. This meant that she excelled in English. She made good marks in Science and Math as well. After Grade 13, she was accepted to train as an x-ray technician at St. Michael's Hospital in Toronto. She was there just four months when she realized that dealing with sick and wounded people was not appealing. She came home to go to university.

Debby enjoyed sports, especially Track and Field. Skating for six weeks each summer meant that she was in the best of shape. In particular, she could run! She played some Badminton. She was too short to play basketball.

In high school, each class could volunteer to organize a one hour assembly which was held twice a month. Debby's class delighted in being in charge. They did skits and musical numbers. She and Patty Elliot memorized and performed routines of The Smothers Brothers. They could bring down the house.

When she was in Grade 13, Debby skipped school one Friday. Yes she did. She had to have a note to get back into class. Sheepishly she confessed on Monday morning. This is the note I wrote—

'Debby finds a five day week tedious. Therefore she skipped school on Friday.'

After all, she was in Grade 13, and the rule did seem out of order. It was a joke between us for some time.

I will digress here to tell you about JIMMY YOUNG.

Swimming

Jimmy Young was retired from the Royal Navy where he had been a fitness instructor. He dedicated his skills to develop a swimming programme for the kids in town. He owned beach property on Eagle Lake and gave swimming lessons at a minimal cost. Erla was a good swimmer. The object was to become good enough and strong enough to swim across the lake, a distance of about a mile, (2 kilometres).

The day Erla made her swim, I accompanied her in the row boat.—Yes, at one time I could row a boat.—Will, who was about 4, was with me and there was no one to leave him with on the shore. A life jacket? Not considered a necessity. So I warned him, "You sit here behind me and don't move! If you stand up you could fall out."

"O.K." he agreed. "I guess my feet won't touch the bottom out here."

Debby was also a strong swimmer. Not to be outdone, she swam from the docks to the narrows and back—a distance of 2 miles!

By the time Jill was a teenager, the swimming program at Eagle Lake was discontinued. She took her lessons in Sundridge at Lake Bernard. This was Red Cross sponsored so she earned several badges and qualified for life guard when she finished.

Will was just past two when the girls started to swim. He would stand on the dock, dive in, and swim under water for 15 or 20 feet before coming up for air. "How do you do that?" his Aunt Jean asked. "Do you hold your breath?"

"No," he answered, "Me just don't breathe."

Will was 12 or 13 before he really learned how to swim. He was good friends with the Whitehead boys who lived at the hydro dam. They swam in the overflow pool by the Whitehead house. He managed to get the idea, but it was never one of his favourite sports. Years later, when he joined the Armed Forces, and swimming was a must, he managed to pass the requirements with a sigh of relief.

We were living on the farm when Paula wanted to learn to swim. She took lessons in Sundridge, earning her Life Saving and Canoeing badges. She taught swimming and canoeing at the summer programme at Hockey Opportunity Camp on Eagle Lake for two summers. She taught Greg deVries (an NHL hockey player) to swim when he was a little guy.

During the heat of summer evenings, as soon as the store was closed, we would pack into the station wagon and head for the Narrows at Eagle Lake to swim. There weren't any docks or rafts there, so the kids would take the step ladder with them. Held on the edge of the deeper water, it made a great substitute for a diving board.

Figure skating

Jimmy Young was also the supporter of figure skating. Not only did he see that a good programme was set up in town, he arranged bus trips to North Bay to see some of Canada's best skaters of the day. Kids had a chance to meet Don Jackson, The Jelnick's, Barb Underhill and Paul Martini, and other noted Gold Metal Canadian skaters of that time.

The girls had figure skated in Leamington so got right into the programme in South River. The arena was primitive, hardly more than a shell over a natural ice surface. Pot bellied wood stoves heated the dressing rooms, but not very warm on cold windy days.

Even with these conditions, the coaching was better than in Southern Ontario. Mrs. Leigh came up from Huntsville to give lessons. You know how you like to brag about knowing someone who knows someone. Well . . . . Mrs. Leigh is Doug Leigh's aunt, and Doug Leigh is coach for Elvis Stojko and Jennifer Robinson who competed for Canada in the 2002 Olympics in Salt Lake City. Debby took figure skating lessons in

Huntsville when Dough Leigh held Canada's Junior Men's title. We knew him well. O.K. Enough of that.

Erla, Debby and Jill all figure skated. Jill's feet died in skates. She valiantly persevered in spite of the pain. Most of the fathers were involved with hockey, but Mac dedicated his interests to figure skating. He was constantly raising money to help out with the Figure Skating Carnivals each year. He built props, looked after playing the music and kept the fires going in the dressing rooms. I sewed costumes, not only for my own girls, but for others whose mother couldn't sew. There were no patterns for these outfits, so one had to be creative in design and construction.

(back to Debby)

Debby was the one who became 'hooked' on figure skating. She was only 13 or 14 when she went to Tam O'Shanter in Toronto for summer skating. Then an excellent summer programme was set up in North Bay, so she skated there for 4 summers. The best of coaches were brought in from Germany, and top dance instructors from Canada.

It takes a lot of money and dedication on the part of the skater and parents to develop a figure skater. Debby carried a full time table at high school, and figure skated in North Bay five times a week. The year she was in Grade 13, I would pick her up at school, drive her to North Bay, and she would spend an hour doing figures on the ice. At that time skaters spent tedious hours drawing specific patterns on a section of ice. The control and edges had to be perfect. Skaters today do not have to do figures Then she would go to the dressing room, loosen her skates, eat a sandwich for supper, and do homework before she went back on the ice for another hour to free skate. She earned her 7th figure, her gold free skate, and 3 of the 5 gold dance tests before she quit skating. Jim White from town was figure skating, too. I took them to practice 3 times a week, Mac took them early, early, Sunday mornings and Jim's Dad took them back Sunday evening. Debby skated Jim through his dance tests.

The figure skating club in Leamington was having a hard time keeping up interest and making enough money to keep the club going. Mary Sova, whom we knew well, invited Debby and Jim to come down as guest skaters for their carnival. She did an excellent job of promoting the two. The event was sold out for two nights in a row! Deb and Jim did solo numbers, then a dance routine followed by a pairs skate. Yes, they were still definitely amateurs, but we were some proud of them, and the crowd in the arena gave them a royal reception.

Costuming was always a challenge. Skating dresses for women must fit the body contours without wrinkles. The skaters bottom had to be covered by a short circular skirt. By this time, I had made several for Debby, but she wanted something distinctive for the show. We bought a black athletic body suit made of stretchy material (It was probably nylon), added a triple row of black, silk fringe for the skirt, and loosely sewed black sequins around the neck. With her blonde hair, this looked sharp on the ice.

The second night, after the show, two women knocked on her dressing room door. "Would you please settle an argument for us?" they asked. "Tell us how you get into that beautiful, black, skating outfit. I say there has to be a zipper somewhere. My friend says there's not."

"Would you believe that I crawl in through the neck," Debby answered, "And if I have to do it many more times before it is laundered, it may fall right off my shoulders."

Debby and Jim did guest appearances two years in a row. The club was back on its feet, interest had ballooned, and Leamington Figure Skating Club produced many fine skaters after that.

Debby showed great promise in her skating. She was chosen to compete in the Junior Women's division for Northern Ontario in Sudbury. During the warm-up, she was spectacular. People were applauding her skating and jumps. Then they cleared the ice and she stood alone waiting for her music to begin. Now came the nerves. You would have thought she had never been on skates before! Her jumps left her, leaving her flat on the ice. Even so, she had made such an impression during warm-up that she was given the bronze medal. Now when commentators talk about the mind set and that special inner focus that it takes to win, we understand all too well what that means.

Had it been a widely known sport at the time, Debby would probably have been a great speed skater. There was rivalry between the hockey players and figure skaters in every rink. In South River, Larry Tebby was the fastest hockey player. At public skating one night, an argument was made as to who was the faster. Debby took Larry on in a race, five times around the rink "And," said Debby, "I will skate backwards." If betting had been popular, the odds would have favoured Larry. The ice was cleared. The 'go' was given. The race was on! Four times around the rink and Debby had lapped Larry! That brought a lot of respect for figure skating. Soon after, stroking became basic training for hockey players. When Debby skated in North Bay, the hockey coach introduced stroking as a skill to practice. He had to convince the boys that this made them faster, better skaters. He chose the fastest young man and asked him which figure skater he wanted to race. "Any body but Debby Drummond," he said.

Debby taught figure skating and stroking for several years at the local arenas.

Because she figure skated every summer when she was in high school, Debby didn't have summer jobs. Although it was not her favourite thing to do, she would help out in the store when she was home.

Debby was good friends with Janie Bray and Patty Elliot. These three dreamed of having ponies to ride. Janie's Dad, Pete Bray, built a little red stable in their back yard and promptly filled it with three ponies. The girls had to keep the stable clean, the ponies fed, and the tack in order.

The three girls were inseparable. They lived to ride. There was a large area of bush to the west of town. They had trails all through it. One day they got lost. We were just about to send out a search party, when they returned. They were scared. Janie kept her head. "Drop the reins and give the ponies free head. They will take us home," she reasoned. It worked. Three very happy girls were glad to be home for supper.

Debby would come home stinking of the barn. "Oh, Debby," I complained. "You smell like a horse. Go take a shower."

"I know, Mom," she replied, "Isn't it great. When I grow up I'm going to have someone invent pony perfume."

Boy friends? Yes Debby had a few. Darrel Wilson seemed to keep coming back. Darrel had a car and a reputation for driving too fast. He picked Debby and Jill up one Saturday night to go to a dance in Powassan. The next thing we heard was a phone call from Debby,

"I called you so you wouldn't worry, Mom. We've been in an accident, but we're all right. Nobody is hurt."

Darrel had lost control of the car driving through Trout Creek. It rolled end for end, then slid on the roof down the middle of the pavement. Describing it later, Debby said, "I was on my hands and knees on the roof. The glass and sparks rolled in through the wind shield. I thought we were never going to stop."

Talk about an angel on your shoulder! The three of them walked away with a couple of bruises and minor cuts. The car was a total write off.

There wasn't a bit of glass left in tact. When Mac talked to the police the next day, they told him that they had never seen passengers walk away from a vehicle so badly smashed. It scared even Darrel. When he got his licence back six months later, he became a responsible driver.

-ERLA-

Erla worked hard in high school to carry the advanced subjects and participate in sports as well. Her time table was full, eight subjects each day, with no spares. She was exceptional in Track and Field, holding the record for triple jump for many years.

She was passionate about basketball. To be a member of the team, you not only had to be good enough to be chosen, you had to keep up your marks as well. Before you could miss classes to play in a game, you had to get the assignments from each teacher the day before the game, and turn in all the double assignments to all eight teachers. Sometimes she would do home work for four or five hours before a game to have everything completed so she could play basketball. Between Grade 11 and 12, she was chosen to attend Leadership Training Camp with emphasis on basketball.

Between Grade 10 and 11, Erla was chosen by luck of the draw, to join students from across Ontario to go to Nova Scotia. She was to catch the train in South River where she would meet up with a chaperone and other students. This was pretty scary for a 16 year old from a small town. How would she find the others on the train? How would they know her?

Debby, Jill and their friends solved that problem. Without telling Erla, when the train pulled into the station, they popped up with 'Bon Voyage' signs, balloons, and flags. Everyone had a great time giving her a royal send off. The group on the train certainly knew who she was. This was a great experience for her.

Erla also liked to dance. The current fad was go-go dancing. It was taught in phys.ed. as part of creative dancing, which made it respectable. She and Lynn Kidd were considered to be among the best.

Erla worked one summer as a waitress at a resort on Lake Nipissing, owned and operated by Mary Craven. This woman hosted a woman's talk show on the North Bay TV station. She was well known and respected as far as we knew. Ah, but working for her was another story.

Air conditioning wasn't thought of in Northern Ontario. Through the heat of July, the crowded, attic, sleeping quarters were unventilated and hot. The girls worked 10 hour days. They started at six in the morning and finished at nine at night. They had two hours free after breakfast, and three in the afternoon. The hour for lunch was hardly ever given. They got one day off a week.

Mary was a demanding boss. She drove her waitress without praise for their hard work. The practise of tipping was not established, and minimum wage legislation had not yet been enacted. The pay cheques were pretty skimpy. She managed to save a little for nurse's training. She stuck it out.

Erla enrolled in Nurse's Training at the Salvation Army Grace Hospital in Windsor. This was a strenuous training at that time. It was for three years. The students went to work making beds, giving bed baths and back rubs within a couple of weeks of beginning. They worked six hours every day in the hospital followed by four hours of classes in the evenings. This demanded stamina and determination. But you know, a Drummond kid never gives up!

The students got one day off a week. Erla could only get home on a long week end. She visited a lot with the relatives in Wheatley.

ENTERTAINMENT

I N Sundridge, Johnstone's dance hall was on the shores of Lake Bernard. Every Saturday night, live bands came in to play. It was *the* place for young people to go. It wasn't necessary to have a boy friend. I often took the girls and their friends to the dance. Drinking was done behind the building. Driving drunk was not uncommon. They always got strict orders not to climb into just anybody's car to get a ride home. All they had to do was call, and I would come and get them. They showed good judgement. I brought them, and everyone else who could pack into the back seat, home most of the time.

A young Percival girl did not have the same advantage. She got into a car with a drunk driver who decided to head for North Bay instead of coming home. He lost control of the car at the rock cut at Powassan. They were both killed. That left a lasting impression and made sense of calling for a ride home.

South River and Burk's Falls had movie theatres, so kids and adults had access to movies. The number of prints made of a movie were limited. We had to wait sometimes for the good ones to come to town.

North Bay and Sudbury were the two television channels available. Programming was definitely in its infancy. The girls, who had watched several channels in Wheatley, found the limited choice easy to turn off.

THE BOOMERANG KIDS

R AISING TEENAGERS WAS A TIME far more challenging than toilet training. Our five did their best to bring us up to speed. However, trouble began when they left home and kept coming back.

Erla and Dale Tebby were a couple from Grade 11 on. Dale spent a lot of time at our house. He was a good student who helped Erla keep up her marks while she played basketball. There were times when Dale got a wondering eye and strayed off with other girls. Erla was always willing to take him back.

We encouraged Erla to take her nurse's training in Windsor, hoping that distance between them would help her get some perspective. She had only six months before graduation when she gave us the news—she was pregnant with Dale's child. We went to Windsor and brought her home. Dale and his parents were very upset about this. They wanted her to have an abortion.

Bravely, Erla faced the town alone. She got a job as an RNA in North Bay and worked until she delivered a beautiful boy.

This was the most heart breaking time of my life. It seemed that Mother's story was being repeated. To give away your first born grandchild was not a solution in my mind. To keep him at that time, meant that he would have to withstand gossip, discrimination and taunts from adults and his peers. The Tebby's would not accept him. For these reasons, Erla decided to give him up. In spite of how I felt, I had to respect her wishes. With many tears, Will, Paula and I gathered up baby clothes to bring him home from the hospital. We turned him over to Dr. Laing who had arranged a private adoption. With tears, I tried to explain to Will and Paula, "When you grow up and find someone special, get married and provide a home for your babies. Don't ever give them away."

Erla went back to Grace Hospital, finished her course and graduated. She was hired by Sick Kid's Hospital in Toronto. The next year she and Dale were married. This was a union doomed from the beginning. The baby they had given up stood between them. The marriage lasted less than a year. Dale had taken up with another woman, and they separated. Erla walked away, making no demands from Dale. She got the relic of an old car that burned oil by the quart as it rattled down the highway.

To help her re-establish her self esteem, her Dad encouraged her to learn to ride a motorcycle. She bought a 350 Honda. That summer, we planned to take a trip to the Calgary Stampede. We had a little Triple E trailer which would sleep five. Erla decided to take the trip with us, but she would ride her motorcycle.

It was good to see Erla's eyes twinkle again and the ready giggle return for simple pleasures. She rode that bike through all kinds of weather, delighting in every mile. It was a great trip. We all attended the Calgary Stampede pretending to be cowboys. On the way home, we left her in Sault Ste. Marie that morning. She was going to ride alone back to South River, pick up her car, and go to Toronto the next morning to return to work at York Finch Hospital. We crossed over into Michigan, planning to go down to Detroit and over to Windsor. We wanted to visit Mother to see how she was doing. Dad had died just 2 months previously.

There seemed to be no hurry. We stayed overnight in Northern Michigan and decided to cross over at Port Huron so that Will and Paula could see the big ships going down the Blue Water Highway. (The Blue Water Highway was part of the St. Lawrence Seaway connecting Lake St. Clair with Lake Erie.) It is a beautiful drive along the St. Clair River. We took our time, stopping to enjoy the sights. We drove into Mother's drive about 6 o'clock the next night. She met us at the door. One look and I knew something was wrong. Erla had an accident. She was in intensive care in North Bay. When I called to get a report, I was told, "How long will it take you to get here? We will try to keep her alive until then." We wasted no time. Mother was packed to come with us. It was a torturous trip. Pulling the trailer behind us slowed us up. We arrived at the hospital about 4 o'clock in the morning.

We were not prepared for the unconscious girl we saw. Our Erla's face was swollen and bruised, almost unrecognizable. Tubes ran out of her body. The heart monitor would beat radically, then almost stop. She flopped on the bed uncontrollably. When her Dad took her hand and spoke to her, she would quiet down. The doctors told us there was no hope. Debby, Phil and Jill were called home.

Miracles do happen. God put the right people in the right place at the right time. Dr. McKenna came up from Toronto. She was moved by ambulance to St. Michael's Hospital where he had interned. He knew the right people and could pull strings. As soon as she was stabilized, five specialists operated at 6 o'clock on a Friday night. Besides a broken collar bone and pelvis, her kidney was split in three. Only a blood clot was holding it together. The kidney had to be removed.

Then she lost the sight of her left eye. Damage to the side of her head had injured the nerves to her mouth and her lower eye lid drooped. Dr. McKenna called in a plastic surgeon who repaired the nerve damage and found a blood clot behind her eye. When this was removed, her sight came back.

Erla was in a coma for nearly four weeks. When she 'woke up', she wasn't able to speak. She had partial use of her left hand. The prognosis—she would probably never walk and her mental capacity would be that of a three year old.

Well, no way! From the time she was moved to Toronto, either Mac or I stayed with her. We became like ships passing in the night. He would take the train home and somewhere along the tracks, I would wave as I took the train to Toronto. Every three or four days, we would repeat the ride. Slowly, Erla came back. By the first of September, she was moved to York Finch Hospital where Dr. McKenna and the nurses she knew took over, challenging her to talk, remember, and walk.

On her Dad's birthday, September 22, we brought her home. She required a lot of physiotherapy. The hospital told us what was needed. I was teaching, so during the day, Mac would come up from the store several times and get her walking. If she had known how far from being normal she was, I don't think she would have made so much progress. Her saving grace was laughter. One day, while her Dad was walking her up and down the living room, she stopped. "What are you laughing at now?" he asked. With a giggle, she replied, "I can walk and talk at the same time."

She progressed to the place where she wanted to help. Getting supper seemed like a good thing to do. She had lost the ability to calculate time and quantity of food. She would start a meal at 4 0'clock although we didn't eat till six. When she dished it up, there wasn't enough to feed six people. Many times we finished up with bacon and eggs (they were quick to fix). Will and Paula were fantastic. They were the soul of patience, never once criticizing or grumbling.

The next spring, we bought the farm on 124. Erla was still fighting to get back her vocabulary. The doctors said it was 'the recall syndrome' that needed retraining. After we had bought some chickens and turned them loose in the barn, she came to the house, laughing, "Dad isn't going to be happy. The chickens went to roost on the . . . (beam) . . . . you don't call it a banister, do you?"

She took a summer course offered by Nipissing University and taught in Burk's Falls that summer. She was allowed to tape record the lectures and bring them home to transcribe her notes. What she heard on the tape and wrote in her book was disconnected and made little sense. She would bring me what she had done and we would go over it together. The red ink said more than the blue. She would do it over, and over, and over, sometimes six times to get it right. Such patience! She got the credit for the course.

In September, 14 months after the accident, York Finch Hospital took her back to retrain her nursing skills. She spent a year there before they sent her home. The conclusion was—the lapse between recall and action destroyed her effectiveness for nursing. Determined, she went to Nipissing University. The staff there was fantastic. The Librarian and several of the professors patiently worked with her. She brought home her last essay for me to check before turning it in. After I had read it, I cried. There was nothing to correct. What an achievement!

To get back into nursing, she took an intensive three week nursing course in California. She passed this with flying colours. She has been on her own with a nursing career ever since.

She married Ron Pacaud in February, 1981. An adorable baby grandson, Troy Ivan was born July 21, 1981. Troy spent a lot of time with us when he was little. He was a great kid to have around. I was afraid he might wander out to the road. I took a can of green spray paint and drew a line across the end of the lane. "If you go over that line," I explained, "you will have to get off your tricycle and come in the house."

Out the lane he would scoot, stop just short of the green line, turn around obediently and ride back to the garage. Then we had a heavy rain storm. When it dried up enough, Troy pulled on his little red boots to ride his trike. I watched to make sure that he didn't go out on the road. Oh, dear, he didn't stop! Out I ran to pull him back. "You didn't stop at the line'" I scolded. Then I realized that the rain had washed out any trace of the green paint. That was soon repaired, and Troy rode safely again.

When Troy was ten or eleven, he went on a motorcycle trip with Mac. I made him chaps, lent him my leather jacket and helmet. He climbed on behind Mac with a grin a mile wide. They were gone five days, travelling to Southern Ontario to visit relatives in Wheatley. They saw the first oil fields at Oil Springs, an air field with antique planes outside of London, the Blue Water Highway from Sarnia to Chatham, and many places in between. It was a trip Mac remembers fondly.

Troy has grown into a fine young man with many talents. His tricks on the snow board and skate board are breath taking. It is a thrill to watch him on the hill. These skills have made him a valuable asset to Legit Trix, where he works.

. . . .

Debby graduated from high school and was accepted at Wellesley Hospital in Toronto for training as an x-ray technician. She moved to Toronto and took up residence in an apartment with her cousin Dee Ann and a friend from school. Handling very sick and injured people without knowing what happened to them later was not what she had in mind.

She came home before a year was up and in September, went to Nipissing University. She stayed at home and rode to North Bay to class with a high school teacher's wife. This teacher was suspected of dealing drugs. Imagine our surprise to find two RCMP Officers in the living room questioning our daughter about her involvement with marijuana. She had been under surveillance. They knew when she left home each morning, when she arrived at school, who she talked to, where she went after classes,—in short, they knew about every movement she made for a period of several weeks. They knew that she had bought a 'joint' and from whom. Because she talked openly and honestly when questioned, she was not under suspicion. It proved to be a valuable lesson about 'keeping one's nose clean'.

When classes were out in the spring, Debby took a job at Lake Louise with CP Rail. Her trip was paid out. Return fare was guaranteed when she had finished at the end of the summer. Well, she didn't stay. She left with a group and toured Alberta and B.C. She hitched-hiked home in late August. Oh, my dears, she was a sight. Our Debby was a hippie! She wore a bright pink, broad brimmed, felt hat, ragged jeans dragging on the ground, and she smelled. She spent her time sitting cross-legged on the bed with incense burning, stinking up the whole house. Everybody said, "Be patient with her, Ruth. She's trying to find herself." I tried. After a week I blew up. She got an ultimatum, "Shape up or ship out. Either go back to university or get yourself a job, kid." She cried most of the night. In the morning she showered and came to the breakfast table, "I've decided to shape up Mom. I'm going back to university."

Nipissing U only taught first year courses. She continued her studies at Laurentian in Sudbury. Things went fine until school finished in the spring. Debby didn't come home. I had no idea where she was or what she was doing. Terrible things go through a mother's head when her daughter is missing. It was six weeks before I found out she had hitched a ride to Prince Edward Island and was working in a restaurant there. The news was delivered by two young men who rode in on motorcycles one Saturday afternoon.

That is when I met Phil Aubin and Giles Godin.

We packed up the trailer. Mac, Paula, Will and I took our vacation in P.E.I. Why were we not surprised to find Phil and Giles there also? When we left the island and toured Cape Breton, they travelled with us on their motorcycles.

Mac talked the camp owner into letting the boys stay at our camp site. They pulled out their sleeping bags and slept on the ground. In the middle of the night, it stormed—a crash, bang, thunder, lightning wrath of heaven storm. Phil woke up and crawled into the car. Giles rolled under the trailer and didn't miss a wink of sleep. The next day, we all piled into the car to do The Cabot Trail. We stopped at a swank restaurant for lunch. Mac and I, with Paula and Will, all nicely dressed, walked in first and were seated at a window table. A few minutes later, Debby, Phil and Giles came in—yes looking like hippies—and sat down with us. I can still see the looks we got and could imagine the conversations behind our backs. The poor little waitress was very flustered. Mac paid the bill. Later, down the road, he pulled it out. "I think there must have been a mistake in this bill," he said. In checking it, the waitress had neglected to put in the three extra dinners. I hope she didn't have to pay for them from her salary.

Well, Debby came home and decided to go to Teacher's College in North Bay. Jill was going to College there too. We pulled the Triple E into a camp site on Lake Nipissing for them to live in until they could get into an apartment the first of October. Finally, hopefully, the girls are all set and knew where they are going. The first week end, Friday night, 6 o'clock, the telephone rings. "Mom, it's lonesome up here. Can you come and get us?"

So, we drove to North Bay after supper to bring them home. "How did your week go?" I asked. Jill was enthusiastic about her courses. Debby was not offering much. "How did your week go Deb?"

"I quit. I'm not going back," she said.

"What do you mean, you quit. You haven't had time to get started. What are you going to do?"

"I'm going to get married."

"What! When?"

"Next Saturday"

"To whom?"

"Phil Aubin"

And she did. On Saturday, we returned to The Bay for white bridal satin for Debby and a pretty dark green velvet for Jill. That week I made the dresses. We made arrangements in Sundridge for a reception for the immediate families to be served at Caswell's in Sudbury. Debby married Phil September 19, 1970. She and Phil then finished their third year and graduated from Laurentian. Phil took a summer course and came to teach at Almaguin. Debby taught typing on a letter of permission because the teacher who had been hired didn't show up. They lived in one of our apartments.

They bought a run down farm on Cloverdale Road, just off 124. There Benjamin Gerald was born May 2, 1973 and Justin Philip came along January 17, 1975. Sadly, our hearts ached when little Xavier was stillborn Dec. 15, 1983.

Then came the saga of the log house to be built on the Paul farm. Fall came. The weather was already cold and rainy. There was no roof to put over their heads for the winter. Phil took a job teaching at a community college in Ottawa. Debby joined a day care group to look after children in her own home. A couple of years of that, and the dream of a log house drew them back to Paul's.

Now, this was a house!? The only thing it had going for it was the view from the top of the hill, in a field, about a kilometre from the main house and barn. It was built 6-sided, on posts. This let the cold winds and frost creep under the floors. The wood and logs were not completely dry, so the place was damp and hard to heat. A kitchen wood stove and a central fireplace were totally inadequate, especially when the wood was too green to burn. As the wood dried out, it shrunk, leaving space between the boards.

We gave them a horse named Dakota, to help carry the boys, groceries and wood up the hill to the house. We spent Christmas Eve and Christmas Day with them. Phil had to hook up the horse to get wood to cook the dinner. This was truly the inexperienced city boy who had no idea about country living. The horse's collar was put on upside down, chocking the poor animal. The harness was held together with baling twine which gave way when hooked to the sleigh.

Ben started to school in Magnetawan the next September. He had to walk all the way down the hill, across a narrow walkway over the spillway from a big deep pond, past the big house, down a long lane, to catch the school bus. This was quite a trek for a little guy. In the winter, when it turned cold with lots of snow on the ground, it could be a treacherous journey. The water in the spillway didn't freeze, but ran swiftly all winter. A slip on the walkway could mean a very cold dip at the least, and death if no one were there to help you out. Debby thought Phil was taking Ben down each morning, when in fact, he was watching from the top of the hill. It was just a short time later, that Debby went down after dark, one night, to have a bath at the farm house. She slipped crossing the walkway, dropping into the bitterly cold water. Thankfully, she was able to grab a root and pull herself up on the bank. By the time she got to the farm house, her clothing was frozen stiff. Early the next morning, a new bridge with railings was built over the water.

By spring, Debby had had enough of pioneer living. We had bought the farm from Jack Austin, just across the road. The house was between renters. Debby, Phil, and the boys moved in and took over the mortgage.

Debby did not like to sew or mend. The boys would walk over with pants to patch or shirts that needed buttons. I sewed overalls for both boys when they were small. When Ben was eight or nine, he wanted a soldier's uniform like his Uncle Will's. I found some kaki coloured material, Will sent brass buttons and a name tag to make it look authentic. The pants were complete with all the pockets, and pleats. The shirt had shoulder straps to hold the Canadian flash. How proud Ben was of that outfit!

What a joy it was to have Ben and Justin so close and to watch them grow into fine young men.

Mac bought the first red soap box and then made a second from scratch. Ben rode in the blue Mac's Box and chose number 99, Wayne Gretzky's hockey number. Justin rode the red cart and chose number 66. Mac took the boys to race in soap box derbies for 3 years. They finished 3rd and 4th in Ontario. Circa 1985

I believe I left Jill in Toronto looking for a job. Although she was exceptionally good at what she knew, she was unable to get work in Radio/Television working behind the scenes because the union was closed to women. She took a job working in secretarial temp-staff, using the typing skills from high school (which she hated at the time) to eke out an existence in the city. Basic computer machines were new at this time. She was in on the ground floor, learning to use many programmes as they were developed. Like her Dad, she could bluff, saying, "This is a little different than the one I have been using. Give me a few minutes and I will be fine with it." The computer skills she learned from the bottom up have stood her in good stead all her working career.

Then she decided to go 'west, young lady'. She hitched a ride to Alberta. She came through South River while I was at school. Although I knew where she was headed, I felt bad that I hadn't a chance to see her and to wish her well. It was several days before we heard from her again. Employment wasn't much better in Edmonton. A few times it was necessary to send her a few dollars to keep her going. She decided to come home in the spring. She got a job working on a summer project for the East Parry Sound Board of Education.

I enjoyed having her home. We had some good times. I taught her how to drive. (That's why she is such a good driver). When the summer was over, she got a phone call from a young man in Lethbridge. That was the first I had heard of Ian Campbell. She returned to Alberta.

The next spring I received 20 yards of beautiful white bridal satin in the mail. "Mom, could you make my wedding dress? Here is a sketch of what I want it to look like, and my measurements."

Talk about trusting your Mother! I had made many dresses, but never had I lacked a body to fit them on. I knew that if I made it to fit me a little snugly, it should fit Jill. I looked at the length and was sure it would not be long enough so I cut the skirt four inches longer than the measurement. I sent the dress back three weeks before the wedding with the rest of the material and a note to take it to a tailor to have it hemmed.

The tailor was abrupt, "Surely whoever made a dress that fits you so perfectly could put a hem in it."

"Mother made the dress," Jill explained, "and she lives in Ontario."

The tailor was impressed. It was lucky I had cut the skirt four inches longer. He had to face it to hem it.

The family made the trip to Lethbridge when Jill and Ian were married July 9, 1975. Our first granddaughter, Elizabeth Kathleen Campbell was born June 18, 1982.

When distance separates, you make the most of it with pictures, phone calls and trips west. Jill and Beth came home for Christmas in 1984, and Beth came by herself one summer when she was 10 or 11.

Wonderland, in Barrie, had just been opened. When Mac went to Toronto to pick up Jill, I stopped off with Beth and Troy to enjoy the rides and sites of this new amusement park. That was a great experience. Beth had no fear of the rides, and didn't want to miss a thing. Troy preferred to keep his feet on the ground. (What a switch from Troy doing stunts in the air today!). He was a little worry wart. He would see her get on a ride at the gate, then hurry around to the exit to wait for her so she wouldn't get lost in the crowd. We had a great time.

Beth takes after my heart with a love for music. She plays the flute beautifully and is learning the piano. Her interest and talent in sewing can be traced back for five generations. I am very proud of her creative abilities.

Will stayed with the military. He served as a Peace Keeper in Cyprus. Later he transferred to the Air Force and Trades. He met and married Louis Snider August 2, 1980. They were stationed in Cold Lake, Alberta when Deborah Anne was born, June 9, 1984. Mac and I rode out to see the new baby on our motorcycle. Security on the base was very strict, so Will said to call him when we were near and he would meet us at the gate with the necessary papers. Everything worked out well. We were introduced to the guards and drove on in. Will handed us the papers and told us to have them ready at all times for we were likely to be asked to identify ourselves coming and going. We stayed a week and then planned to go down to Edmonton to visit Jill and Beth. As I was cleaning out my pockets, I came across the papers. I held them up and asked, "Why was it so important to carry these? We have been in and out through the gate all week and no one has asked to see them."

"Really, Mother," he replied, "everybody on base knows who you are. How many grandparents come to visit on a motorcycle!"

Two years later, a little, blonde, Katie Louise joined the family on May 16, 1986. This gave us a great excuse for another motorcycle ride to Cold Lake.

In the summer of '88, Louise left the family, giving Will custody of the little girls. He applied for transfer to North Bay where we could help with them. They flew home for Christmas. The girls stayed with me. Mac went back with Will to help him pack and move in January. When they got back to base, they found that Louise was suing for custody of Debbie and Katie. She won in court. I was given 48 hours to return the girls to her. Sometimes hard things have to be done. My eyes were so red and swollen when I bought the airline tickets in Toronto that the airline attendant asked, "Is this a compassionate flight?" At the time, to me, it felt as if some one had died.

After delivering Katie and Debbie to Louise, I went to Cold Lake, helped with the last of the packing, and climbed into the little space in the back seat that was left for Jake the dog, and me. Will was driving a station wagon with his boat and trailer hitched behind. We had packed what was left from the freezer and any other odds and ends into the boat. Here we are, travelling across the north of Saskatchewan, Manitoba, and Ontario, pulling a boat, in the middle of January. The snow around Dryden was piled 20 feet high. We stopped for gas. The attendant asked, "What are you going to do with the boat?" Will answered with a grin, "Go fishing as soon as I can find some open water."

Louise kept the girls just twelve days, then flew them back to Will. He had lost his housing at the base when he lost custody. Grandma and Granddad open their arms and welcomed them in.

Debbie and Katie lived with us for three months. Will had to live in barracks, but came home on the weekends. We had good times together. Every morning we dressed up to go to the barn to feed our dinosaur. This was a snow covered bit of tree branch out by the drive shed. One day, coming back to the house, we ran into a blizzard, and we were explorers in the Arctic.

Once a week I went curling. When I got home, Debby would ask, "Did you win Grandma?"

"No," I would answer, "but I had fun." She would smile and go on playing. One day, when she asked the question, I was able to say, "Yes, I did." Then, what a whoop and holler. You won, you won! I had to smile and look at reality. Even a four year old knows it's more fun to win than to lose.

When Will got base housing in North Bay, we looked forward to seeing them nearly every week end. The yard was too small for Jake. He stayed with us. Then, I introduced Will to Jane Webster, a teacher whom I had met curling. Will had a favourite saying about the girls, "They are like American Express. I don't leave home without them." I guess Jane liked his express card, and signed up with him. They were married May 2, 1992.

Will was transferred back to Cold Lake early that summer. The two households, including Jane's car, were packed on a big moving van. The station wagon and boat were crammed full. There was no room for Jake. He remained with us. They had hardly got settled in Ardmore in August, when they were hit by a snow storm. Welcome to Alberta!

Jake was a wonderful pet. He loved to go to the mail box and carry a piece of mail into the house. He always dropped it in front of the sink. He was a smart dog. He knew that his treats were stored there.

Jake seldom let the truck leave the yard without going with it. He would run and jump into the box even when the truck was moving. However, when it pulled back into our lane, he would stay there for hours until Mac put the tail gate down for him to get out.

Jake seldom came into the house without jumping up on his box to have his feet wiped off. He loved to be bathed, and knew how to get his nightly shower. He would swim in the creek, then roll in the garden. What an unsightly, muddy mess! Of course, he couldn't come into the house for the night in that condition. He would sit beside the rain barrel where I kept the sprinkling can and a large bottle of cheap shampoo. After a good rinsing, he would go out into the yard, shake himself, and wait at the door to come in. His spot atop the box was just the right height to be rubbed down and brushed. Occasionally, I would rub a bit of perfume into his hair. He was not impressed with this bit of personal pampering.

Jake would be tempted to roam when Blondie, Ben and Justin's dog, came to call. He knew he shouldn't go, but, oh dear, the call of the wild was just too strong. One night the two dogs didn't come home. The next morning, our neighbour, John MacLauchlan, found Blondie caught in a beaver trap, with Jake standing guard to keep the wolves away. Blondie's paw was bruised, but not broken. As soon as John released her, the two pets high-tailed it home, never to roam again.

When Will's family moved west, Jake missed seeing the girls every week end. He quit eating; his coat got coarse; he lost interest in the mail and going to town. We took him to the vet who could find nothing wrong with him. Then Jane came for a visit with Debbie and Katie. Jake was like a puppy again. When they were ready to fly back to Ardmore, we crated

Jake and put him on the plane with them. He lived to be an old dog, in happy contentment with his family.

We went west to welcome our sweetie, Sarah Jane Ruth when she was born December 11, 1993. Will and Jane's family became complete with four daughters when Valerie Grace arrived, May 13, 1998. We visit when we can, but not nearly often enough to watch them grow up.

Then our baby came home. I think I left Paula graduated from Humber College. She got a job working with Jay Hayes who competed for Canada in the International Equestrian Show Circuit. She thought she was to exercise and train the young horses in his barn. Instead, she never got beyond cleaning the stables and tack. The pay was so poor that we had to sent her $50.00 a week so she could afford a place to live. After three or four months, she came home.

She looked at her talents and decided to open a dress shop with Lexi Osborne, a high school friend. We owned a building in South River which her Dad renovated to make a suitable store. Paula was in her element. She learned to go to Toronto, make good connections and brought back very good merchandise. To help get the business started, she did mending and alterations. She made wedding dresses and put on a fashion show. Lexi, however, was not a business woman. Although she had accounting training, she couldn't, or wouldn't keep books. She knew nothing about a sewing machine, and made no pretence to learn. The store stayed open a little over a year when it became clear that it had to take another direction. Lexi wasn't holding up her end of the work and felt she should be taking more out of the business. She refused to sell her share to Paula. They sold out with considerable debt left on the books. Lexi refused to take responsibility for her share. Paula went back to Toronto to work at the track, paying off everything owing to clear her name and credit rating.

We helped Paula move back to Toronto. She got a job with John Burns grooming and exercising horses at the track. John soon came to respect her knowledge and handling of the horses. She met Barbara Wilson again, who also worked at the track. The horses raced at Mohawk and Greenwood. The girls had good accommodation at Mohawk, but at Greenwood, they had to sleep in a tack room in the barn. That made it very difficult to keep clean and healthy. No matter what you did, you still smelled of barn and disinfectant.

Paula got very homesick. John gave her a week off to come home. She enjoyed hot showers and good food until Friday morning. "I have to go back to the track," she told us. "Leroy is racing in a big race tonight. He won't run if I'm not there."

So we bundled her up and headed for Mohawk, arriving in the barn about 5 o'clock. The instant that horse heard Paula's voice, he stuck his head out of the stall and whinnied until she came to rub his nose. We watched while she fed and watered. We had a bite to eat in the track kitchen, then back to the barn.

It was something to watch the horse and groom together. Paula showed him each piece of tack before she put it on. When it came time for the training hobbles, she started at the right front leg which he lifted on command. This was repeated with each leg as she moved around until the left front leg was lifted.

Now Maple Grove Leroy was not a beautiful horse. His head was too big; he was tall and lean; he moved with disjoined movement. He looked more like an old Holstein cow than a race horse. "What do you think, Dad?" Paula asked. In typical Mac encouragement, he said, "Well, Paula, if he holds together long enough to get to the track, he might get around before he falls down." In true race track optimism, Paula replied, "He's going to win tonight, Dad. He'll race for me."

With that, Mrs. Fernandez, the owner came into the barn. Leroy was in the fourth race. This was a big one. A horse had been imported from New York State. It was the favourite to win. We had to stay to see Leroy run. She gave us two passes to the stands. What could we do? It would mean we got home late, but who could pass up free admission to a race!

We gathered up the money we could afford to bet—$18.00, which we put on Leroy to win, place, or show. What a race! Leroy lead the whole race, finishing four lengths ahead of the horse from New York State. Our payout was something like $54.00

Paula met Paul Vella. This was a mismatch from the start. Paul had been born and raised in Toronto. He hadn't been north of Finch Avenue. He was really green about living in the country. Paula had fun pulling his leg. Before she brought him home for a visit, she told him we had no electricity or running water, and that he would have to go outside to the outhouse. It was eleven o'clock at night when they got off the train and out to the farm. It was a moonless night. His eyes were big as saucers. Every sound was strange to him. Someone flushed the toilet and the water pump came on. "What's that?" he asked. It took me ten minutes to explain about water from a well that was pumped into the house and put under pressure to give us water on tap. Every sound was frightening to him. I'm sure the frogs kept him awake most of the night.

The next morning, Paula and I were busy in the kitchen talking up a storm.

"What is there to do here?" he whined.

Paula laughed. The idea that there wasn't anything to do on the farm was foreign to her. "Go to the barn to see the animals," she suggested. Animals were not in Paul's experience.

"Then go for a walk," Paula suggested.

"Where would I walk," he questioned.

"Down the road, or along the creek bank," Paula offered.

"But I'll get lost," Paul complained. The country scared him sh . . . . less.

Paula and Paul were married at Zion Church on May 16, 1987. A thunder storm raged during the ceremony. Paula cried throughout most of the vows. It seemed to be an omen of the times ahead. Paul was not happy having Paula work at the track. She gave it up and got a job 'running', i.e. taking letters and documents from one office to another across Toronto. He didn't like that either, fearing that she would get mugged. Then she got a job at The Royal Bank, starting as teller. She liked working at the bank, took courses and soon moved up. It wasn't long until she was making more money than Paul. He began saying late at the office. When Paula found out his 'late' work was spending time with another woman, it was the end of the marriage. She got a transfer from the bank to the office in Huntsville, and moved back home.

She decided to be a teacher so she went to Nipissing University to get her BA. She got an apartment in North Bay. She didn't want a student loan hanging over her head, so she worked a 40 hour week as waitress while carrying a full course load, graduating with a 79% average. It took 80% to get into teaching. In spite of making a good argument, she was refused.

That's when she met Kelly MacCarthy. A partnership was formed and they opened "Gun Slingers", a western themed bar in North Bay. It was a classy place. They were doing a good business. However, she had teemed up with another person who didn't, or wouldn't pay attention to the accounts. Kelly began to drink where it became a problem. Money was disappearing from the cash registers. By the time she realized that there was no way to save the business, they had to declare bankruptcy. This was a terrible blow to her.

She went back to waitressing. On the way home from work one night, she was attacked and beaten by a patient who had been let out of the psychiatric hospital. It took her weeks before she could leave her apartment alone after dark. She needed to get out of the Bay.

Go west, young lady seemed like a good idea. She moved to Edmonton and met Pierre Ferreira. Here was a fellow who fit into the family. They were married September 6, 1997. Now they have a beautiful family. I was privileged to be there and to be the first one to hold Gloriana Irene when she was borne February 24, 1998 and again when brother, Antonio Mac, joined her April 9th, 2000.

LIFE GOES ON

M ANY CHANGES TOOK PLACE WHILE we were getting the five offspring grown up. In 1970, Mac sold the store business, and finally the building in 1972. We bought a farm outside Sundridge on Highway 124. This is mainly where Will and Paula grew up.

The farm was a whole new experience. Will could hardly wait to get some animals in the barn. He and I went to South River to the cattle sale and bought a small, white head Herford calf for which we paid $85.00. I knew this was really too much money, but we loaded him in the truck, brought him home, and put him in the barn. "Don't tell your Dad how much we paid for this critter," I cautioned Will. The pat answer was, "Never mind. It's paid for." Will and Paula named the calf Joseph.

To make a long story short, Joseph didn't grow. He was either stunted or a dwarf. When it came time to slaughter an animal for meat, Joseph was the prime candidate. He was loaded into the truck and returned neatly wrapped in brown paper packages marked steak, roast, hamburg, etc. and packed into the freezer.

It was still a farm family tradition on Sunday to put dinner into the oven before going to church. I pulled out a rolled roast from the new supply in the freezer. We had gone to South River to church that Sunday. Rev. Huntley, a former minister was there. Wonderful. We invited her and her friend to join us for dinner. The table was nicely set for some eight people. Grace had been said. Dishes of food were passed. When everyone had their plate full, Paula looked up over hers and asked, "Momma, is this Joseph?" That roast of meat lasted several days! From that time on, the animal raised for the table was called meat.

Will saved his money to buy a sow, (that's a female pig). He bought Ezmerelda from Mr. Pink in Burks Falls. Will waited anxiously for her to have her piglets. It was the last day before Christmas Holidays. Rather than wait for me to ride home from school, he caught the bus. When I arrived an hour later, he ran to the house.

"Mom," he said, "Ezmerelda's having her piglets. What do I do?"

Mac was still away on the school bus. I changed my clothes and followed Will to the barn. He had put up a board to block off a corner of the pen and had the heat lamp hung over it.

"Everything looks fine to me," I assured him. "Just stand by and let nature take its course." I went back to the house to get supper.

Mac went to the barn as soon as he got home. When supper time came, Will stayed in the barn with Ezmerelda. It was nearly eight o'clock when he came in.

"How did it go?" I asked.

"Oh, Mom," he said. "I thought they were never going to stop coming. She had eighteen piglets. Five were still born. There are thirteen living. She doesn't have enough teats to feed them all. What do I do now?" Unhappily, Ezmerelda laid on one of the piglets. However, she did raise twelve which grew into a nice bit of money for Will.

As usual, in the Drummond house, there was never a shortage of other kids. Jack Austin, a retired RCMP pilot, owned the farm across the road. The family lived in Toronto, but spent holidays and summers at the farm. Ray, Karen, Doug and Robert spent a lot of time between the two houses. They had a small motor scooter. Their long lane, across the road, down our lane to the barn, make a u-y, and back again made a great race track. We were constantly watching when they crossed the road because they sometimes forgot to stop and look for traffic. Mac took over as policeman, threatening to fine them and/or confiscate the bike if they didn't stop before crossing the highway. I'm not sure they always did. At least we escaped without an accident worse than a couple of skinned knees when they lost control in the gravel.

One summer as the Austin's left to return to Toronto, Mac gave Robert a small rabbit which they concealed in a box in the back of the station wagon. When they were well down the road, Robert said to his Mom, "I'm a magician, Mom. I can pull a rabbit out of a hat."

"Where did you get that idea?" his Mother replied.

"Yes, I can," Robert continued. He'd pulled the box out of the back and covered it with his hat. He reached in, took the rabbit by the ears, pulled it out with an "Abbra Cadabbra". Jean was a very good sport. As soon as she got home she was on the telephone telling Mac what she was going to do to him when they came North again.

Robert was my favourite. Even after we bought the farm from Austin's, Robert came to visit on holidays. For two summers while Jack and Jean were in Northern Manitoba, Robert stayed with us. I affectionately referred to him as my summer son, (sun).

The Chapman's rented the house from us. They had four boys, all nick-named: David was Crow, Don was Crane, Gordon was Luigi, and the little one, Richard was Goober. These boys were at our house a lot, especially Luigi, who like to spend time fixing things in the garage with Mac. I taught Don one year in Grade 10 Math. All year I was very careful not to call him Crow. I was so pleased with myself. The last day of class when I was handing out marks, being relaxed with my comments and compliments, in a lapse of control, I called him Crow. I was embarrassed and apologized. Don on the other hand, thought it was a big joke. "I was waiting for you to do that," he generously responded.

There were five young teenage neighbours Will's age who spent a lot of time at our house. They were: Paul Donnelly, Crane and Crow Chapman, John and Bernie Hicks. Along with Will, the six were a work force to tap into when bringing in hay. The machinery on the farm was not new so there were often break downs. It seemed that if anything broke, one of the boys, especially Will, would be driving. The six became known as "The Buster Boys'.

Rivalry and competition, being second nature to boys, didn't help much. Who could build the biggest load of bales in the shortest time? The wagons were old and not meant to be challenged. More than once they would break down, have to be unloaded, repaired, and reloaded before the bales got stacked neatly in the mow.

Our kitchen seemed to be the home base for the boys. I never knew how many were staying for dinner or supper. I became an expert in stretching food for six to feed ten. One summer, Fred Johnstone got the boys to help him bring in hay. It seemed that the Johnstones knew nothing about the etiquette of neighbourly exchange of labour. Not only did he not provide them with lunch, he sent them home at 6 o'clock without giving them supper. Six irate, hungry, young fellows stomped into my kitchen determined never to help him again. It was lucky that the Drummond table could quickly provide food!

You remember me telling Paula that someday we might have a farm, and when we did, she could have all the four-legged animals she wanted to take care of. What a great memory that kid had! She wanted a pony! Her Uncle Harold Dundas gave her Pixie, a pony that their kids couldn't ride. Off she and her Dad went with the truck to Wheatley. What a pretty pony, part hackney with wonderful movement. She was quiet around the barn and in the pasture. Oh, but don't get on her back! In spite of everything we tried, that animal was not going to be ridden.

Fred Johnstone, next door, was raising racing ponies. His breeding stock was growing too tall. Pixie looked like a perfect addition to his stable. She was traded for a brown and white pinto pony who Paula named Chico. Chico was an ideal pony. Paula soon learned to ride, both with and without a saddle. Chico and Paula won many ribbons in the western classes at the fairs.

Soon, one horse wasn't enough for Paula. When she was about 15, she and her Dad bought six more ponies and started a trail ride business. That didn't last long. Paula was upset at the way her customers mistreated her animals. The ponies were sold off in the fall.

We didn't know that one of the pony mares was in foal when we bought her. The colt was born while she was tied in the stable. Because she was young and couldn't get to the baby, she refused to accept it. How do you raise an orphaned foal? We got mare's replacement dried milk formula from the vet, and bottle fed the little waif. This was a lot of work that fell on my shoulders. Chimney Sweep imprinted on me, thinking I was his mother. The formula gave him a terrible smell, which the other horses would not tolerate, so he could not be kept in the pasture with the rest. Instead, he wondered about the yard on his own. When he saw me outside, he whinnied and ran to me. He followed me everywhere. When I sat down he almost tried to sit on my knee.

When winter came he was tied in the barn off by himself. One night Rebel got loose and jammed him into the manger. The bone in his leg was cracked leaving him in great pain. It was impossible to save him.

Paula grew too tall to ride Chico, so she had the mare bred to raise a foal. The result was Dakota, a rather homely, but very gentle animal who also imprinted on me.

It was Thanksgiving. A phone call from a family below Burks Falls was returning to the city for the winter. They had a horse to sell. Were we interested? We piled into the car and went to see what they had. 'Rebel', a palomino horse 14 hands tall, was running in the pasture. Before we really had a chance to look at him, the owners agreed to sell him, saddle, bridle, and all his tack for $125.00, just to be rid of the responsibility of looking after him.

Mac, Paula, and a neighbour went down to pick him up. We had just bought another animal that didn't want to be handled. I think he must have been mistreated. When he was finally tied in the stable, he resisted being handled, especially any touching of his head. Paula worked with him all winter in the stable. By spring he looked forward to seeing her and enjoyed their rides.

An English Riding Instruction course was being offered in Powassan that spring. Paula decided she wanted to go. What horse would she take? Chico was too heavy with foal to ride. Rebel was about to become a hunter/jumper. He loved it so much that Paula changed his name to Revel. For two summers they went to courses in New Liskeard. At the last one, they won every event they entered. English riding and jumping events were added to the fair programmes. Paula collected another box of ribbons and trophies.

Paula owned Revel until she went to college. He was sold to Gay & Dan Collins who had a riding school. One of the students fell in love with him and bought him. Revel and his new partner continued to win ribbons. The last we heard he had been retired to pasture to live happily ever after.

Chico didn't have that opportunity. One foggy night the horses got out and went to the road. She was hit by a car and died from shock. The whole family mourned her loss. She is buried on the farm. Dakota was given to Debby who sold him and we lost track of him for several years. One day, Jack Bolschulte, a friend in Sundridge, called to say he had something I might like to see. It was Dakota. After all that time, the horse remembered me. He came to the fence and laid his head on my shoulder like he did as a colt. Jack used him not only to work in the bush, but also on trail rides and in therapy for handicapped children. His gentle nature made him a favourite, a treasured pet, with everyone.

There were many other horses that came and went on the farm, all of them special for Paula. It was dangerous for her and her Dad to go to a sale or to hear of an animal that was looking for a home. I never knew what was coming and going from the barn.

Cows, pigs and horses were joined by dogs and cats. Many came and went, but a few were special.

GLADYS—WONDER DOG!

N O FARM IS COMPLETE WITHOUT a dog. It was January when Will and Mac took the notion that we should have a pup. A pup to house train in the dead of winter? I don't think so, guys. Why was I not surprised to come home from school to find a tiny, runt of the litter, black puppy of mixed origin? She learned so quickly it was impossible not to love her. "What are you going to name her, fellows?" I asked.

"Gladys."

"Gladys? That's an odd name for a dog. Why would you want to call her Gladys?"

The answer—"When I take her hunting and call for her to come, I don't want every dog in the country to come running." You know something? He was right. I've never heard of another dog called Gladys. She was such an eager puppy that Will and Paula nicknamed her Happy Bum. You get that, don't you?

I house trained Gladys by making her sit in a cardboard box, taking her out every hour or so. She learned to sit in her box with very little coaxing. It got so that, every time you set a box on the floor, she got into it and waited for further orders. After she grew up, Paula would put down a box much too little for her and say, "That's your box, Gladys. Get in." The poor dog would gather up her four feet, scrunch them into the box and look so sad. Paula would say, "Sit". Gladys would lower her bum to the edge of the box, her tail wagging out on the floor, and stay like that until Paula told her she could move.

Because she was so small as a puppy, Gladys shared the space with me in a big arm chair in the living room. Even after she grew to a mid-sized pet, she insisted on her share of the chair. She was a friendly licky pup. Her long pink tongue could slurp your face from chin to cheek bone in an instant. Once we got settled into the chair, I would warn, "Don't you lick."

She would sit up politely, with that look of—I wouldn't think of it. The minute my attention was relaxed,—slurp. When I glared at her accusingly, that innocent look would seem to say, "See how nicely I'm sitting. Is there a problem?"

Gladys sat on the high stool against the wall at the end of the counter each night as we cleared the table. When the scraps made a bowl full, Paula would say,

"Give me an S," Gladys would give a short, sharp ARF.
"Give me a U." . . . . "ARF"
"Give me a P" . . . . "ARF"
"Give me another P" . . . . "ARF"
"Give me an E" . . . . "ARF"
"Give me an R" . . . . "ARF"
"What does it spell?" . . . . . . .ARFFFFFFFFFFFFFFFFFFFFF"

One night we had eaten out. We forgot to feed Gladys when we got home. She bugged and bugged as we sat in the living room reading the paper. "What's wrong with that dog, tonight?" Mac asked. Then I realized—I said, "No one fed her S. U. P. P. E. R" With that, Gladys let out her ARFFFFFFFFFFFFFFFFFFFFFFF howl.

Gladys could almost speak. She had a short, crisp bark that sounded like 'Ruth'. More than once I went to the kitchen window to see who wanted me. There sat Gladys, tail wagging, wanting to come in. The family said that they always knew when I came home from school. Gladys would announce me with "Ruth's home! Ruth's home!"

We had a man who came once a month with cookies, kindly known as 'The Cookie Man'. In no time at all, Gladys would let us know when he was at the door. One day I caught the action through the kitchen window. The Cookie Man drove into the yard, Gladys met him with a wag of her tail, he gave her a broken cookie from his pocket. No wonder he had so many doggie friends.

We never thought of Gladys as a watch dog. However, neighbours told us that, if we weren't home, she pressed herself against the door, hair standing on her neck, with a threatening growl. Even speaking to her did not coax her to move. Apparently, no one felt brave enough to try to come in.

Mac spent a lot of time teaching Gladys tricks. She liked to sit at the table—well her chair was pulled back. He would say, "I don't like you on that chair. Sit over here." She would slide off that chair and move onto the one he indicated. "That won't do either," he'd say. "Try this one." Down she would get and move to yet another chair. It didn't seem to matter how many times he asked her to move, she would move. Finally a quizzical expression would seem to say, "Make up your mind, Man!"

I had taught Gladys to say 'Please' with a short quiet bark. Mac taught her she wasn't to speak if he shook his head 'No'. Imagine the poor animal's predicament. I would tell her to say 'Please", Mac would shake his head 'No'. In her effort to please both of us, she would open her mouth and a breathy non-sound would escape her throat. When Mac chose to let her talk, he would shake his head 'yes' and she would bark 'Please".

Gladys went to town with Mac. She never required a leash. She would wait at the door outside a store as long as it took, never moving from the spot where he told her to sit. Even a cat strolling across the street couldn't persuade her to budge. He took her to have his hair cut. The barber had no patience with animals and distrusted dogs. Gladys, however, was allowed into the barbershop, sitting politely on a chair, waiting until the job was done. She was the talk of the town, everyone thought her a remarkable pet.

Gladys reigned for ten years. Then a usurper entered her domain. This was a feather-brained Red Bone Coon Hound named Lady Di. This puppy lived by her nose, which I suppose made her a good hound, but left her one brick short of a load when it came to fitting into a family. Gladys tried by example to teach her how to behave. The pup would put her nose to the ground and take off running without looking up. More than once she hit the fence, bounced back and hit it again before she realized it was a fence.

We had inherited three rabbits that grew from cute little bunnies into furry monsters. The farm seemed like a good place to find them a good home. Mac got tired of looking after them in cages, so he let them out to run. They made a warren under the machine shed and proceeded to multiply. We had rabbits running everywhere. When you put a coon hound in the middle of this, you are in for many laughs. Gladys and Lady Di would take off around the barn chasing rabbits which ran every-which-way. The rabbits would trick the dogs and pop up behind them as they raced by. The dogs would turn and run the other way. When the rabbits had had their fun, they would disappear in their warren. The dogs never did catch one.

We were never sure why Gladys quit eating or coming to the house. The vet couldn't find anything seriously wrong. I bought baby food to try to encourage her to eat. Was she unhappy about sharing with Lady Di? That really wasn't her nature. Perhaps she was simply old and tired. Mac found her one morning in the barn, curled up in her bed of straw, deep in her last sleep. It was mid winter. There was no way we could bury her in our animal cemetery. We made a funeral pyre and cremated her. In the spring, her ashes were scattered on the front yard where she could watch for me coming from school. For a long time, I would think I heard someone call my name and look out the kitchen window expecting to find her asking to come in.

One spring, Paula inherited a small fledgling crow which she named 'Jekyll'. I think I laid down the law about Jekyll in the house. The bird was never caged. He lived in the yard waiting for someone to come out to play. He would sit on your shoulder or arm coaxing to be hand fed. Then he would take the food, fly to the rail fence, cram the morsel into a hole, and be back for more. He particularly liked my head. By looking down into my face, he could see himself reflected in my glasses. Then he would peck at the bright metal rims. If he had got them off, I'm sure he would have flown away with them.

Jekyll was a conversation piece all summer. When fall came, he began to notice the other crows gathering for the winter. Finally, the call of his brothers became too strong. The last we saw him he came down out of the flock, perched on the fence, cawed a farewell, and left for the south. Although we missed him, we were happy that he had found the freedom birds are meant to have.

One March, we inherited 12 little turkeys. Bud Payne had saved them from destruction in a turkey hatchery. By the time they were dropped off at the farm, they were a couple of days old, and matted with the pabulum he had bought to keep them alive. We had no facilities to raise baby turkeys so a pen was set up next to the furnace in the basement. The little guys imprinted on me, thinking I was their mother. When the weather warmed up and they had grown sufficiently to live in the barn, they still came running to me no matter where I was in the yard. That summer, they followed me up and down the garden rows picking off bugs and flies. The only vegetable they ate were the onions. They kept those nibbled off about two inches. I teased the family, saying that come time to put them in the freezer, all I would have to do is feed them some stale bread and sage and they would be ready for the oven.

That same summer, we had an uninvited red fox who thought we should feed him too. He became very bold, coming right up to the back step to carry off the chicken bones left for the cats. Early one Sunday morning, I heard him screaming at the cats outside our bedroom window. Then he headed for the barn where the little turkeys were scratching for morning worms. He sat down on the lane as if needing time to decide which one would make the best breakfast. By this time, Mac was up and had the gun loaded. The fox heard the door open and decided to make a hasty retreat to the road. Mac's poor aim barely scared him. The fox returned twice more that summer. Having escaped the third time with his life, he decided to search for food in less dangerous pastures.

One year Mac decided to grow potatoes. After all, the Potato King of Canada was Wilmer Bow, in South River. Wilmer had won the top prizes at the Royal Winter Fair for several years in a row. So why not grow potatoes! Mac worked up ten acres of sand knoll and planted potatoes. He fertilized, cultivated and hoed. He had a bumper crop. He bought a potato digger to help with the harvest. Then, horrors of horrors! It rained . . . . and rained . . . and rained. The field was so wet that the tractor and digger got stuck in the mud. Still it rained. The season was getting late and turning cold. In desperation to get the crop harvested, he started to dig them by hand. To get the bags to the barn he borrowed Joe Hornibrook's team and wagon. In this way, he managed to save about half the crop.

The morning he was finished, he harnessed the team to take them home. Suddenly, those horses became very stubborn. What was wrong? After several attempts to get them to step over the tongue of the wagon, it hit him—he had them hitched wrong side out—that is, he had the horse used to working on the left, hitched on the right. There was no other solution. He had to change the harness on each horse and rehitch them. Whenever Mac was tempted to be critical of another's ineptitude, we didn't let him forget this boo-boo.

Brother Ray had laughed at Mac for thinking he could grow potatoes so far north. We went to Wheatley for Thanksgiving that fall. Mac hand picked 50 potatoes and put them in a 50 pound bag. That bag of potatoes weighed exactly 50 pounds. He took them to Ray and Leola.

"I've brought you a bag of potatoes, Brother," he said. "These are some that were too small to sell." Ray never missed an opportunity to brag and to show the neighbours Mac's potatoes.

Having harvested the potatoes, the next problem was selling them. Mac peddled them door to door all winter until they were all sold. That was his one and only experience as potato king.

Then, there were the chickens. Mac had bought a dozen, year old, Rhode Island Red, laying hens. He made a pen for them in the stable where they could stay warm during the winter. If a hen lays two eggs in three days, that is considered very good. Sometimes these ladies laid three eggs in two days. So, of course, Mac had to brag in the coffee shop in town about gathering 15 eggs from 12 hens.

In the spring, he decided to raise 18 Rhode Island chicks to take their place the next winter. They grew well all summer. It began to grow cool in the fall. Time to move the hens into their new headquarters in the barn. We decided to band them (put a ring around each leg) so we could tell the young ones from the old. It made them pretty flighty, so it seemed reasonable to wait a day before putting them in the barn. The next night, after dark, we went to the chicken house, and there they were, all but five, gone! Someone had stolen our chickens.

Word got around. Now the jokes in the Coffee Shop centered around fried chicken and red feathers. Sid Boyes, in particular, like to rub it in. Not to be outdone, Mac put an ad in the Almaguin News—'Pullets for sale. Too young to lay and too small to fry'.—Then he put in Sid Boyes' telephone number. The other fellows quickly picked it up and bombarded Sid with calls. The whole banter was good until after Christmas.

It was a Sunday morning, April Fool's Day when Mac noticed a bag hung from the mail box. Where did that come from? He brought it to the house. Inside was a tub of Kentucky Fried Chicken. Now, who could have left that? We roared with laughter when we opened it and found red feathers. We figured the chickens were worth about $5.00 each and calculated we had more than got our money's worth with the fun and foolishness they provided.

Your Granddad was creative in many ways. He played trumpet in the Wheatley Community Band and was an excellent banjo player.

Every town had its band. Mac played trumpet in the Wheatley community Band. Look for him, 3rd row, 2nd trumpet in from your left. Two or three times each summer, I was asked to be a guest vocalist at a Saturday night concert.

He loved to build something from nothing. This horse was welded from scrap metal and soon became a landmark on Hwy. 124. He put it up on his 70th birthday, September 1990.

Ruth, the teacher. Photographers started to come to the schools every year. The teacher's photo was free. I have so many that it was difficult to choose which one to include. This one was taken about 1975.

RUTH, THE TEACHER

WHILE ALL OF THE ABOVE was going on, I also had a full time job as a teacher. In South River, three buildings were used to accommodate all the students. Grades 1 and 2 were taught on the ground floor of the old red brick building: Grades 3 & 4 in a yellow frame old continuation building; and across the street, grades 5 to 8 were in a new yellow brick building. The first year, I taught a split Grade 1-2, the second year a full Grade 2. I loved my little students. They did well. But my preference was for older children. When the offer was made, I willing took over teaching art and music to Grade 8 for two hours each week. I wasn't paid extra for this, but that was OK. It was a fun thing to do. In May, the second year, Mac's Dad died. I took three days off to attend the funeral. When I got back, I found that I had been docked three day's pay because in-laws didn't count for time off for bereavement. I was insulted and mad. My extra time and commitment meant nothing to the board. They even rubbed it in by saying, "We know we have good teachers, but you women all live in town. You aren't going to drive to teach somewhere else." Ooo.

Those were fighting words. The next day, I reassured them I could and would drive. Here is my resignation, Gentlemen! I had no idea where I might get a job. I just knew that I was worth more than that.

South Himsworth had just completed a new school outside of Powassan. They were looking for a Principal. The inspector strongly suggested that I apply. My application offered to teach grades 7 & 8, plus music to the other grades for a salary of $4,200. I got a call from the chairman of the board. He frankly told me that, although I was the only applicant the inspector would approve, this was more money than they wanted to pay, unless, being a woman, would I consider working for less. I don't think so!

A South River teacher, David Harwood, taught at the high school in Powassan. He learned that I wanted to teach older students and suggested to the board that they consider me. They seemed impressed by the interview. I was hired, but because I was not qualified to teach high school, they would have to apply for permission to hire me, and the contract couldn't be signed until after June 1. I would start at the entry point of their pay scale—$4,800.

The 28th of May, I got a second call from South Himsworth—the Inspector had told them to pay me the money. "Sorry, Gentlemen," I almost laughed, "Powassan District High School has offered me a job at $4,800. Unless you are willing to meet that salary, I'm not interested."

"My God," he exploded through the telephone, "Are you worth that much?" Yes! You better believe it!

South Himsworth hired a male principal and ran him out by Christmas. Was I ever fortunate that I didn't get that job.

The Powassan District High School Board was one of the best boards that I worked for. The secretary/treasurer dropped in at least once a week to see if there was anything we needed. Any reasonable request was granted immediately.

Apparently, there had been some negative discussion about hiring a teacher from 'out-of-town'. When I got my first pay check at the end of the first week, I went to the local Bank of Nova Scotia, opened an account, and deposited the money. Then I went to the Red & White Store and bought my week's groceries. When I walked into school the next Monday morning, Charlie Driscoll, the Principal, greeted me with, "You're O.K. The whole town knows you opened a bank account and bought your groceries at the Red & White." It was true. I was accepted as 'one of them'.

Being the low man on the totem pole and not really qualified, I got the subjects that were left over. Class streaming had not yet come to the high schools. Every student studied from the same curriculum. At one time or another, I taught everything but French and Latin. That first year I taught, at the Grade 9 level, 2 classes of Mathematics, 1 class of English, and 1 class of science, plus all the girls' phys ed. That was 8 periods a day, no spares, no preparation time. That didn't seem to be a problem. Elementary teachers were used to working such a demanding schedule.

The first week of October, the Inspector came to see how I was doing. He sat in on my first period class, Science. This was an overflow class that had to be taught outside the science room. The lesson was the electrolysis of water to produce oxygen. I had brought in the necessary equipment before class, and had it on my desk, set up on boxes so the students at the back could see everything as it happened. Ah, yes. I produced oxygen, collected it in a test tube, and lit it afire (it was just a puffy little flame) to prove the success of the experiment.

After the class, the Inspector stayed to give my evaluation. "You have come from the Elementary Panel, haven't you?" It was more a statement than a question.

"My goodness," my insecurity answered, "does it show that much?"

"Your enthusiasm does. I don't often find that at the high school level," he said. Whenever I was criticized for my lack of certification after that, I hoped that I had made up for it with a delight in learning in front of my class.

By Christmas that first year, I realized I was pregnant with Paula. I resigned. The board asked me to stay until Easter. I resigned at Easter. The board asked me to stay until June. Paula was born on the 5th. The day I brought her home from the hospital, I received a bundle of exam papers to mark. Two weeks later, I sat in on the promotion meetings. I resigned a 3rd time. The board suggested I take a year's leave of absence. I never did know whether this was because teachers were really scarce, or they thought that I was really good.

When the year was up, the board contacted me again. They wanted me back. I talked it over with the family. Going back to teach at the high school level meant taking at least one university course each year to have a letter of permission renewed. The girls were getting older and were a great help in keeping the house running smoothly. "Go," they said, "you're a lot easier to live with when you go to work."

So I went back to Powassan, still teaching 8 periods a day, but also taking my first university course. Laurentian University in Sudbury had started a satellite campus in North Bay. There wasn't much choice so I elected to take a 1st year Introduction to Philosophy Course because it was lectured 3 hours on Friday Night and 6 hours on Saturday, twice a month. The course was lectured by Dr. Nimo, a Presbyterian Church Minister with a heavy Scottish accent. He was a very learned man who shook his head at the naivety of taking philosophy as a first course. The old argument—if a tree falls in the forest, and no one sees it, or hears it fall, did the tree really fall?—was a frustration in semantics, as far as I was concerned. My saving grace was the third of the course made up by Logic. Logic uses the basis of Mathematics in argument. This made sense to me. In the final exam, I wrote a perfect Logic section, receiving the top mark in the class—75% and a $50 cheque. Wow! I would never have believed I could do that.

The twelve members on staff (including me) at PDHS were great to work with. The Principal, Charlie Driscoll was a man of few words and rules. Just don't break them! Repercussions were swift and to the point. He ran a tight ship and was respected by both students and parents. He stood at one end of the long hall each morning as the students got off the bus. He greeted each of them by name. He watched as they went to their lockers. If any shenanigans broke out, one bellow would echo over the confusion. Every kid froze in his tracks. Charlie didn't have to yell many times.

We had the Donnelly's and the King's who came from families who had feuded for many years. They knew better than to fight on school property. However, when they went down town at noon, the store owners were concerned that they might kill each other. It was expected that Charlie could fix this. He did. The King's were allowed to go down town on Monday, the Donnelly's on Tuesday, alternating days for the rest of the school year. Charlie had such respect, that none of the boys challenged his ruling.

We said the staff was The United Nations. Ray Novacowski was from the Czech Republic, B.D. Dhamaraj was East Indian, Ethan Mings was black from Barbados, Sy Yoshida was Japanese, Jerry Wilcox was Irish, Richard Beaudoin was French, Edward Wiens was German. The male teachers, of course, outnumbered the female. Mrs. Alice Erickson was Norwegian, an excellent teacher of English who got the same respect as Charlie. The rest of us, Ruth Pike and Gwen Froud, just mixed in.

During my time at PDHS, I always taught Girls' Phys Ed. There wasn't a gym in the school, so one had to be creative when it came to exercise. There was no problem in the spring and fall when the weather was good. Track and Field events were always popular. In the winter, I was given a basement room where the noise wouldn't disturb other classes. We would push the desks to the outside and do callisthenics, and relay games in the middle of the room. Mr. Mings, who taught the boys' Phys Ed., decided that we should flood a rink in the yard so that our students could get some healthy winter exercise. This was quite an undertaking on Mr.

Ming's part. Coming from Barbados, he really felt the cold, and had never skated. He and the older students persevered after school and early in the morning until they had a good sized outdoor rink that served us well for three or four months. I augmented the Health course by teaching St. John's Ambulance First Aid. The society came, tested the girls, and gave them a certificate. They all passed, of course.

While I was still at Powassan, a new gym was added to the school. Now I had to learn the basics of basketball, volleyball, and several other sports that I had no experience with. I studied the rule books, but that is no substitute for having played the game.

I was taking my required university course each winter in North Bay. More subjects were being lectured which gave a bit more choice in what you could study. I enjoyed a Geography and then an English course. I became excited when I learned that Guidance and Counselling was to be offered in high schools. The board was supportive when I mentioned becoming qualified, and offered me half time Guidance, half time Phys Ed. Part One Guidance was offered in North Bay in a six-week summer course. I was sure that I had found the area I wanted to pursue in Secondary School. There was a catch—isn't there always—one couldn't get a Guidance Specialist without first having an university degree.

If that's what it took, I'd better get down to work. I started taking two subjects each winter and one in the summer. I took a lot of verbal abuse from people, especially other women, at this time. "A women with a good husband and a family has no business going back to school. What are you trying to prove?" they'd sneer. "Do you want to be the smartest woman in town?" Support from Mac and the girls gave me the courage to continue. Like a pup sticking to a root, I stuck to it, and six years later following that first Philosophy course, I graduated at the Fall Convocation, Laurentian University, in 1971. It was just in time. Letters of permission were discontinued September, 1971. At last I was fully qualified for Secondary School. I didn't feel like a prostitute any more.

I taught at Powassan District High school from September 1962 until June, 1967, when I moved down to South River/Sundridge High School.

The Ontario Government reorganized school boards in 1968. Powassan and Port Loring High Schools were closed, Burk's Falls students came in the next year. An addition was built onto the South River/Sundridge High School. It was renamed Almaguin Highlands Secondary School. Schools now had shops, commercial departments, gymnasiums, home economic rooms, and libraries. Three levels were taught, Advanced, General, and Occupations.

With just one summer course in Guidance, I was given Math to teach, with one period of Guidance per day. That first year, I taught four periods of Grade 9 Math in a row, followed by Grade 10, 11, and 12 commercial math to all girl classes. I found repeating the same lesson four times in a row made it difficult to remember what you had covered with each individual class. Many of the girls in the commercial group were brain washed to believe that women didn't do Math. It took me a month to convince them that I was a woman and I could do Math. When we got over that hurdle, it was amazing how they could grasp concepts, working with speed and accuracy. In time, I was given more Guidance, and less Math, but I taught all the Commercial Math Courses for seven years. At the last, I had almost as many boys in my class as I had girls.

With my degree under my belt, I concentrated on completing my Guidance qualifications. This meant University of Toronto Summer Courses in Toronto. Here I was introduced to Adlerian Psychology applied to counselling. This was what I had been looking for. It worked! Two more summer courses and I had my Specialist Certificate in Guidance and Counselling. I was doing the two things I loved—Math and Guidance.

Salaries were raised every year. When more young men entered the profession, they were not content to work for less as a teacher than they could make in business. As I earned my degree and specialist certificate, I moved up accordingly in the pay grid. Only those teachers with Master's degrees made more than I did. When I retired, I was making about $45,000 a year.

Earl Zurbrigg, Head of Guidance retired in 1980. I applied for the position. It was still thought by the board, that heads of departments should be male. The Principal, John McDermott recommended me. The board agreed to hire me if I produced a complete course of study including aims, objectives and delivery. This bothered me a bit. No male applicant had been asked to produce such a document.

"When does the board want this?" I asked John.

"I don't think there's any hurry," he replied. "If you have it when school opens in September, that will probably suffice."

I thought this might be a loop hole where the board could say, "See she hasn't got it done. She's not capable of holding the office."

So I got busy immediately. I worked nights and all week end. If I say so myself, what I produced was impressive. When I walked into school on Monday morning, John came to me with an apology. The Board was meeting that night. They wanted to see my course outline before they would approve hiring me. Could I have it on the Director's desk by 4 o'clock that afternoon?

"I have the draft completed," I smiled. "Do you think the secretary can have it typed for presentation by then?"

I had learned lesson #1. To deal with the administration, you had to keep one step ahead of them.

This was a time when Guidance was major in the secondary school. It was an advantage being the only high school in the district. We were able to implement many good programmes that couldn't get off the ground in North Bay where they had to coordinate five schools. We developed an overlay of lessons that corresponded to topics in English. These included resume writing, and interviews, subject planning and course requirements. I prepared and taught a Grade 12 Guidance Credit course which included topics such as: educational planning, job search, budgets, and family harmony. This course became so popular that I had to have another teacher take some of the classes. I went for training in giving and interpreting the General Aptitude Test Battery (GATB) which the Ministry of Employment used widely. This test was time consuming, but the results were valid and very helpful in encouraging students to find and develop their natural talents and interests. I ran the first Co-op credit course in the area.

When my grandson Ben was in Grade 6, he wanted more art instruction than he was getting at that level. I arranged with the Sundridge Principal to release him from class for one hour each day, and with Jim Buchan, the art teacher at Almaguin, to accept Ben in a Grade 9 art class. His mother took him up each day. So, Ben got a Grade 9 Art credit when he was in Grade 6.

With so many programmes running, we were the envy of the North Bay schools.

In counselling, I soon had students coming to me who were physically and mentally abused. I was fortunate in having the best support from the police and Children's Aid workers. When they were called, there was no nonsense. They took it from there. They listened carefully, getting the story quickly and acting immediately.

The teachers soon began to watch for signs in their classes of students who were being abused. They would refer students to me. The students came to feel that they could trust me and that I would work for them. The sexual abuse cases were the hardest for me to deal with. That is the worst kind of abuse. With the support I had, I didn't back away from anything. A couple of times I was threatened, which gratefully didn't go beyond words.

I held the position of Head of Guidance and Counselling for five years. Teachers were now plentiful. I was 58, and had been teaching for 33.6 years. We 'older' teachers were encourage to retire to make room for the younger ones, who, the boards felt, had more energy and newer methods. When one's experience and age added to 90, you qualified for a pension. I had that magic 90, a $5,000 incentive to go, and accumulated sick leave that qualified for one half a year's salary. I had always felt that I wanted to retire when I was still good at my job and loving what I was doing. I had seen so many people hang on until they weren't, and I wanted to quit while I was still on top. So in June, 1985, I happily retired from teaching.

It's true! I became a 'Motorcycle Momma', leathers and all. Mac and I made several trips west, east and south. This was an exciting way to see the world.

MOTORCYCLE MADNESS

M AC NEVER LOST HIS LOVE for motorcycles from his years in the Service. The children were grown up and left home. Mac bought a 750 Honda, a beautiful road bike. There was no way I was going to be left behind. I bought a helmet, a leather jacket, and made myself a pair of chaps from deer hide. Yes, my darlings, I became a Motorcycle Mamma.

I'm not going to tell you about all the trips we made, only some of the unique experiences we had on the bike. For one thing, it was unusual to see two 'old' folks riding a motorcycle. Some of the remarks were priceless.

Standing under the overhang of a service station, in pouring rain, in Thunder Bay, a smart mouth asked, "Are you getting wet?"

Only my face was exposed beneath the yellow rain suit I was wearing. "Just on the outside," I grinned back. In truth, my boots were full of water, but who would admit that!

In the beginning, it was often difficult to find a motel who would rent a room to motorcycle riders. We stopped in Russell, Manitoba, at a nice motel along the Yellowhead. The lady looked at Mac with some misgivings, but finally gave us a room away at the back, asking him to park the motorcycle out of sight. We had a shower, changed into street clothes and reappeared in her office asking where we could find a nice restaurant for supper. "Are you the same couple who just rented a room?" she asked. I always enjoyed answering, as if it were the most natural thing going, with a drawn out "Yes".

We took the Yellowhead across the Western Provinces. We were out in the middle of nowhere in Saskatchewan when Mac realized we had to have gas. Up ahead was a farm machinery business with a rusty, old, gas pump out in front. Mac wheeled off the highway and into the lot. "Could I buy a couple of gallons of gas?" The young man who waited on us was very friendly, filling the tank. Noticing our Ontario license plate, he asked what part of Ontario we were from. There was no way I was going to try to explain to a fellow in the middle of Saskatchewan where Sundridge was, so I answered, "We live in a little town about three hours north of Toronto."

"That would be up Highway 11 toward North Bay. I've travelled that road many times," he said.

I was surprised, so thought I would be more specific. "Actually we are from Sundridge. Do you know where that is?"

"There's a beautiful lake there and a big hotel. It's a pretty place," he remembered.

Curiosity made me ask, "How do you know so much about Ontario?"

"I was raised in Ontario," he explained. "My wife is from Saskatchewan. She won't live in Ontario, so I live in Saskatchewan."

"Where did you grow up?" I asked.

"In Southern Ontario, not far from Windsor," he offered. "Do you know where Leamington is?"

With a grin I asked his name. "FROESE," he said. I proceeded to spell his name for him. "How do you know how to spell it?" he asked.

"When we lived down there," I explained, "there was a trucking company called FROESE."

"That was my Uncle," he said. "What's your name?"

"DRUMMOND," we told him.

"Drummond. Um, when I was home a year ago there all these Drummond Real Estate signs everywhere," he recalled.

"That's our nephew," we told him. Even in the middle of Saskatchewan, it's a small world!

We thought we were really doing well on that trip. We crossed Saskatchewan in one day's ride, pulling into Lloydminster after 6. The motels were all full. We pulled into a Husky Station to have something to eat. The waitress was very friendly. When we asked if there was any place to stay, she got us a room at a new hotel. It was posh and expensive, but at that stage of the game, we would have paid almost anything.

This hotel was built down by the railroad, a rather doubtful location to leave a motorcycle parked for the night. As we were out for a walk, we stopped to chat with an RCMP Officer. Mac mentioned the motorcycle and asked if he would keep an eye on it for us.

"I can do that," he said. "How far have you folks come today?"

Brightly, I told him, "We left Russell, Manitoba, this morning and came across Saskatchewan today."

"Then don't cross the street," he laughed, "or you'll be back in Saskatchewan" We hadn't realized that main street in Lloydminster forms the border between the two provinces.

We barely slept that night although we had a beautiful, king sized, expensive bed. We could hardly wait to get to Edmonton. We were up, dressed, and at the restaurant by 6 o'clock. As we were pulling off our helmets, a young fellow coming to work approached us with a big grin. "This is wonderful," he said, "to know that age is no barrier."

It was still very foggy when we left the service station, but we decided to push on anyway. A little after 8, we began to look for a place to have breakfast. There was simply no place to eat. We met a fellow in a pick up who was stopped to pick up his mail. "You have to cross the tracks to find anything open," he told us. Ahead we could see the ever present elevators. We crossed the tracks and found a place that looked worse than South River when we moved in. There was, however, a two storied brick building with a plate glass front that sported a sign—RESTAURANT-. Mac stopped the bike, got off, and walked over to the window, pressed his face against the glass, then called to me, "They're open".

There were a half dozen farmers sitting with their coffee mugs who quickly exited the premises when they saw two leather clad motorcyclist in yellow rain suits and helmets, whom, I'm sure they felt were there to rob the place.

The proprietor was a young Chinese lad who was glad to see someone from the outside world. He seated us at one of his best tables, poured coffee and offered us everything on the menu. While we ate, he talked. He had immigrated from China, just a year and a half ago. He came first to Toronto, but didn't find any opportunities there. So one morning, he packed his bag and hit the road. His plan was to travel by foot and hitch hiking until he found a place that needed a restaurant. You had to admire his courage. He was about half way between Lloydminster and Edmonton. Sure enough, there wasn't any competition at this rail stop. He was open from 7 in the morning until 10 at night. He lived above the business. His face proudly beamed when he announced that he would have enough money to bring his wife and son to Canada for Christmas. We tipped him generously and wished him happiness in his life journey with his family.

We crossed the Prairies four times on the bike. In 1988, we toured the mountains from Jasper, stopped at the Athabasca Falls and the Columbia Ice Fields, Lake Louise, Banff, down to Radium Hot Springs where twice in the pool healed some nasty insect bites that had been bothersome, and as far as Cranbrook. Then we turned east through the Crowsnest Pass. What a shock it was to come upon the giant rock slide where a third of Turtle Mountain had crumbled burying the town of Franks. This was a beautiful, at times awe inspiring trip.

We also rode to the east coast with three couples from the Nipissing Voyagers Touring Club in North Bay. No, we were not connected to the Hell's Angels! We rode through Quebec, New Brunswick, Nova Scotia and Prince Edward Island. The Cabot Trail was a wonderful ride. We came home through Maine, Vermont, and New York State. I wanted to go to Newfoundland, but never did make it that far.

Riding a motorcycle through Montreal is a real experience. Ivan Bouchier, who was born and raised in Quebec, knew the road. As we climbed on our bikes, he said, "Follow me. I mean keep right behind me, and go like H . . . ." He knew what he was talking about. Trucks to the right of us, cars to the left of us, vans ahead of us, buses behind us, raced as they tooted. A little red Volkswagen scooted across four lanes of traffic on two wheels to get off on a ramp to the right of us. I'm sure we would have made good footage as stunt riders in a movie.

From the back of a motorcycle you see, hear, and smell like you have never sensed before. The grandeur of the mountains is that much more real. The heights are greater when you round a bend on the outside of the highway and feel you could ride right out into the sky. Your insignificant size is even more dwarfed when you look up from a narrow valley to the top of snow capped mountains. On the sides of the mountains, the big horned sheep watch you pass by as they cling to a narrow ledge without fear. Great birds soar over head, paying little attention to mere man rooted to the ground below.

The Prairie skies are bigger. One day we watched the moon overhead, clearly visible in the deep blue sky above. We followed dust devil whirl winds as they scooted ahead of us in a black frenzy. Along the sides of the road, you saw mice and other little critters scurrying out of the way.

The waters in the streams and rivers of the mountains run more swiftly. They boil and churn over the rocks and falls with such anger. You can hear them roaring long before you come upon the rapids. If you stop to admire and dip your toe, you can still feel the chill of the ice that has just melted above. Winter never seems to leave the Ice Fields. Though it was the middle of July, we pulled out our heavy sweaters and still shivered in the gray, damp morning.

Now the smells! I soon became very discriminating about smells. I could tell you the difference between red and yellow clover, and a pig farm from a horse or dairy barn. I found the smell of Canola in bloom extremely powerful. It made me think of Dorothy going to sleep as she travelled through the field of poppies in *The Wizard of Oz*.

Even with the noise of the motor, the sounds were in stereo. Have you ever followed beside a train and experienced the tremors in the air when the whistle is blown to signal a crossing? That's surround sound. Because we could hear and see so well, we were able to manoeuvre the bike out of the way safely when a run-a-way semi lost its brakes coming down the hill at the Agawa River bridge. That was scary!

We had variations to the motorcycle. One summer we rode with a side car attached. I refused to ride in it, preferring to sit straddle behind Mac. It did hold the suitcases nicely. We drove this to Wheatley to celebrate Ray and Leola's 50th anniversary.

Then Mac built a three-wheeled trike from the back wheels, axle and motor of an old Volkswagen car. He used the front wheel from a motorcycle. He customed a smart body which was painted red and white. I rode in a seat behind him. He got it properly licensed through the Department of Transport in North Bay. This was a real conversation piece on the road. I think every Policeman from North Bay to Huntsville stopped him at one time or another. After going through checking licence and insurance, they really wanted to know more about the trike.

Whenever we stopped, there would be people gathered around to see this oddity, asking questions and taking pictures. Coming back from Kingston after visiting Will at the base, we were travelling along the 401, easily keeping up with the traffic. Cars would follow, then pass, passengers grinning from ear to ear as they pointed at this unique vehicle. One car was loaded with teenage boys. As they passed us, a lad in the back seat was leaning out of the window taking pictures. There's no telling how many walls we may be hung on.

The motorcycle did get us into trouble with Paula and Debby. One Sunday morning, we took a little tool with the Club over to Parry Sound. The day was perfect for riding, so we decided to slip up to Sudbury, back to North Bay, have supper together and then return home. It was a little farther than we had planned to go, so it was well after dark when we drove into the lane. Two angry daughters met us at the door.

"Where have you been? Don't you know we were worried half to death. You never stay out this late at night. Wasn't there a telephone where you could have called?" they scolded.

Well, they were right. Somehow, it hadn't dawned on me that THEY might be worried when WE were late. This was the shoe on the other foot. From then on, we made sure to call home and let the girls know where we were and when to expect us back.

We enjoyed riding until 1994 when Mac suffered a heart attack. From then on, riding was limited to trips into town to have coffee with 'the boys'.

In 1990, we severed from the farm the seven acres on which the house 'across the creek' was built. We redecorated it, and moved in on the 24th of May. A few years later, we sold the farm to Ray and Shirley Gates. We like our little house, yard and gardens. We plan to live here as long as possible.

FAMILY PHOTOS
AFTER 50 YEARS

ERLA'S FAMILY

Erla with her son, Troy

ERLA WITH ME AND MAC

DEBORAH'S FAMILY

Ben, Grandma (Momma too), Mac, Deborah, Justin

JILL'S FAMILY

Jill, Me, Mac, Elizabeth (Beth)

WILL'S FAMILY

L.R.: Me (Grandma), Mac (Granddad), Deborah Ann, Sarah Jane,
Jane, Katie and Will

WILL'S GIRLS

Top to bottom: Deborah, Katie, Sarah Jane and Valerie

PAULA'S FAMILY

Paula's husband, Pete Ferreira, Paula, Me (Grandma);
Gloriana and Tony

PHOTO: OUR 50TH WEDDING

Our 50th Wedding Anniversary.

Mac and Momma Too still dancing.

MY FAITH

Praise God from whom all blessings flow,
Praise Him all creatures here below,
Praise Him above ye Heavenly Hosts,
Praise Father, Son, and Holy Ghost.

I WAS TAKEN TO CHURCH nearly every Sunday from the time I was a baby. As I have told you, I could carry a tune from the time I was 2 years old. At that age, because I couldn't read, I learned the words by rote.

When I was about 5, I came home from church one Sunday and asked Mother, "What's that song we sing about praise Father, Son and down the hole he goes?"

It took Mother a little time to come up with Holy Ghost. God the Father and God the Son were easy concepts for even a 5 year old who went to church every Sunday to understand. But who is this Holy Ghost? "It's part of the Trinity," Mother replied. To a 5 year old, that sounded reasonable, and I accepted it on the value of her word. The invisible world that surrounded me when I played alone in the corn crib, the wood pile, or swung from the Manitoba Maple in the front yard, was part of 'The Holy Ghost'. No, I didn't talk to it, nor did it talk to me, but I never doubted that it was there.

For some reason, I was not baptized when I was a baby. I was about 8 years old when Mother decided I should 'be done'. The minister, Rev. Champion, came to our house for dinner. In the afternoon, in the parlour, I was baptized in the name of The Father, and of The Son and of The Holy Ghost. There it was again—The Holy Ghost. From that day on, I began a quest to find The Holy Ghost. As I look back on it now, I sense that from that day on, the Holy Ghost led me through life in many miraculous ways that I could only see in retrospect.

One short verse in Luke 2:40 tells of Jesus growing up. Translated for children in Sunday School, I memorized the paraphrased version: "And Jesus grew in stature, and in wisdom, and in favour with God and Man." I am sure that this is the verse that drove my desire to learn. The Holy Ghost provided teachers and opportunities to help me overcome a learning disability, and fuelled a desire to read, learn, and study, to expand and capture as much of the knowledge and wealth of the universe as it is possible for a limited human mind to comprehend. (At age 75, I just wish I could remember more.)

By age 8, I had been to Sunday School for more than 300 Sundays, studying the Bible, not as stories, but as a remarkable history of the development of mankind. (Today, being politically correct, that would have to be person kind. That has never bothered me. In my mind there has never been a sexual division in God's thinking.) The Bible is full of ghosts, spirits, angels, and the devil. These are accepted as part of God's Word—but don't ask questions or expect to discuss the topic in any depth. Somehow, this associated one with the occult, and the evil, scary world of things unseen. Don't be foolish enough to mess with those ideas.

So, as children do—if adults can't give you a satisfactory explanation, you have to find the answer yourself. This became a lengthy search. It was not until years later that I realized that the Holy Ghost, Spirit, or whatever one wanted to call it, strengthened, guided, shoved, pushed, and sometimes kicked butt to move me in the direction that my life was meant to take. I thought I wanted to be a nurse. He wanted me to be a teacher. I was happy to stay in the elementary grades. He wanted me to counsel teenagers. When I was floundering in how to raise my children, He introduced me to new ideas. When the doctors told us that there was no way that Erla could survive the accident, He put the right people in the right spot at the right time. He answered the prayers of those who prayed and gave us the strength to sit by her side day after day providing hope and encouragement.

The Bible tells us that we each have at least one guardian angel, and in times of great need, we can call upon 10,000. When I was seriously ill with a bad gall bladder, I think most of the 10,000 comforted me at one time or another. I also felt their presence when I was operated on for

Spinal Stenosis. Only afterward did I realize the risk of being permanently paralysed if the surgeon's knife had slipped.

The Wind

I saw you toss the kites on high
And blow the birds across the sky;
And all around I heard you pass,
Like ladies' skirts across the grass—
Oh wind, a-blowing all day long,
Oh wind, that sings so loud a song!

I saw the different things you did,
But always you, yourself, you hid.
I felt you push, I heard you call,
I could not see yourself at all—
Oh wind, a-blowing all day long,
Oh wind, that sings so loud a song!

O you that are so strong and cold,
O blower, are you young or old?
Are you a beast of field and tree,
Or just a stronger child than me?
O wind, a-blowing all day long,
Oh wind, that sings so loud a song!

Robert Louis Stevenson

Like the unseen wind, God as Holy Ghost, can be seen in the works of His hands, in the beauty of the trees, the grandeur of rocks, the strength of a germinating seed, the myriad of stars in the sky, the wonder of the moon, the miracle of birth and the mystery of life after death, the creator of all things great and small. Are the things that we attribute to luck or coincidence, really just that, or are they set in motion by unseen spirits? I choose to believe in the spirits and praise the Holy Ghost that miracles happen today, as they did 2000 years ago.

The more I studied and taught math, the more I found my faith in God expressed. The concept of infinite numbers can be interpreted as the infinity of God. Count as long as you want, left, right, up or down, and you won't come to the final value. That is infinite.

Look at zero (O) as a beginning point, the Origin of all numbers. Zero is a circle with no end and no beginning. All numbers radiate from zero, the Origin. This is another description of God—'In the beginning, God created heaven and earth . . . '(Genesis 1:1). Another interesting concept is 'Division by O has no meaning'. Perhaps this is why, when we try to break God down into smaller pieces that we can understand, we distort the whole, and lose the meaning.

Between any two numbers, there is another number. This is easy enough to understand. Between 1 and 2, there is 1.5, 1.25, 1.125, 1.0625, 1.03125 and on to infinity. As earthlings, we can only measure according to the discretion of the instrument we are using. Isn't that interesting. It means that there is always that part that is left unmeasured. For more than 50 years, in the desert in Arizona, scientist has been attempting to build the perfect clock to measure time. Have they succeeded? No. They are still fractions of seconds out—that portion of time between any two measurable quantities.

Then there are interesting fractions. One half (1 divided by 2) is 0.5—neat, easy to compute. It terminates. One third (1 divided by 3) is 0.333333 . . . . a repeating decimal. Before we can use this quantity, we must decide to what degree of accuracy we wish to measure, realizing that we will still be slightly off the true value.

This need to 'round off' the value of fractional numbers, to reduce them to sizes that fit our computers, is often forgotten. We think we have the right answer, when in reality, the best that we can hope for, is a close approximation.

Too often, organized religions try to define God with the tools of their exposure. They try to put God in a box where they can study, define, and manipulate the full understanding of an infinite, omnipotent being. Mathematics shows us that this is impossible. No matter how we measure, there is always that part which escapes our comprehension. Perhaps this is what Jesus was referring to when he said, "Judge not, that ye may not be judged." Remember, our yard stick doesn't measure like God's.

God and science? I have never seen a problem between the two. Science can do nothing but define God. Think of it this way. Science never creates, it discovers. To discover something, indicates that it was there all the time waiting to be 'discovered'. It is man's drive to discover the 'secrets of the universe' that drives the human imagination to search for answers.

Science is built on empirical knowledge based on experiment and observation. Before a hypotheses can be accepted as true, it must be repeated over and over, always producing the same results. From these results, empirical definitions are written. Example: the definition of energy is—that which can neither be created nor destroyed. In other words, energy is infinite. How interesting that this fits the definition of God as the energy of creation!

The 'Big Bang Theory' required an energy, a spark if you will, to create the big bang. The great Albert Einstein was convinced that the more he discovered the secrets of the universe, the surer he was that such an ordered, defined, infinite creation could only come about through the universal intelligence of a creator.

I enjoyed a real laugh when the probe sent to Mars reported that that planet was made of the same minerals and rocks that we have on earth. Of course it is. Even the 'Big Bang' theory should have expected that.

New technology is constantly re-enforcing biblical records that have been passed off as folk lore. A plane flying over Mount Ararat using modern photographic technology took pictures of 'something' buried on the top of the mountain with the exact shape and dimensions of Noah's Ark. A human skull has been found that is older than any ape skull previously unearthed. God must have a real sense of humour. I can hear Him chuckle saying, "Hey, folks. Your theories are a little off. I'll just tuck in an older, humanoid skull here for you to find. to help you get it right."

The Bible says that after six days, God rested from His creation. It doesn't say He retired. So why should we be surprised that the world continues to evolve with black holes, super novas and the birth of whole new universes that have been photographed by the Hubble Space Telescope. Every day, I am amazed at the possibilities of new scientific discoveries, as great as the exploration of the heavens and as minute as the mapping of the genes in our DNA.

Jesus, the Son of God, completely, totally, fulfilled his mission on earth. Pope John Paul ll, speaking to the youth in Toronto (2002), expressed it this way, "Jesus did not proclaim His faith, He lived it." For me, without the teaching and example of Jesus, we couldn't know God's love and how we are to express it. If you read nothing else in the Bible but the Ten commandments, the four Gospels, Matthew, Mark, Luke and John, and

1 Corinthians13, you will have direction for any situation in your life. In this regard, my Quaker roots are showing, i.e. the Bible is timeless. It contains the answers *you* need for *your* life. You find those answers through study, contemplation and prayer. The answers and plans given to you may be different from those given to someone else. That is as it is meant to be. Each soul, going through the measure of his/her days must find the path he/she is meant to take on life's journey.

The Bible tells us that we are made in God's image. Jesus taught that each of us is a child of God, that the Holy Spirit is within each of us. Psychology divides each person into body, mind and soul (spirit). This recognizes the trinity within every living person. The problem is of course, that we are not holy. In our earth journey, we must nurture the Spirit, allowing it to grow in stature, and in wisdom, and in favour with God and man. As a teacher, I found I could teach anyone except the student with a closed mind. To learn and to grow, requires an open mind, a willingness to read and study, and to consider possibilities and choices, for as long as you live and have your mental capacities.

I hear the expression 'blind faith'. It is my experience that faith grows through questioning, considering, and application of good choices. Faith, then, is informed, reliable, and trustworthy. It is never blind.

I don't know where I heard this story. I will include it here to illustrate the meaning of faith.

A famous aerialist had won his acclaim by successfully walking a tight rope over scary, dangerous, places. He came to Niagara to walk a tight rope over the Horseshoe Falls and over the streets and highway to the top of a skyscraper. This was to be the longest, highest, tightrope walk ever to be completed. The media soon got hold of the exploit. Discussions followed as to the pros and cons of a successful walk. The strength of the wire, the stretch extended by his weight, the direction and force of the winds, the possibility of distraction that would cause him to lose balance. These and every variable they could think of were all taken into account. The conclusion was—he'll never make it!

But, there was one young reporter who had read and studied all he could find about the tightrope walker. He asked to interview him. The aerialist asked the reporter: Q: The general consensus is that I can't do this and that I will fall, splattered on the ground Why are you interested in what I have planned?

A: I have read about and studied every daring feat you have completed. I believe that you can do this too.

Q: You believe I can do this. What makes you so sure?

A: I just really believe.

To which the aerialist responded, "If you truly believe, climb up on my shoulders and come across with me"

I believe that free will is God's greatest gift to each soul. Jesus' life's mission was to show us how to love. He laid out the blue prints for making good choices so that we can show that love. Choices come with inescapable consequences. Forgiveness when a poor choice has been made and the opportunity to try again with a better choice is always available. The hardest words to say are, "I made a poor choice. I was wrong, I'm sorry. Please forgive me." The sweetest words to hear are, "You are forgiven."

The power of prayer cannot be measured. As a child, it seemed impossible to me that God could hear my small voice. Thirty years later, as I was watching and listening to the first moon mission. someone asked, "How big a radio transmitter is built into the module so that messages can be sent back to NASA?" The answer was enlightening. "The size of the transmitter is irrelevant. It is the size of the receiver that counts." My conclusion—if this is what man can do, consider how much greater is God's receiver. Of course He hears and answers prayers. When the answer is 'no', the Holy Spirit can redirect your steps. When you are hurting from circumstances that were beyond your control, He can *Turn Your Scars into Stars* (Dr. Robert Scheuller).

My dears, I did not intend this to turn into a sermon, but rather an insight of faith as it has been revealed to me so far. At 75 years old, I believe that God the Father, God the Son and God the Holy Ghost have not finished with me yet. Hopefully, I'm still growing.

My prayer and hope for each of you is that you develop your own statement of faith, and draw from it. Build on your God given talents to realize your possibilities. Follow your dreams. Never forget to laugh *at* yourself and *with* others. And may the Force be with you.